University of Plymouth
Charles Seale Hayne Library
Subject to status this item may be renewed
via your Voyager account

http://voyager.plymouth.ac.uk
Tel: (01752) 232323

European Economies in Transition

Also by Oliver Fabel

THE ECONOMICS OF PENSIONS AND VARIABLE RETIREMENT SCHEMES

INSURANCE AND INCENTIVES IN LABOUR CONTRACTS: A Study in the Theory of Implicit Contracts

Also by Francesco Farina

ETHICS, RATIONALITY AND ECONOMIC BEHAVIOUR (*co-editor*)

Also by Lionello F. Punzo

THE DYNAMICS OF A CAPITALIST ECONOMY: A Multi-Sectoral Approach (*co-editor*)

ECONOMIC PERFORMANCE: A LOOK AT AUSTRIA AND ITALY (*co-editor*)

CYCLE, GROWTH AND STRUCTURAL CHANGE (*co-editor*)

European Economies in Transition

In Search of a New Growth Path

Edited by

Oliver Fabel
Professor of Management Studies
University of Konstanz
Germany

Francesco Farina
Professor of Economics
University of Siena
Italy

and

Lionello F. Punzo
Professor of Economics
University of Siena
Italy

First published in Great Britain 2000 by
MACMILLAN PRESS LTD
Houndmills, Basingstoke, Hampshire RG21 6XS and London
Companies and representatives throughout the world

A catalogue record for this book is available from the British Library.
ISBN 0–333–79461–3

First published in the United States of America 2000 by
ST. MARTIN'S PRESS, INC.,
Scholarly and Reference Division,
175 Fifth Avenue, New York, N.Y. 10010

ISBN 0–312–23224–1

Library of Congress Cataloging-in-Publication Data
European economies in transition : in search of a new growth path / edited by
Oliver Fabel, Francesco Farina and Lionello F. Punzo.
p.   cm.
Includes bibliographical references and index.
ISBN 0–312–23224–1 (cloth)
1. European Union countries—Economic conditions—Regional disparities. 2.
Europe—Economic integration—Social aspects. 3. Monetary unions—European
Union countries. 4. Fiscal policy—European Union countries. 5. Labor policy–
–European Union countries. 6. Public welfare—European Union countries. I.
Fabel, Oliver. II. Farina, Francesco. III. Punzo, Lionello F.

HC240 .E83613   2000
338.94—dc21

00–021163

This book is printed on paper suitable for recycling and made from fully managed and sustained
forest sources.

10   9   8   7   6   5   4   3   2   1
09   08   07   06   05   04   03   02   01   00

Printed and bound in Great Britain by Antony Rowe Ltd, Chippenham, Wiltshire

To the memory of our friend Bruno Miconi

Contents

List of Tables

List of Figures

Acknowledgements

Research leading to the writing of the papers published in this volume was largely financed by the European Commission, through contracts no. ERB CHR XCT 930231 and ERB CIP DCT 940015, establishing a Human Capital and Mobility network called EUCompEcs and its extension to Central Eastern European Countries. Laboratories involved were: Department of Political Economy (Siena, co-ordinator), LATAPSES (Nice), PREST (Manchester), Department of Economics (University of Madgeburg), CNR-IDSE (Milan), Instituto de Analis Economica (Valencia), and in the extension, Charles University (Pargue), IBSPAN(Warsaw), and Budapest University of Economics.

Introduction

The emergence of the European Monetary Union (EMU) certainly represents the most significant recent development in the transition towards European economic and political integration. Thus, the monetary and financial aspects of the ongoing process have come to dominate public debate for a time, its focus being distracted away from the issues of convergence in real terms and social cohesion. After a substantial chapter devoted to the monetary issues, this book concentrates on some of the real aspects of the process of continental integration. These, as the title implicitly suggests, share the complexities of other parallel processes, technically denominated 'transition'.

While after December 31 1998, the EMU being 'done', the debate has returned to convergence and cohesion, it is nevertheless appropriate to begin with some comments on monetary issues. This major change, the launching in earnest of the EMU, presently involves the establishment of irrevocably fixed parities among the currencies of the Euro-11 and the introduction of Euro-denominated financial assets. The main boost to European integration is expected to come on January 1 2002. Following this date, all transactions of the EMU countries – which, including the four countries that have not joined yet the common currency, form the widest productive area of the world – will be settled in Euro. Since the European Central Bank (ECB) has definitively established a reputation for giving priority to monetary stability, incentives for government authorities within the Euro area have radically changed. Upon experiencing an asymmetric shock, a country can no longer rely upon beggar-thy-neighbour policies. It cannot provoke an inflationary process ending in the devaluation of the currency in order to maintain competitiveness at an unchanged level of economic activity. In fact, the ECB will conduct a European monetary policy, which will intentionally oversee any differences between the business cycles of the member countries.

One such common monetary policy can then be expected to accelerate the move towards more specialization at the regional level and more uniformity in specialization at the national level. This should sensibly reduce the risk of asymmetric shocks. Therefore, the single currency is envisaged as the new institution which should accompany the emergence of economies of scale within the most dynamic industries of the EU area – thus fostering both homogenization of business cycles among the

European nations and real convergence among European regions. However, such exclusive commitment to monetary stability raises doubts concerning the capability of the ECB to cope with the need to push the continental productive system towards a higher activity level. The whole burden of sustaining employment expansion and growth in the Euro area will in fact fall upon fiscal policy. Yet, the Stability Pact and the commitment to zero public deficits within the transition period to the Euro are bound to lead to the loss of all classic 'automatic stabilizers' aimed at cushioning declines in demand. Moreover, resorting to an increase in public expenditure – as is allowed in particular cases to counteract a recession – will prove almost impossible for governments compelled to run large primary surpluses to service their public debts.

One might then ask for the rationale of a Stability Pact, which could only further depress growth rates in Europe. The official tenet stresses the moral hazard problem of a 'free-rider' country that may be tempted into excessive public borrowing which will eventually be paid for by higher interest rates in all other countries. This implication is at least questionable. In the liberalised and fully integrated international financial market a 'risk premium' would be imposed upon the assets of such 'divergent' government. Hence, the true reason behind this general ban against public deficits more likely aims at preventing national authorities from servicing their public debt by continually increasing tax revenues instead of proceeding to its rapid reduction through radical cuts in public expenditure. Drastic downsizing of public sectors is conceived as the main route to achieve considerably lower levels of taxation in Europe. This, in turn, is thought to provide the prime supply-side measure urgently needed to boost private investment and to definitely unleash the demand for labour in Eurolandia. In fact, the shrinking of the Welfare State in the EU countries – necessarily reducing the present high level of social protection – is considered as one of the reform instruments that can improve the incentive structure in the labour market.

However, the likely shortcomings of full capital mobility and, in particular, of the increasing mobility of highly educated and generally skilled workers, should not be underestimated. Fiscal competition among European countries – competing with each other through tax cuts in order to attract more corporate investment and highly productive human capital – runs the risk of producing a chronic underprovision of social insurance. Moreover, less regulation and lower levels of social expenditure may aggravate the significant inequalities in income distribution already existing as well as the abnormally high unemployment rates – thus endangering the EU long term growth rate. In the light of these considerations, the main problem faced by European governments is to find ways to reconcile the rapid strengthening of market forces triggered by globalization and privatization processes on the one side, and the efficient functioning of the public institutions aimed at guaranteeing social cohesion on the other. In order to prevent a stiffening competition from further increasing income disparities at the personal as well as at the regional levels, co-ordination among the fiscal policies of the European countries – and possibly their thorough harmonization – will have to figure high among the priorities in the agenda of the institutional arrangements to come.

It is worth noting that, at least up to now, the process of monetary integration has hardly closed the gap between the countries in the so-called Core and Peripheral Europe. In his contribution in Chapter 1, Francesco Farina questions the conventional wisdom according to which, during the EMS, the low credibility of the central banks of the Peripheral Europe countries would be explained by their time-inconsistent monetary policies. Evidence for a high real wage rigidity in Europe suggests that monetary authorities could not have relied upon a 'surprise inflation' to temporarily improve income and employment levels. Farina's alternative interpretation instead highlights the low degree of credibility of the peripheral countries' fixed exchange rates as the consequence of the Bundesbank dictating tight money creation to the whole system. Excessively high real interest rates thus determined very low growth rates. Inflation was eventually defeated at the cost of high unemployment. If the monetary stance of the ECB will pursue a 'zero inflation' target, the condition of a lower real wage rate – which in the peripheral countries is the pre-condition to improve activity levels – will not be obtainable by means of a monetary expansion. As a result, aggregate demand will continue to be depressed. Hence, convergence to the target levels of the Core Europe will obviously not be realized.

It is with the emergence of the new growth theory that the issue of convergence within and among national economies has received increased attention. Being predominantly preoccupied with the dynamics of economic aggregates, however, the fundamental structural and institutional changes which do take place over the transitional phase and are integral parts of its realization are not at the heart of such analyses. Yet, persisting institutional and economic structures obviously govern the adjustment processes and mark their unfolding and exits – affecting their speed, nature, and possibly even the very success in achieving their implicit goals, among them 'macroeconomic convergence'. This applies to processes ignited by policy reforms that are designed to achieve such a goal – as is the case with the institutional changes enacted in the course of

European political and economic integration. However, it is also equally true for the current developments in the former socialist countries, which have been initiated by exogenous, fundamental changes in their general political system. In this respect, two basic issues are at stake then. First, any policy for institutional reform is bound to alter the incentive structure in an economy. Hence, the decisions induced on the part of the economic agents may well counteract the intentions pursued when implementing a regime change. They may generate other – sometime undesirable – consequences as well. Second, it is necessary to keep track of the actual time paths of institutional and structural economic adjustments in order to understand the nature of the overall transition process.

Reflecting their applied nature, the studies collected in this volume are certainly diverse in their choices of analytical subjects. Nevertheless, on the whole they provide exemplifying approaches towards addressing these two issues associated with investigating the characteristic features of economic transition. Furthermore, all contributions are to be noted for their consistently selecting a comparative outlook. This in fact constitutes a truly unifying element beyond the fact that the particular methodologies employed – ranging from simulation and empirical work, theoretical incentive models, purely conceptual discussions to, finally, policy assessments – appear to even add more diversity. It also contrasts sharply with more conventional analyses that are based on what can be called a set of continuity-assumptions between the old and the new paths emerging through the transition process. Given the fundamental changes of policy regimes involved, only a comparative conceptual framework promises to reach (tentative) conclusions about the ultimate economic state(s) that will be attained and the manifold processes leading towards them: the 'attracting path', if there is one, of the transitional phase(s). These comparative perspective manifests in analysing theoretical steady states associated with different institutional regimes, investigating historical economic developments as reference models, or contrasting policy-contingent time-paths of adjustments.

In order to serve an exemplifying purpose, applied work must further be restricted in scope and concentrate upon a selected number of general topics. Hence, contributors to this volume were asked to supply studies that would fit under three themes: general structural adjustments following the process of European economic integration, consequences of specific legal/institutional changes, and characterization of national systems of industry and technological innovation. This thematic distinction combined with an attempt to also provide the necessary links between topics, explains the organization of contributions. Hence, following the opening discussions on monetary and financial issues, the focus shifts towards the real aspects of the European integration.

The production systems of the Euro area are under pressure to put themselves in pace with the transformations that developed in the last two decades. In fact, after the recent structural changes, such as the lean production overtaking the Fordist model and the huge technological revolution brought about by the new sectors of informatics and telecommunications, process and product innovations have emerged as key factors propelling productivity growth. How they combine with the processes of capital accumulation, and to what extent the related figures really capture the ongoing dynamics in production (and in the services sector) still constitutes an open, challenging question. Hence, Bernhard Böhm and Lionello F. Punzo provide an investigation of the dynamic changes in the industrial structure as national economies are merged to form an integrated European economy. The focus is on how reciprocal integration interacts with technological change and capital accumulation to determine the observed cross-country dynamics. A set of data on the development in the last two decades of four European countries, and in addition of Japan and the US, is analysed with a novel framework proposing a critical reconstruction that highlights fundamental changes at the levels of the dynamics of the industrial structures. The time evolution of the economies under scrutiny exhibits certain 'dynamic discontinuities' that need to be taken into account on the eve the continental unification to understand the pace and the peculiarities of the latter (for example, *vis-à-vis* other integration processes). The analytical method to tackle the issues involved, departs from neo-classical and modern growth theories as it focuses on irreversible changes that on one side affect long run sectoral performances, while on the other substantially determine the forms and possibilities of mutual economic integration.

The parallel experience in Japan and the US is used as a benchmark in the study of European industrial adjustment. The case of the US also provides an interesting benchmark to evaluate perspectives of the service industry. Compared to the recent US experience, the development of the latter has doubtlessly not yet attained similar significance in Europe. Hence, Jacques De Bandt addresses the issue of the emergence and the development of the service industry, a nearly new event in European history. In order to assess its economic potential, against opposing views from an 'industrialists' side, the author reviews a wealth of empirical material, coming to highlight the central position already occupied by and becoming increasingly central of the banking and business service activities in the European panorama.

Introducing to the analysis of specific institutional changes, Oliver Fabel and Bruno Miconi study the incentive stability of policies designed to limit the scope of government itself as the national states are replaced, respectively amended, by supra-national authorities. Going beyond popular criticism, an extensive survey of the literature aims at identifying the political and economic essence of current reform proposals in the provision of public services. This review by itself yields a clear warning against implementing only partial reforms. To strengthen the argument, a simple analytical model comparing a two-layer and a three-layer bureaucratic organization confirms that an isolated 'flattening' of the decision hierarchy – as is on the agenda of all approaches to lean government – may in fact increase the overall size of bureaucracy. The decisive incentives to downsizing in fact hinge on the degree of integration, which is achieved within the decision process. In consequence, the threat of developing 'Eurocracy' in the course of European political integration must be associated with the subsidiary principle contained in the Maastricht Treaty which precludes the full assignment of residual decision rights to the respective European authorities.

National systems of social transfer clearly also face growing competitive and harmonization pressure. Despite the ongoing controversy over implementing the Social Charta, the German government stepped foreword in 1995 and, by introducing public long term care insurance, even added an entirely new scheme to its already highly developed social security system. In doing so, it responded to demand from the growing number of elderly relying on Social Aid paying the high cost of care which – as in all other developed countries – appears to reflect inadequate private insurance coverage. Employing a comparative theoretical analysis based on the strategic bequest hypothesis, Oliver Fabel and Daniela Georgus investigate the induced behavioural changes in the parent-child relationship. As it undermines the strategic importance of bequests, public insurance is predicted to eventually crowd out private savings. At the same time, the reduced risk of exhausting private wealth is bound to increase the provision of care by children for parents with health deficits. Yet, averaging over all families including those with healthy parents the amount of attention devoted to parents will decrease. These results highlight the conceptual deficit involved when emphazising solely fiscal problems in addressing social security policy issues.

The above theme already touches upon the issue of existence, character, and adjustment capabilities of the national and local systems of innovation. In this respect, Michel Quéré provides a critical conceptual discussion of the two approaches to the role of institutions in the process of innovation enhancement and promotion of growth. Such a role is essentially seen in the establishment of incentive schemes that are able to confine co-ordination failures, if and when they occur, within an acceptable viability corridor that is still able to support long run growth.

On the other hand, Mario Maggioni investigates the impact of European economic integration on national systems designed to propel and diffuse technological progress. By means of a network approach, Germany and Italy as well as the two industrially most advanced regions of Italy – Lombardy and Piedmont – are compared. Under the assumption that technological leadership requires a high degree of systemic connection, Germany appears to be better prepared to cope with the increased competitive forces exerted by European economic integration. The German network of innovative links can be shown to be significantly more tightly knit. Furthermore, innovations primarily diffuse through the production process itself, while technological progress in Italy predominantly aims at reducing the resource cost in production. Similar reasoning leads Maggioni to conclude that Lombardy acts as the 'engine' for the Italian technological innovation, whereas Piedmont's industries are rather isolated from external innovative links.

Distinguishing efficiency gains in resource use from the effects of technological innovation constitutes the main point of interest in Jan Gadomski and Irena Woroniecka's paper on a technically defined transition path, the one associated with Poland. Their simulation analysis of the country's transition towards a market economy demonstrates the efficiency-enhancing virtue of privatisation – generating the most significant increase in labour productivity in the agricultural sector. Nevertheless, due to simultaneous technological change the Polish economy is expected to also experience a fairly dramatic structural shift towards the manufacturing sector. In consequence, employment in agriculture will further decrease, well beyond the point in time when aggregate employment begins to increase again.

The final contribution, by Ugo Pagano, fundamentally questions whether institutional rules can be actually imported via the pursuit of privatization policies. Disputing the neo-classical view that property rights govern the productive environment, the author argues that insider knowledge potentially induces high agency costs. Thus, already existing hierarchical structures in the production entities may also allocate property rights. The emergence of the postwar Japanese firms is thoroughly analysed as a support to this assertion. Emphasizing the similarities between Japan's initial situation and the current state of the former socialist countries, the convergence of institutional rules is therefore not likely to occur in the latter cases neither. However, as many Western firms today attempt to imitate the contractual environment associated with a Japanese firm, economic performance may also well be improved by developing even more national institutional diversity.

On the whole, the research effort exposited in this collection of studies can be usefully compared to the literature on growth and convergence which has dominated the discussion over the nineties. While the demise of the State-rule, along with privatization, has boosted growth in Central Eastern Europe, the slowdown in growth experienced by most Western European countries has been attributed to the negative influence exerted by income inequality. The median voter is induced to press for a high redistributive tax rate with the result of reducing incentives to private investment. The idea of a link between inequality increases and higher redistribution, which in turn would gravely hamper growth, *de facto* locates the growth enterprise led by market forces and public institutions on two opposite sides of the economic arena. The contributions in this volume depart from the traditional way of accounting for economic institutions which assumes that they are external to the market game, and of looking at the public economic institutions – such as the Welfare State – as fundamentally antithetical to the efficiency-enhancing functioning of the market competition. The unifying feature of the book lies in the attempt look at the complementary roles of public and private sectors in promoting the widening of technology and human capital as the main recipe for growth and convergence. In pointing at the strategic importance of public as well as of private institutions as providers of financial and organizational support to the stability of the market mechanism, the contributions contend that the interactions between the State and the market is far more complex than is hypothesised by mainstream economics.

Therefore, as the central message conveyed by the volume, the process of institutional reforms in Central Eastern Europe should not forget the historic lesson of the importance of social cohesion for incentive stability. On the other hand, Western European countries should sensibly orientate their institutions to balance a stronger incentive structure aimed at fostering growth with the smoothing of income and regional disparities, the fundamental condition for convergence.

List of Contributors

Bernhard Böhm is Professor for Economics and Applied Econometrics at the Institute of Econometrics, Operations Research, and Systems Theory of the University of Technology, Vienna, Austria. He directs a postgraduate programme in applied economics at the Academia Istropolitana Nova in Slovakia. He specializes in econometric model building, structural change, and environmental economics.

Jacques De Bandt is Research Director at the Centre National de la Recherche Scientifique and Professor at the University of Nice-Sophia Antipolis. He is editor of the *Revue d'Economie Industrielle*. He is a specialist in industrial economics. He has been concentrating his research progressively on informational business services, and on the knowledge economy.

Oliver Fabel until 1999 professor of management, in particular labor and industrial organization, at the Otto-von-Guericke University, Magdeburg, and since 1999 professor of management, in particular firm policy formation, at the University of Konstanz. His main research interest focused on the theory of the firm and incentives and risk shifting in organizations.

Francesco Farina has taught at the Universities of Naples, Perugia and Toronto, and is presently professor of economics at the University of Siena. He is the author of books and articles on monetary economics, social choice and economic integration.

Jan Gadomski is senior researcher in the Systems Research Institute of the Polish Academy of Sciences (SRI PAS). With SRI PAS from 1974 till now. Between 1980 and 1991 was also involved in the Center for Vocational and Social Studies of the 'Solidarity' trade union (from 1990 to 1991 its deputy director). From 1997 to 1998 worked in the Department for the Financial Policy in PKO BP bank. From 1997 lectures on introductory economics at the University of Information Technology and Management in Warsaw (linked to the SRI PAS). His main field of research is the dynamics and structural changes in economies in transition.

Daniela Georgus has since 1996 worked at the Ministry for Justice, Federal and European Affairs of the Länd of Schleswig-Holstein in the section for budget planning and control. She is also a lecturer at the 'Verwaltungs-fachhochschule' (administration academy).

Mario A. Maggioni is a lecturer in economics at the Catholic University of Milan, and was a research fellow at IDSE-CNR between 1989 and 1997. His main field of research is industrial and spatial economics. His research interests focus on the relationships between technological change and economic development at both local and national level.

The late *Bruno Miconi* was Professor of Economics at the Department of Political Economy, University of Siena, and served a number of years as department chairman and as active member of the university's board for foreign relations. A key member of the EUCompEcs network, and a visiting professor in foreign universities of two continents, he contributed to the debates on value theories, game theory and growth theory, and finally to the discussions on the restructuring of government and bureaucracies. His broad interests included the economics of arts and culture, the study of which he initiated on the Siena campus.

Ugo Pagano is Professor of Economics at the University of Siena and Recurrent Visiting Professor at the Central European University (Buda-pest). He is the author of *Work and Welfare in Economic Theory* and has recently co-edited the books *Democracy and Efficiency in the Economic Enterprise*, *The Politics and the Economics of Power* and *The Evolution of Economic Diversity*.

Lionello Franco Punzo, Professor of Economics, Department of Political Economy, University of Siena, and Director of the University Diploma in Economics of Tourism, University of Siena at Grosseto; co-ordinator of the EUCompEcs and LACompEcs HCM research networks (1996–8). Visiting professor in a number of Universities and research centres abroad. Currently involved in IDEE, a EU research project financed as part of the Targeted Socio-Economic Research within the Fourth Framework Pro-gramme for Science and Technology. His interests are in the field of the study of structural change from the point of view of industrial and production dynamics, mathematical modelling of economic dynamics, and mathematical methodology.

Michel Quéré is research fellow at CNRS-IDEFI/LATAPSES. His main field of research is economics of innovation and, more specifically, the analysis of R&D strategies of companies, inter-firm partnerships and science-industry relationships.

Irena Woroniecka is a research worker in Systems Research Institute of Polish Academy of Sciences, Ph.D. in economics (Warsaw University Faculty of Economics). Her main field of research is modelling of the national economy with particular emphasis on modelling of the Polish economy in the transition period, inflation processes and macroeconomic policies.

PART I
Money and Industry

1
The Economics of European Monetary Integration and the Convergence Problem

*Francesco Farina**

In this paper, the New Classical Economics appraisal of the low credibility faced inside the EMS by the monetary authorities of the peripheral countries has been challenged. The time-inconsistency of the monetary policy cannot be taken as an explanation of the wide differentials of interest with Germany, because from the second half of the 1980s real wage rigidity has prevented a 'surprise' inflation be considered a successful strategy by a peripheral country. In the EMU a real divergence might arise between the core and the peripheral countries. The paper maintains that if the ECB continues with the monetary stance fully oriented to price stability, an inflation rate close to zero will make more difficult the reduction of the real wage rate and the peripheral countries would be doomed to bear the burden of excessive deflation.

1.1 Introduction

From its inception in 1979 to its 1992 crisis, the EMS *de facto* evolved into an exchange rate agreement between two groups of countries. On one side, the *core* EMS are the countries grouped around Germany (the so-called DM zone including the Benelux economies and Denmark, whose financial markets were integrated with that of Germany since the inception of the EMS and whose trade with Germany already represented most of their current account), and France (although at the beginning a high–inflation economy, this country can be regarded as part of this first group from the second half of the 1980s). On the other side, the *peripheral* EMS includes Italy and the late entrants – the two large economies of Spain and Great Britain, and then Ireland, Portugal and Greece.

The functioning of the EMS from 1979 to 1992 can be divided into two phases: the first, 1979–86, can be labelled the regime of 'managed' exchange rate mechanism (ERM). During this first period, initially characterized by many realignments, nominal devaluations became progressively less frequent and smaller than compensation of the competitiveness loss due to persistent, although shrinking, inflation differentials.[1] The problem was that the opposite responses to the oil crises had created a divergence of the high-inflation peripheral EMS countries with respect to the low inflation core EMS countries. In fact, the inflation differentials with Germany were determining divergent price trends in the peripheral countries with respect to that of Germany.[2]

The second phase, 1987–92, was characterized by exchange rate stability, which can be considered the effective implementation of the fixed, although adjustable, exchange rates regime. After implementing more effective deflationary policies, the widening of interest differentials with Germany became a substitute for the progressive abolition of capital controls in allowing peripheral countries to stay inside the limits of the bands of their bilateral parities, so that no realignment took place until the September 1992 crisis. However, the tight monetary stance impinged in many peripheral countries both on the employment level and on the credibility of the exchange rate, so that the further widening of the interest differentials in 1990–92 caused the peripheral countries' currencies to be involved in movements which led to the EMS collapse.

This paper considers the question of convergence in European monetary integration process. Sections 1.2–1.4 deal with the interpretation of the lack of credibility of the fixed exchange rate regime, in relation to the sluggish nominal convergence by the peripheral countries to Germany as the best low inflation performer. It will be asserted that the need to cope with the credibility problem, in the presence of the asymmetric functioning of the EMS, led to a too restrictive monetary policy which provoked a slow growth rate and an increase in the 'natural' unemployment rate in the peripheral countries. Section 1.5 deals with the tendency towards real divergence between the core and the peripheral countries which might show up in Europe after the introduction of the single currency. If the credibility problem draws the European Central Bank (ECB) towards 'zero inflation' targeting, it is argued that the real adjustment process might be undermined and the employment hysteresis in Europe be prolonged.

1.2 Exchange rate credibility in the EMS

The division between the core and the peripheral EMS corresponds to the observation of highly correlated supply and demand shocks in each of these two groups of countries.[3] The divide can be traced back to the large differences reached at the end of the 1970s in the inflation rates in Germany and the DM zone, on the one hand, and in many peripheral countries and France, on the other. In fact, divergent responses to each of the two oil crises had been observed.

Germany reacted to the uneasiness of the inflation situation by increasing labour productivity and improving its non-price competitiveness.[4] Since the Bundesbank put money creation under strict control, its anti-inflationary reputation caused wage-setters and firms to consider credible its announcements of the German monetary growth rate. The target for monetary growth announced by the Bundesbank was always considered credible by economic agents. The reason was the high reputation reached by German monetary authorities. However, in other large European countries, such as France and Italy, firms rapidly transferred onto prices any rises in import costs and workers managed to obtain wage rate indexation.

Exchange rate devaluations following monetary expansion did not bring about benefits in terms of output and employment in the high-inflation countries of the peripheral EMS. In fact, anticipation of further monetary acceleration led to demands for higher nominal wage and prices, so that the struggle between wage-setters defending the workers' standard of life, and firms unwilling to squeeze their mark-ups ended up in a wage–price spiral. The peripheral countries' central banks pursued a strategy to react with monetary accommodation of the augmenting costs, and this led to nominal wages chasing price increases. Rising costs stemming from the stagflation process, such as higher uncertainty impinged on investment decisions, soon exceeded benefits in terms of boosted competitiveness. Since the expansionary effect of large devaluations was rapidly fading, these nominal adjustments no longer seemed an efficient tool to avoid losses in competitiveness. The central banks of most high inflation countries realized that they had to gain an anti-inflationary reputation and decided to put an end to the wage–price spiral by moving towards an anti-inflationary monetary stance.

The origin of the EMS at the end of the 1970s can be traced to the convergence of national interests based on a commitment to monetary stability as a necessary public good for Europe.

The peripheral countries shared the view that the EMS had to function as a 'disinflation engine'. The turn to tight money creation was meant to discourage firms from making price increases, to convince unions to accept income policies and de-indexation of the nominal wage rate, and to oblige governments to turn to the market for the financing of the public deficit, and eventually to start cutting the public debt. As is well known, the high-inflation and weak-currency countries used to peg their currencies to the DM, in order to align themselves to the Bundesbank's reputation for low inflation and to thus foster their monetary policy credibility. The $(n - 1)$ problem of any fixed exchange rate regime was solved by virtually assigning to the DM the role of nominal anchor of the system. Germany was allowed to set its money stock independently, so that the Bundesbank was able to dictate monetary policy for the whole system.[5]

The German interest in the asymmetric solution given to the $(n - 1)$ problem was strictly linked with German competitiveness with respect to other European countries. The Bundesbank has usually been oriented to drive the DM towards real appreciation with respect to Europe, in the fear that a growth rate of the German economy lower than that of her European competitors could negatively affect its competitiveness in manufacturing. To achieve this, monetary authorities have also traditionally tried to impede downward trends of the US dollar exchange rate with the DM, but with European competitors following the US dollar, the competitiveness of German manufacturing in European exports would have been significantly undermined.[6]

The theoretical debate around the nominal convergence process between the core and the peripheral EMS countries is rooted in the analytical framework of exchange rate credibility. In this section, this framework will be applied to the EMS in order to clarify alternative views on the factors which determined incomplete convergence and the 1992–93 collapse of the ERM.

In Figures 1.1–1.4, the trends of the short and long term interest differentials with Germany for France, Italy, Spain and the United Kingdom are plotted against their inflation differentials with Germany. In measuring the exchange rate credibility of the EMS, it is possible to overlook that part of the variation in the exchange rate of peripheral countries which applies to depreciations within the band.[7] Therefore, the interest differential can be taken as a measure of the expected change in the exchange rate. The trends in Figures 1.1–1.4 show that the correlation between the interest and the inflation differentials improved continually from the inception of the EMS, especially in the case of France, Italy and

Spain (less for the UK, since it joined the ERM only in 1990). However, the slow decline of the trends in the 1987–92 second phase of the EMS confirms that EMS credibility has also been low during the period of exchange rate stability.

Let us express, in equation (1), the difference between the peripheral country's interest rate differential with the 'leader country' $(i - i^*)$ – where i is the internal interest rate, and i^* is the 'leader' country's interest rate – and the expected depreciation of its weak currency with respect to the DM over a consistent horizon $({}_tE_{t+1} - E_t)/E_t$ as the sum of two terms: the first is the difference $[(i - i^*) - (F_t - E_t)/E_t]$, non-zero values of which indicate the existence of the 'country risk', that is the risk borne by the investor due to the presence (or to the future introduction) of currency controls. The second term is the difference $[(F_t - E_t)/E_t - ({}_tE_{t+1} - E_t)/E_t]$, which indicates the possible existence of 'currency risk', that is the compensation for holding assets denominated in the weak currency (where $(F_t - E_t)/E_t$ is the forward discount of the weak currency with respect to the DM, that is the

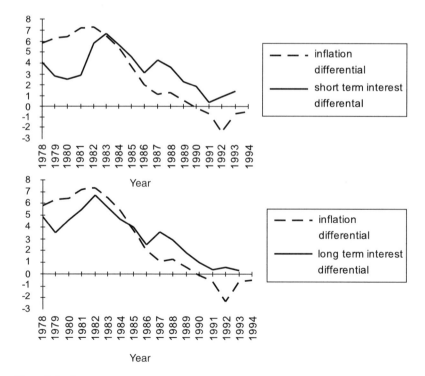

Figure 1.1 France
Source: Own elaboration on data from *European Economy*, EEC Commission.

market expectation of the future spot rate, and $({}_tE_t+1 - E_t)/E_t$ is the expected depreciation of the exchange rate).

$$(i - i^*) - ({}_tE_{t+1} - E_t)/E_t = [(i - i^*) - (F_t - E_t)/E_t] + [(F_t - E_t)/E_t \\ - ({}_tE_{t+1} - E_t)/E_t] \tag{1}$$

If the rational expectations hypothesis is assumed to hold, in equation (1) the unknown value of the expected change in the exchange rate of the weak currency (the second term on the left-hand side) can be approximated by the *ex post* depreciation of the currency with respect to the DM. In the period from the inception of the EMS and the first half of the 1980s, for many European countries the equation has shown a negative sign, as the interest differential has been lower than the expected and *ex post* (realized) depreciation. This negative value can be traced mainly to the negative values of the first term on the right side, that is the 'covered' interest differential. The fact that the forward discount of the peripheral country with respect to the DM – which roughly corresponds to the interest differential in international financial markets (offshore rates) – has been exceeding the domestic financial market's interest differential (onshore rates), can be explained by the presence of capital controls. By virtue of these 'country barriers', the peripheral country's monetary authorities have been able to bargain on realignments measures and to postpone the nominal convergence, thus permitting coexistence between small devaluations and large inflation differentials. In the first phase of the EMS, capital controls determined that the current account balance was negative (due to an inflation differential higher than the currency depreciation with respect to the DM).

By limiting the free movement of capital, controls have been shielding the internal currency from foreign capital markets by reducing the need for a huge rise of the onshore rates to defend the currency's ERM parity grid and by creating a wedge which permitted the onshore interest rates to be lower than would have been required by the devaluation expectations.[8] In the vicinity of devaluations of a weak currency provoked by speculative attacks, its offshore rates have shown a large spread relative to the onshore rates. Any time a positive forward discount of the weak currency appeared in the European financial markets, a wedge χ between the onshore and the offshore interest differentials was created internally by capital controls, as the interest rates did not react much in the domestic market:[9]

$$(i - i^*) = (F_t - E_t)/E_t - \chi \tag{2}$$

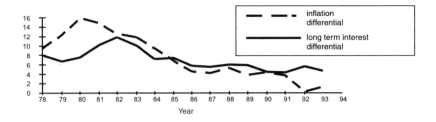

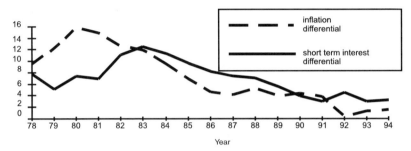

Figure 1.2 Italy
Source: Own elaboration on data from *European Economy*, EEC Commission.

Market efficiency was then advocated, for the EMS members to join the Anglo-Saxon financial markets in the complete liberalization of capital movements. The tenet was that the larger and deeper the monitoring of the macroeconomic performance of the high-inflation and weak-currency

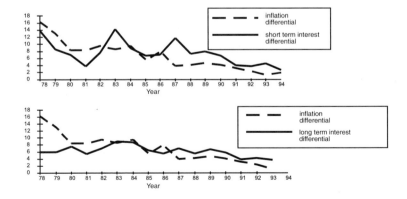

Figure 1.3 Spain
Source: Own elaboration on data from *European Economy*, EEC Commission.

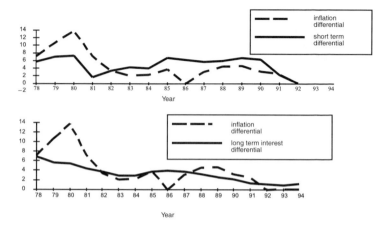

Figure 1.4   UK
Source: Own elaboration on data from *European Economy*, EEC Commission.

EMS countries performed by financial operators, the more precise is the signal transmitted by asset prices as to the credibility of the central banks' commitment to low inflation. The 'discipline effect' related to interventions in foreign exchange markets is justified by the perfect market hypothesis that financial markets know best about fundamentals. The forward discount reflected by the peripheral countries' interest differentials with Germany might be considered the rating of their nominal convergence process to the best performer for low inflation. The complete liberalization of the capital markets achieved within the first half of 1990 by most peripheral countries caused a progressive disappearance of the wedge between the interest differential and the forward discount, so that the negative value in the 'covered' interest differential (the first term on the right side of equation (1)) disappeared.

However, after the annulment of 'country risk', the problem of exchange rate credibility became apparent, since in the large peripheral countries the difference in the left side of equation (1) – between the interest differential and the expected change in the exchange rate with the DM – turned out to be positive in the 1987–92 second phase of the EMS.

Equation (3) indicates a possible error in the exchange rate forecast (a divergence between the forward exchange rate F_t and the future exchange rate E_{t+1} as the sum of the possible difference between the forward exchange rate and expected exchange rate (the first term) and of a forecast error caused by the presence of a market's erroneous expectation, that is by the absence of rational expectations in financial markets (the second term):

$$(F_t - E_{t+1})/E_t = (F_t - {}_tE_{t+1})/E_t + ({}_tE_{t+1} - E_{t+1})/E_t \qquad (3)$$

Once the rational expectations hypothesis is assumed, the second term on the right side $({}_tE_{t+1} - E_{t+1})/E_t$ is equal to zero. Due to the equality between the expected and the realized exchange rate, the first term on the right side represents the divergence of the forward exchange rate F_t with respect to the realized exchange rate E_{t+1} and corresponds to the second term of the right side of equation (1). Therefore, the difference: $(F_t - E_t)/E_t - (E_{t+1} - E_t)/E_t > 0$, explains the positive value shown by the left side of equation (1): $(i - i^*) - (E_{t+1} - F_t)/E_t > 0$.

During the late 1980s in the peripheral countries there appeared a positive difference between the interest differential with the DM and the (realized) change in the exchange rate and this can be traced back to the positive, although shrinking, difference between the forward discount and the *ex post* exchange rate in the second term of the right side of equation (1) (the 'currency risk').[10] To explain this persistent excess of the interest differential with respect to exchange rate variations, two interpretations can be considered: either a time-varying credibility of the exchange rate regime, or a risk premium,[11] that is a compensation for risky domestic assets (for instance, government debt). Since the evidence suggests that the risk premiums are negligible,[12] the excess interest differentials with respect to Germany that were observed in peripheral countries should be traced back to a degree of credibility of the exchange rates lower than a subsequent depreciation would have justified.

The reason that the interest differentials with Germany remained wider than the (realized) change in the exchange rate is that the progressive abolition of capital controls was leaving the peripheral countries with no shield against the consequences of a sluggish nominal convergence. During the 1987–92 period of exchange rate stability, the convergence of inflation rates to the German level was even slower than in the 1979–86 phase of the EMS. The result was a persistent and widening price level differential of the peripheral countries in relation to the core EMS countries. From this a trend of real appreciation, and then of current account imbalances ensued in most peripheral countries (see Tables 1.1 and 1.2), and in Italy and Spain in particular, price competitiveness was severely undermined (see Figures 1.5a and 1.5b).

However, Germany has taken advantage of the asymmetric functioning of the EMS by sustaining its exports by means of the real depreciation of the DM, and thus smoothing the price competitiveness of its manufacturing sectors (see Figure 1.5b). The real depreciation has long allowed Germany an output growth sustained by an export-led demand pull in the

12

Table 1.1 Balance of current transactions

Year	Germany	Spain	France	Italy	UK
1978	1.4	1.0	1.4	2.1	0.5
1979	−0.5	0.5	0.9	1.6	0.2
1980	−1.7	−2.4	−0.6	−2.4	1.5
1981	−0.6	−2.7	−0.8	−2.4	2.5
1982	0.8	−2.6	−2.1	−1.8	1.5
1983	0.9	−1.8	−0.8	0.2	0.8
1984	1.4	1.2	0.0	−0.8	−0.3
1985	2.4	1.4	0.1	−1.0	0.3
1986	4.3	1.6	0.5	0.4	−1.1
1987	4.1	0.1	−0.2	−0.3	−2.2
1988	4.3	−1.1	−0.3	−0.8	−4.9
1989	4.8	−3.2	−0.5	−1.5	−5.6
1990	3.5	−3.7	−1.0	−1.6	−4.9
1991	0.7	−3.6	−0.5	−2.1	−2.7
1992	1.5	−3.6	0.1	−2.4	−2.6
1993	1.9	−1.0	1.0	1.0	−2.5
1994	2.0	−1.2	1.0	1.5	−2.1

Source: *European Economy*, EEC Commission.

Table 1.2 Terms of trade of goods and services

Year	Germany	Spain	France	Italy	UK
1978	102.8	95.3	101.3	82.3	92.7
1979	99.3	97.3	99.9	81.1	94.5
1980	93.5	83.8	91.6	78.8	98.2
1981	88.5	76.3	87.7	76.3	98.8
1982	89.1	77.0	87.8	79.4	98.7
1983	90.0	74.0	88.9	80.7	98.8
1984	88.5	74.6	88.4	80.7	97.8
1985	88.6	77.9	90.7	81.7	98.8
1986	98.6	89.7	100.8	92.6	94.8
1987	102.5	91.2	100.9	95.1	95.2
1988	102.6	93.0	101.0	94.1	96.3
1989	100.2	95.0	99.3	93.9	97.8
1990	100.9	97.7	99.3	96.9	98.8
1991	100.0	100.0	100.0	100.0	100.0
1992	102.8	101.8	101.0	100.4	101.7
1993	104.7	99.9	102.0	98.1	102.0
1994	105.0	98.6	102.4	95.7	100.9

Source: *European Economy*, EEC Commission.

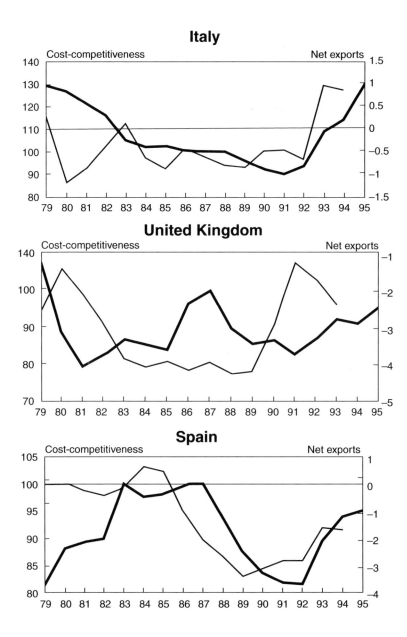

Figure 1.5a Competitiveness
Cost competitiveness[1]; Net exports[2]
[1]Inverted real effective exchange rate (ULCE).
[2]Net intra-EUR 15 exports of goods excluding energy as percentage of GDP.

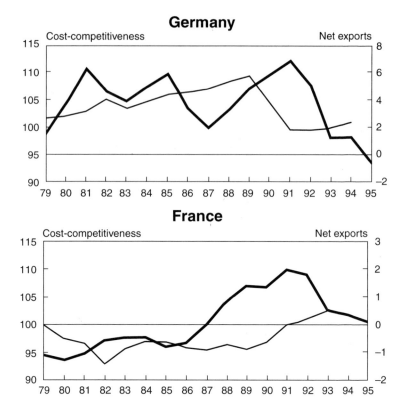

Figure 1.5b Competitiveness
Cost competitiveness[1]; Net exports[2]
[1]Inverted real effective exchange rate (ULCE).
[2]Net intra-EUR 15 exports of goods excluding energy as a percentage of GDP.
Source: *European Economy*, EEC Commission.

anti-inflationary environment created by the Bundesbank's tight money regime. During the 1987–92 period of exchange rate stability, the German real exchange rate depreciated by virtue of negative inflation differentials, which was a consequence of the current account surpluses caused by lower domestic prices in relation to the peripheral countries. In fact, a correlation between the German competitiveness index worldwide and the German competitiveness index inside the ERM switched to negative values just for the 1979–92 EMS period.[13]

Equation (4) describes a simple version of the equilibrium flow condition of the balance of payments, in a world composed of a peripheral country and Germany. The first expression is the trade account balance and the second expression is the capital account balance:

$$(e + p^* - p - e_N) + [(i - i^*) - ({}_t e_{t+1} - e_t)/e_t] = 0 \qquad (4)$$

where e is the log level of the peripheral country's exchange rate with respect to Germany, e_N is the long-term value of the real exchange rate, ${}_t e_{t+1}$ is the expected exchange rate (which forms the expected depreciation with respect to e_t), p^* and p are the log values of the German and of the peripheral country price levels, and i and i^* are the interest rate levels of the peripheral country and of Germany.

As for the first expression of this condition, the competitiveness loss determined by a widening price-level differential with Germany causes a real appreciation, so that the real exchange rate $(e + p^* - p)$ goes below its e_N value, thus expressing a current account deficit of a peripheral country. However, the second expression, the capital account balance, corresponds to the left-hand side of equation (1), which is a specification of the interest parity condition. It can then be said that the positive value of the second expression of equation (4) at the same time shows the low exchange rate credibility of the EMS and the peripheral countries' need to re-equilibrate the balance of payments by attracting capital inflows, thus offsetting the negative value of the first term of the equilibrium condition. In other words, the peripheral countries were able to cope with their current account deficits in the short term because the compensation to foreign investors in the peripheral country's financial assets was larger than the devaluation expectations would have required (under the no risk premium hypothesis).

However, the balancing of current account deficits by capital inflows was not a guarantee of long-term equilibrium in the balance of payments, as these foreign financial investments were mainly short-term positions in search of speculative profits. The low exchange rate credibility of the EMS ended in the 1992–93 ERM collapse. Figures 1.1 to 1.4 show that the 1992 crisis was clearly anticipated by trends of the interest differentials and inflation differentials, which, starting from 1990, switched to an inverse relationship in Italy and Spain (and also in the UK, for the long-term interest differential).

1.3   The 'monetary discipline view' and the nominal convergence problem

The appraisal of the nominal convergence problem in the EMS, proposed by the New Classical Economics, will be presented here as the 'monetary discipline view'. According to this view, the excess of the interest differential with Germany *vis-à-vis* the change in the exchange rate, has to be traced back to the low degree of credibility of the peripheral countries' central banks. We will now reconstruct the analytical framework by which a 'representative' peripheral country participating in the EMS can be modelled according to New Classical Economics.

The 'natural' rate of unemployment can be defined by means of the traditional expectation-augmented Phillips curve equation, containing the inflation rate π, the expected inflation rate π^e, the unemployment rate U, the 'natural' unemployment rate U_n, and the parameter α, that is the slope of the curve:

$$U = U_n - \alpha(\pi - \pi^e) \tag{5}$$

The parameter α indicates the response of unemployment to unexpected inflation. The higher α is, the flatter is the Phillips curve, so that a large increase in employment will be brought about by an inflation acceleration. This means that there is the opportunity for successful 'surprise' inflation. Figure 1.6 depicts a series of short run Phillips curves whose flat slope expresses the view that in the 1970s the peripheral countries' monetary authorities were prepared to accept a certain increase in the inflation rate in return for a significant reduction in unemployment derived from a 'surprise' inflation. Therefore, the assumption of an inflationary process boosted by a monetary over-expansion is related to the adoption by the peripheral country's central bank of the following quadratic loss function, containing a target for the unemployment rate (U^*) and a target (π^*) for the inflation rate:

$$L = [\beta(\pi - \pi^*)^2 + (U - U^*)^2] \tag{6}$$

The parameter β indicates the weight given by the authorities to the inflation objective and determines the slope of the indifference curve: a high β corresponds to a steep indifference curve. The loss function of equation (6) is plotted in Figure 1.6 as a series of indifference curves (I), reflecting the aversion of the monetary authorities to inflation and unemployment. The steeper the indifference curves are, as it is the case of I, I' and I'', the more the authorities are inclined to inflate the economy in order to reduce the unemployment level.

The 'monetary discipline view' describes the inflationary process which developed during the pre-EMS 'floating' period as a game between the central bank and the wage-setters. The sub-optimal outcome of this game consisted of a succession of monetary over-expansions leading to the

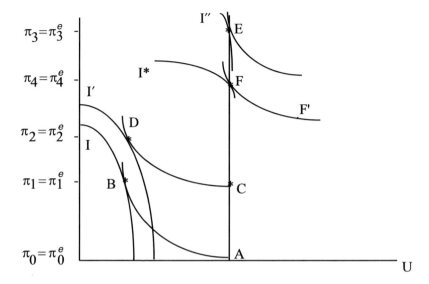

Figure 1.6

formation of an 'inflationary bias'. The following analysis applies also to the 1979–86 first phase of the EMS, indicated as the period of the 'managed' parity grid in which several realignments took place in the peripheral countries. The main difference with respect to the previous period consisted essentially in not very frequent realignments, each of which less than compensated the inflation differential of the devaluing country with respect to Germany.

The rationale of this game between the central bank and the wage-setters can be described as follows. Starting from point A in Figure 1.6, a stable equilibrium at this zero inflation point is not credible. In fact, after the wage contracts are signed at the beginning of each period, the authorities have an incentive to reduce unemployment by a 'surprise' inflation. Had a commitment to zero inflation been announced, monetary authorities would be likely to renege on it by accelerating money creation. In this case, labour demand rises and the economy moves from point A to point B, where the short-term Phillips curve becomes a tangent to the inflation-unemployment indifference curve I preferred by the authorities. The wage-setters are supposed to revise their inflation expectations from π_0^e to π_1^e and switch to a higher short-term Phillips curve. Since the short-term Phillips curve shifted from B to C, the authorities' utility decreases, owing to the return to the previous unemployment level at a higher inflation rate. If the central bank learns from the fundamentals and renounces further 'surprise' inflations, the final position of the system will be at C.

To engineer a 'surprise' inflation does not fall in the domain of rational behaviour, because in the long-term no benefits in terms of higher output and employment levels can be obtained, while a higher inflation rate decreases welfare. However, short-sighted government authorities might impose a monetary expansion on the central bank. Despite the limited duration of the expansionary effort, a further money growth acceleration could then be initiated, in order to augment short-term output and employment. Once a new 'surprise' inflation π_2 is started, a new equilibrium is reached in D, the tangency point between the new short-term Phillips curve and the higher indifference curve I', at a lower unemployment rate. After that, wage-setters will revise expectations from π_1^e to π_2^e and an upper short-term Phillips curve will be reached. While the nominal wage rate will continue to be linked to the inflation expectations π_2^e, another unannounced monetary expansion might be planned by the central bank, and so on. The inflationary process will then proceed, until the incentive to 'surprise' inflation will become zero. This happens on the vertical long-term Phillips curve at the natural rate of unemployment, in the tangency point E between the highest short-term Phillips curve and the inflation–unemployment indifference curve I*, where the inflation expectations reach the level π_3.

The theoretical underpinnings of this analysis are to be found in the well-known time-inconsistency model.[14] Since monetary authorities set their money creation after wage contracts have been signed, the possibility of unannounced monetary expansion makes the zero equilibrium inflation rate not credible, since it is time-inconsistent.

The 'monetary discipline view' applies the time-inconsistency model also to the disinflation process of a peripheral country during the 1987–92 EMS second phase. Following the announcement that monetary accommodation will be denied in case of inflationary wage contracts and budget deficits, the credibility of the peripheral country's commitment not to inflate impinges on its capability to maintain the bilateral parity with the nominal anchor provided by the 'leader' country.

By continuously monitoring the DM pegging of the weak currencies in foreign exchange markets, financial operators check the credibility of the commitment of the central banks of the peripheral country to keep trade flows and capital movements in line with the agreed parity with the nominal anchor. Indeed, the sanction of speculative attacks is considered as a credible threat on high inflation countries, capable of convincing their monetary authorities to raise the weight assigned to the inflation rate in their loss function. Symmetrically, the cost borne by a central bank goes up after any money growth acceleration, because the credibility accumulated is rapidly ruined.

If the 'discipline effect' of the anti-inflationary monetary stance were recognized by agents, inflation expectations will go down, and a peripheral country would enjoy self-reinforcing benefits, mainly with a reduced cost of disinflation in terms of output and employment losses.

The stronger commitment to inflation convergence to the 'leader' country, undertaken by most of the peripheral countries' central banks after the 'managed' EMS of 1979–86, can be modelled by the assumption that a 'conservative' Governor of Rogoff's theoretical scheme is appointed in the peripheral country's central bank. The anti-inflationary stance can be analytically expressed by adding a positive value ω to the weight β placed on the inflation aversion in the loss function:

$$L = [(\beta + \omega)(\pi - \pi^*)^2 + (U - U^*)^2] \tag{6'}$$

Monetary authorities then look for a 'new regime' by attaching a weight to the inflation aversion which is higher than one that the government of the peripheral country would have chosen according to the preference of the 'median voter'. The tightening of monetary policy signals the determination to eliminate the inflation differential with Germany. According to the 'monetary discipline view', the more that commitment is trusted, the more the degree of cohesion of the exchange rate accord is strengthened, the more the central bank will be obliged to comply with the rules. The strategy of pegging the currency of the central bank with the highest reputation for low inflation has then to be viewed as the tool used by a peripheral country to bring about a more rapid fall in inflation expectations. The hypothesis was that the higher weight given to the inflation aversion in the loss function would have ameliorated the monetary policy credibility of a peripheral country, so that complete convergence to the German low inflation level would have followed.

From 1987 till 1990 a significant reduction of the exchange rate and interest rate volatility was experienced in Italy, Spain and Great Britain, the large weak-currency countries. The 'monetary discipline view' drew the conclusion that the strategy of DM pegging had worked and a 'new EMS' was at last in place. The argument was put forward that financial markets had perceived that realignments were no longer possible because the only alternative to compliance with the EMS rules of the game was to opt out from the fixed exchange rate regime.[15]

However, the exchange rate stability which followed the strengthened commitment to anti-inflationary monetary policies was not accompanied by the annulment of the peripheral countries' inflation differentials with Germany. The incomplete convergence to Germany can be sketched in the graph of Figure 1.6. The new inflation-output trade-off preferred by the 'conservative' monetary authorities is portrayed by the new flatter indifference curve I* corresponding to the higher weight $(\beta + \omega)$ attributed to inflation aversion in the loss function of equation (6'). The failure in the attempt to reduce, once and for all, inflation expectations is expressed through a limited downward shift of the indifference curve: the location of the new indifference curve I* is just below I''. After the negligible decrease of the inflation expectations from π_3 to π_4 and of the inflation rate from point E to point F, inflation expectations are stuck. The low money creation causes a significant increase in the unemployment rate in the peripheral country along the short-term Phillips curve (point F' in Figure 1.6).

Let us try to rationalize how the 'monetary discipline view' has amended the inconsistency embedded in its theoretical framework of a steady process of nominal convergence to Germany followed by a 'representative' peripheral country. The peripheral country is assumed to determine a 'target' unemployment rate which is linked to the 'natural' rate by the weight $(1 - \delta)$, where $0 < \delta < 1$:

$$U^* = (1 - \delta)U_n \tag{7}$$

The rationale is that in the judgement of government and monetary authorities of the peripheral country the 'natural' unemployment rate is unduly high.[16] However, according to the 'monetary discipline view', excessive unemployment was determined by distortions in the labour market, such as the rigidity in the labour force utilization and the inflexibility of nominal wage rates. Therefore, a value close to one for the parameter δ means that they are confident in the capacity of 'activist' policies to boost the peripheral country towards a lower unemployment rate.

By substituting equations (5) and (7) into equation (6'), the following loss function is obtained:

$$L = (\beta + \omega)(\pi - \pi^*)^2 + [\delta U_n - \alpha(\pi - \pi^e)^2] \tag{8}$$

where, by assumption, the 'target' inflation rate π^* is equal to zero.

Since the rational expectations hypothesis is assumed to hold, authorities will minimize equation (8) subject to the constraint that agents set inflation expectations so that $\pi = \pi^e$.[17]

The minimization of the loss function yields the equilibrium inflation rate:

$$\pi = \alpha(\delta U_n)/(\beta + \omega) \tag{9}$$

Thus, the equilibrium inflation rate appears to depend on three parameters: positively on the parameter α (the higher α is, the flatter the slope of the Phillips curve, the higher the opportunity for 'surprise' inflation), and on the parameter δ (the higher the desired divergence from the 'natural' unemployment rate, the higher the equilibrium inflation), and negatively on the parameter $(\beta + \omega)$, the augmented value of the inflation aversion, which was supposed to foster the reduction of the inflation rate.

To explain why the more rigid commitment to tight monetary stances adopted by the peripheral countries failed to improve monetary policy credibility, cut down inflation expectations and trigger inflation convergence, the 'monetary discipline view' is led to adhere more closely to the New Classical model. The rationale given for the failure in achieving nominal convergence questions the 'Rogoff proposal' to appoint 'conservative' monetary authorities. The monetary authorities' commitment to disinflate, which in the loss function of equation (6'), was formalized as the passage to the higher $(\beta + \omega)$ weight attributed to inflation aversion, suffered from lack of confidence. Therefore, the time-inconsistency of monetary policy generates an 'inflation bias'. Agents are convinced that a 'natural' unemployment rate raised to an abnormally high level by labour market distortions creates an incentive for monetary authorities to target a 'too low' unemployment rate. In other words, in equation (9), whatever the values of α (the response of unemployment to unexpected inflation) and $(\beta + \omega)$ (the 'inflation aversion' parameter), the value of δ (the monetary authorities' desired divergence of the unemployment rate from its 'natural' level, according to the agents' expectations) is close to 1 and puts a 'bias' on the inflation rate.

After a decrease at the beginning of the 1987–92 period of exchange rate stability, the unemployment rate of the peripheral countries experienced a new upward trend starting from 1990. This was the opposite signal with respect to the one which was needed to switch to lower inflation expectations, as it is instead a reason for resuming monetary policy 'activism'. The higher the unemployment rate, the higher will be the value of a 'surprise' inflation. Whatever the weight placed on inflation aversion, the credibility of the commitment to curb inflation is reduced if the unemployment rate is increasing.

The turn to anti-inflationary monetary policies was then to be considered a necessary but not sufficient condition.[18] The missing condition for a rapid fall in the inflation expectations was indicated in the reputation linked to a fully credible independence of the central bank. Peripheral countries could not substitute higher values of the weights attributed to inflation aversion in the loss function for their central bank's low reputation. Neither was the DM pegging a possible substitute, because in a fixed but adjustable exchange rate regime the commitment to fixed parities is not done once and for all. The strategy to comply with a fixed exchange rate commitment, in order to import the Bundesbank's reputation for low inflation, is not likely to improve monetary policy credibility, because the inflation-unemployment trade-off in the authorities' loss function could at any time be modified and an unannounced monetary expansion be realized.

1.4 A critique of the new classical appraisal of the EMS

The main thesis of the 'monetary discipline view' is that the low exchange rate credibility of the EMS was ultimately caused by the agents' anticipation of an unemployment-motivated 'surprise' inflation planned by the central bank in a peripheral country. This tenet can be questioned from the viewpoint of a too low 'target' unemployment rate as a credible objective of a 'surprise' inflation.

In the New Classical appraisal of the EMS, a high 'natural' unemployment rate at the same time represents the outcome of labour market malfunction, that is of the downward rigid wage rate, and the cause of a high value attributed by authorities to a 'surprise' inflation. Yet, this reasoning contains a contradiction regarding the nominal wage adjustment to price increases. A necessary condition for a 'surprise' inflation to be successful in reducing unemployment is the monetary authorities' expectation of a very sluggish response of nominal wages, that is a high real wage *flexibility*. On the contrary, the assumption of a too high 'natural' unemployment rate caused by labour market distortions points to a high real wage *rigidity* (a low nominal wage rigidity, following a price increase).

The empirical evidence shows that in Europe the upward rigidity of the nominal wage is very low, thus predicting that any price increase by firms is rapidly followed by a proportionally higher nominal wage rate.[19] Hence, in the peripheral countries the short-term Phillips curve's slope should be steeper than is assumed in the 'monetary discipline view'. A much steeper Phillips curve with respect to Figure 1.6 is shown in Figure 1.7, along with the same flatter I* curve (indicating the higher weight given to inflation aversion by monetary authorities, which lowers the inflation rate from E to F). The New Classical interpretation of rigid inflation expectations, as caused by the agents' anticipation of a 'surprise' inflation, suffers from weak motivations: starting from point F in Figure 1.7, any unannounced monetary acceleration would result in much more inflation and in negligible improvements in the output and employment levels.

Therefore, the incentive to engineer a 'surprise' inflation can be assumed to be very small, as the expected reduction in the unemployment rate is limited. The alleged dependence of the European inflationary process on the monetary authorities' propensity to 'surprise' inflation appears far from real. Even conceding that the 'inflation bias' accumulated by the peripheral country in the 1970s was the outcome of a succession of 'surprise' inflationary processes, one may be very hesitant to accept the idea that, during the second half of the 1980s, monetary authorities could have planned to continuously reignite money creation in search of a reduction in the unemployment rate.

It cannot of course be excluded that a central bank might be exposed to short-sighted government behaviour with a high rate of discount for the future and be prone to undertake 'surprise' inflations despite low real wage flexibility. However, every game played by central banks and agents is a

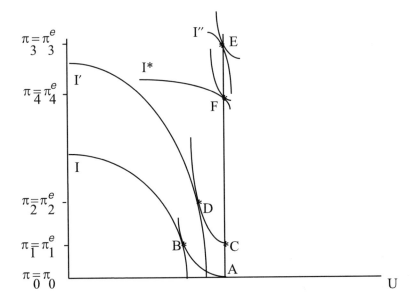

Figure 1.7

repeated game. In a peripheral country, monetary authorities might take into account the fact that agents must have learnt from the experience of previous inflationary processes and be prompted to ask for nominal wage adjustments. However strong the influence of the government, it is then difficult to believe that the explanation of an inflationary process is a game started by monetary authorities, despite the fact that from the start they know they are bound to lose due to the tendency of nominal wages, in case of an unannounced money supply acceleration, to immediately chase after any price increases.

However, empirical evidence of a rising unemployment rate in peripheral countries starting from the second half of the 1980s strengthened the presumption that the peripheral countries' monetary authorities had reason to engineer 'surprise' inflation.[20] Incomplete nominal convergence to Germany, which characterized most peripheral countries during the deflation process of the 1987–92 second phase of the EMS, has been explained with rigid inflationary expectations due to the fear that an unemployment-motivated 'surprise' inflation would have been planned by the central bank. Estimates showing the contextual rise in 1990–92 in interest differentials and unemployment rates has been presented, to sustain the hypothesis of a causal relation going from an increase in the unemployment rate to the increase in the interest differential with respect to Germany.[21]

This interpretation of the low exchange rate credibility of the EMS lacks a sound empirical basis. Econometric tests only signal evidence that a higher unemployment rate is significantly associated with high interest differentials.[22] The thesis of a causal link in 1990–91, going from higher unemployment to widening interest differentials with Germany in the peripheral countries, owing to the anticipation of a 'surprise' inflation and to the concern for a possible realignment, has been disproved.[23] The idea that the inflation bias and the low exchange rate credibility of the peripheral countries could be traced back to a low 'target' unemployment rate reveals that the New Classical approach overlooks a major feature of the EMS, that is its asymmetric functioning.

Owing to the nominal anchor role of the DM, the Bundesbank monetary policy has impinged on the output level in the peripheral countries. If one assumes that an asymmetric shock takes place, for instance, a negative monetary shock occurs in a peripheral country, given that the interest differential remains constant as it is determined by devaluation expectations, the adjustment has to be brought about by a decrease in its money stock. This is the opposite of what should be needed, as the peripheral country will then be facing a recession.[24]

Assume now that a negative demand shock hits the 'leader' country. This asymmetric shock is countered by the Bundesbank by monetary expansion, which is transmitted through an equal reduction in the interest rates of both countries, to the peripheral country's money stock, so that an inflationary process will adversely affect the peripheral country. Symmetrically, a positive demand shock hitting the 'leader' country will induce the Bundesbank to effect a monetary restriction, which in turn will eventually cause the peripheral country to bear the burden of the German disinflation, because the common rise in interest rates will bring about an unwarranted fall of output in the peripheral country.

In both cases the monetary policy reaction to the disturbance is transmitted from the Bundesbank to the central bank of the peripheral country. Therefore, in the peripheral country the output and employment levels depend on monetary policy followed in Germany. Contrary to New Classical presumption, it cannot be maintained that the peripheral countries could target the unemployment rate, as it was endogenously determined by asymmetric functioning of the EMS.

The case of a positive demand shock in the 'leader' country came about in 1990–91, with the inflationary process fuelled by German economic and monetary unification (Gemu). Had the EMS been symmetric, both the 'leader' country and peripheral countries should have coped with the tendency of the weak currencies to move towards the upper limit of their bands with the DM in the middle months of 1992, by symmetric interventions in each other's currency.[25] But the EMS did not function as a true currency area.[26] The Bundesbank did not consider the DM as the nominal anchor but as the German currency. Hence, Germany refused to take responsibility for the monetary stock of the whole system, and so caused a huge rise in interest rates which left the peripheral countries either to accept the restriction of the money stock and raise their interest rates (as in the previous example), thus further aggravating the unemployment situation, or to opt out from the ERM. Both the fundamentals and self-fulfilling speculation[27] were then responsible for the ERM 1992 crisis in 1990–92: on the one hand, the fundamentals of the peripheral countries were continuously deteriorating; on the other hand, financial markets anticipated that in the asymmetric EMS the peripheral countries would have not escaped the consequences of the Bundesbank anti-inflationary stance, and accelerated the ERM crisis.

Therefore, an alternative interpretation of the low exchange rate credibility of the EMS can be put forward. It was not because of the agents' anticipation of 'surprise' inflation that inflation expectations did not decrease in the 1987–92 years of exchange rate stability. Instead,

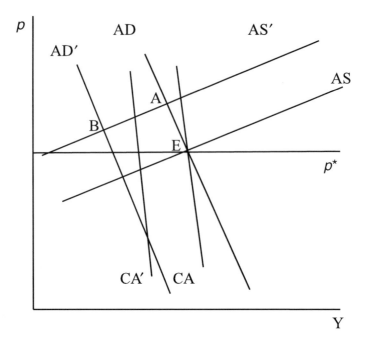

Figure 1.8

agents were aware that the asymmetric EMS functioning – mainly the Bundesbank's refusal to co-operate with the peripheral countries' central banks with regard to the adjustment problem created by the real appreciation of their currencies – was jeopardizing the creditworthiness of those countries. Since the compensation to the current account imbalances warranted by high interest rates which attracted speculative capital inflows was not a credible long run solution to the problem of the balance of payments, the credibility of the exchange rate agreement declined continuously.

In the previous sections, it has been maintained that the widening price-level differential with Germany caused by the incomplete nominal convergence process created inside the EMS a dichotomic structure between the core and the peripheral countries. Figure 1.8 represents the price-level differential with Germany as an aggregate supply shock hitting a 'representative' peripheral country: the aggregate supply curve of the peripheral country is AS', while the aggregate supply curve of the core EMS is AS.

The adjustment process, with the peripheral countries joining the core countries at point E, could have been accomplished through two mechanisms. First, a fall in the wage and price levels; second, monetary restrictions aimed mainly at reducing absorption and restoring the current account equilibrium. However, the standard mechanism of downward variation in wages and prices was not working. Evidence shows that in Europe nominal wage rates promptly react to price increases and, as stressed above, this real wage inflexibility has also impeded a 'surprise' inflation as a viable strategy for targeting a lower unemployment rate. Since the first mechanism was lacking, the burden of adjustment was essentially borne by the second mechanism, that is by the rise in interest rates.

The huge increase of interest rates in the peripheral countries can be traced back to the asymmetric functioning of the EMS. Whenever the competitiveness problem provoked devaluation expectations inside the ERM parity grid, in order to sustain their currencies peripheral countries have often been selling the DM obtained through short-term financing. The Bundesbank, however, never intervened either marginally or intramarginally in the defence of weak currencies, even in the presence of speculative attacks, and instead systematically sterilized, through open market operations, the DM inflows stemming from those interventions.[28] Since Germany did not let the domestic money stock augment, the whole burden of the adjustment in the interest rates was borne by the peripheral countries. If the EMS had been a true currency area, the widening of the interest differential would have been jointly brought about by Germany and the peripheral countries, by manoeuvring the interest rates in the opposite directions. Besides, had Germany allowed domestic demand to be augmented by an increased money stock, the German inflation rate would have risen and both the peripheral countries' price-level differentials with Germany and current account deficits would have improved. The wide interest differential with Germany can then be explained by the German tendency to force the peripheral countries to take full responsibility for the monetary restriction, and provide the full increase in the interest differential.

It is then possible to advance the hypothesis that the impact of this asymmetric EMS functioning on the aggregate demand level was at the origin of the hysteresis which characterized the peripheral countries' unemployment rate starting from the 1980s.[29] The rise in interest rates following the tight monetary policies in the peripheral countries was larger than that needed to further inflation convergence to Germany.

In Figure 1.8, at the initial equilibrium point the peripheral countries share the same price level p^* with core Europe. Let us express the deflation experienced by the peripheral countries by a shift of the aggregate demand curve to AD' (the aggregate demand curve of the core EMS remains AD). The deflationary policies determined also a fall in absorption, thus helping to counteract the current account deficits. The CA line is the trade account equilibrium condition: $p_D Y = p_A A$ (where p_D is the price of domestic good; Y is domestic output, p_A is the average price index of the domestic and imported goods, A is absorption).[30] The reduction in absorption following the deflationary process moves the peripheral countries' CA line leftwards to the position CA'. By construction, the peripheral countries' equilibrium point B, at the intersection between the AS' and the AD' curves, determines a lower output level with respect to the equilibrium point E of the core countries. Point B lies at the left of the CA' line, in order to ensure that the decrease of domestic demand exceeded the decrease in absorption, after the slow growth experienced by peripheral countries in the second half of the 1980s.

1.5   The real convergence problem in European Monetary Union

With the abandonment of exchange rate flexibility in Europe starting from 1999, the convergence question will involve more directly the real evolution of the economies participating in European Monetary Union. The view is often put forward that the European regions, as a consequence both of the Single Market and of Monetary Union, will grow more specialized in production, and their industrial activities will become more concentrated in particular areas.[31] Even if the productive structures resulting at the state level show more sectoral homogeneity among the EMU countries, the danger of an exposure of the European monetary union to asymmetric shocks would not fade. Since industrial specialization and concentration will strengthen production mainly in the countries that rely more on technological than on price competitiveness, in the core EMU countries a process of endogenous growth should be boosted by increasing returns. The productivity differential which might then open between the core and the peripheral countries can be considered as a source of real divergence among the EMU countries, similar to a negative asymmetric shock hitting the peripheral countries.

Therefore, after the nominal convergence of the peripheral to the core EMS countries has been reached and eleven of them adopt a common currency, a real convergence problem might arise inside the EMU among the same two groups of countries. If it is agreed that monetary policy has no real effect, the condition for avoiding a fall in output and employment after a negative supply shock is that the standard market reaction, consisting in full wage and price flexibility, be rapidly in motion. In order for monetary restriction to be effective in lowering inflation expectations and in convincing wage setters that no accommodation of high wage contracts will be allowed, the central bank's credibility is reputed to be the decisive factor.

However, it has been shown in Section 1.4 that the credibility problem of the peripheral countries' central banks has been overstated by the 'monetary discipline view'. While real wage rigidity did not allow any incentive for surprise inflation, excessive monetary restrictions determined very slow growth rates in the peripheral countries. The deflationary process has been larger than would have been required by their competitiveness problem and has brought about in most of them an increase in the 'natural' unemployment rate.

The New Classical approach to possible real divergence among EMU countries again points to the credibility problem. It is maintained that the ECB should establish a tight monetary policy aimed at building up its own reputation whatever the evolution of the real economies of the EMU countries might be. The priority of the credibility problem implies that a 'zero inflation' target (or, more realistically, an inflation rate ranging between 0 and 2 per cent) is acknowledged by agents as time-consistent.[32] In case of an asymmetric shock, the credibility of the European monetary authorities will be aknowledged by financial markets if stabilization policies are opposed and the market mechanism of wage and price flexibility is let alone to perform the real adjustment. However, as was the case during the EMS period, the credibility problem required a strict link to the Bundesbank (magnifying the deflationary effects of nominal convergence in the peripheral countries) in the EMU a 'Hard Euro' strategy aimed at maintaining the European inflation close to zero might have deflationary effects.

Let us describe a 'Hard Euro' strategy by means of a numerical example. Assume a world consisting only of the core and peripheral EMU countries. After an increase in labour productivity in the core countries, labour productivity growth (v) in the 'representative' core country, say Germany, rises to $v_G = 5$, while in the 'representative' peripheral country, say Italy, it is $v_I = 2$. Suppose that in a peripheral country firms and wage-setters agree on the standard adjustment via lower wages and prices, with the objective to fully compensate for the competitiveness loss caused by the productivity differential with the core countries. A price competitiveness recovery should result from prices augmented by firms at a rate lower than the inflation rate targeted by the ECB and, correspondingly, from a nominal wage which grows at a rate lower than the labour productivity growth. Let x be the competitiveness recovery with respect to Germany, which has to be equal to the current labour productivity differential: $x_I = 3$; by definition, x_G is nil. The variable τ represents the inflation deviation from the EMU level (π^*), as it will turn out to be depending on the ECB's monetary policy. In general, this inflation deviation corresponds to the competitiveness loss to be compensated: $\pi_I = \pi^* + \tau_I$. Since Germany has a competitiveness advantage, the German inflation rate π_G does not deviate from the core EMU 'target' inflation rate π^*, and the variable τ_G is nil. We can thus define x_I as the difference $\tau_G - \tau_I$: the variable τ_I will be equal to the competitiveness recovery.

In the case of the 'Hard Euro', a tight monetary stance will permit the ECB to fulfil the zero inflation target $\pi^* = 0$. Since $x_I = \tau_I = -3$, then $\pi_I = \pi^* + \tau_I = -3$. The nominal wage growth rate will now be determined by the usual equality in which the growth rate of the nominal wage (w) is the sum of the price and labour productivity growth rates. The following equations are obtained:

$$w_G = \pi_G + \upsilon_G = \pi^* + \tau_G + \upsilon_G = 5$$
$$w_I = \pi_I + \upsilon_I = \pi^* + \tau_I + \upsilon_I = -1$$

Therefore, after a negative shock a monetary policy, targeting a zero inflation rate suffers from a severe limitation: not only does the need to engineer a competitiveness recovery require a real depreciation in the peripheral country, but the adjustment consisting in a higher inflation that causes a fall in the real wage is impeded. When an asymmetric shock hits a peripheral country, such as a productivity gap which opens with respect to the core countries, real wage flexibility is severely undermined owing to the impossibility of reducing the real wage by means of an inflation rate higher than the nominal wage growth rate. A fall in absolute terms of the nominal wage rate would then be required. However, a nominal wage cut is generally resisted by workers; in this particular case, they might refuse to accept variations in the relative wages among the countries participating in the common currency and ask for a European 'centralized' wage bargaining despite productivity differentials. Contrary to the New Classical framework, labour market deregulation aimed at augmenting nominal wage flexibility might fail to bring about the wage adjustment.[33]

It can be shown that the origin of this failure in real adjustment derives from the constraint put on the monetary stance by the credibility objective. In the EMS case of nominal divergence, the credibility problem suffered by the peripheral countries' monetary authorities was tackled by a tight monetary stance. However, the asymmetric functioning of the EMS brought about an excessive rise in interest rates which provoked a low growth rate, thus pushing up the 'natural' unemployment rate in the peripheral countries. In the EMU case of possible real divergence, the credibility objective of the ECB, that is the 'Hard Euro' strategy, asks for a restrictive monetary stance. If a stubborn nominal wage rate impedes real adjustment, the employment hysteresis might continue in the peripheral country. In both cases, the monetary stance imposed as a result of the credibility problem brings about distorsionary effects in the real sector. As the EMS experience shows, to give absolute priority to the credibility objective can trigger lower aggregate demand. In case of a real divergence arising among the EMU countries, the real adjustment should be eased by supply side policies, but policies aimed at sustaining aggregate demand should also be implemented.

Given the lack of a system of fiscal federalism regulating 'interregional' transfers for stabilization and redistribution purposes and the ban imposed on active fiscal policies by the Stability Pact, the exchange rate manoeuvre is bound to play an important role in sustaining the demand level. In fact, the way in which the Euro will be managed by the ECB can make a difference to the adjustment path which a peripheral country will follow after an asymmetric shock. A 'managed' foreign exchange with the other main currencies (namely, the US dollar), aimed at fostering the flow of exports, might be effective in raising aggregate demand despite the limited openness of the 'Euro area'.[34] Monetary policy will then become more discretionary and the output variance will be reduced at the cost of a moderate inflation.

Assume that the ECB pursues this strategy of a 'Flexible Euro' and targets a positive inflation rate, say $\pi^* = 3$. As in the previous case, given that π_G is equal to π^* and thus τ_G is 0, the inflation deviation needed by the peripheral country is $\tau_I = -3$ and the inflation rate of the peripheral country should then be $\pi_I = 0$. The values for the nominal wage rates are as follows:

$$w_G = \pi_G + \upsilon_G = \pi^* + \tau_G + \upsilon_G = 9$$
$$w_I = \pi_I + \upsilon_I = \pi^* + \tau_I + \upsilon_I = 2$$

With the ECB targeting a positive but moderate inflation rate, the peripheral country will be able to pursue a recovery in competitiveness with the 'Flexible Euro' guaranteeing a higher demand level. Differently from the previous strategy, there would be no need for prices to fall in absolute terms or for a negative dynamics of the nominal wage rate. In addition, the advantages of the 'Flexible Euro' strategy go beyond the fact that variations in the inflation rate allow a reduction in the real wage without a decline in the nominal wage. In fact, it might even happen that the discretionary monetary policy which comes with the 'Flexible Euro' strategy could make more acceptable a reduction in nominal wages. Provided that a higher money creation could convince firms to revise their production plans in the expectation of a higher demand level, an increase in the demand for labour might follow. Since employment expectations are rising, 'outsiders' in the labour market might be more prepared to underbid their nominal wage claims.

1.6   Conclusion

In the New Classical appraisal of the functioning of the EMS, the low credibility of the peripheral countries' central banks, as shown by widening interest differentials with Germany during the 1987–92 second phase of the EMS, is explained by a time-inconsistent monetary policy.

In this paper, the New Classical appraisal of the credibility problem faced by the EMS has been challenged. The interpretation of the time-inconsistency of monetary policy maintained by the 'monetary discipline view' is disproved by evidence showing high real wage rigidity in Europe. This has shown that a 'surprise' inflation could not be considered a viable strategy by a peripheral country's central bank. An alternative interpretation points to the low exchange rate credibility of the peripheral countries, stemming from their persistent and widening price level differentials with respect to the core countries due to the sluggish convergence to the low inflation rate of the leader country. These differentials prompted real appreciation, competitiveness losses and current account imbalances. The peripheral countries were then forced by their low creditworthiness to open wide interest differentials with Germany in order to cope with devaluation expectations and also to offset the current account deficits by means of capital inflows. However, the asymmetric functioning of the EMS, mainly through the excessive increase in interest rates to which their central banks were obliged by the Bundesbank's monetary policy, caused the raise of the 'natural' unemployment rate in peripheral countries.

It was then observed that in the European Monetary Union a productivity differential might arise and provoke a real divergence process between core and peripheral countries. The credibility question, just as it was central to monetary policy in the EMS, might also influence monetary policy in the real convergence problem which is likely to emerge inside the EMU. Whenever a divergence of the peripheral countries in relation to the core countries is determined by a negative supply shock, although the macroeconomic equilibrium must necessarily be restored by a real adjustment, monetary policy can have a real effect and the chosen exchange rate strategy will make a difference. The rationale is the following. As the credibility objective pushes the ECB towards a 'Hard Euro' strategy, so that the monetary stance is oriented to pursue a 'zero inflation' target, a lower real wage rate – which in the peripheral countries is the precondition to improve the activity level – is no longer obtainable by means of a monetary expansion. If the nominal wage will stay rigid in Europe, renouncing real wage rate cuts through a rise in the price level will represent a dangerous setback.

Once this policy instrument is lost, whenever an EMU area is hit by a negative shock, it will be doomed to bear the burden of excessive deflation.

Instead, in order to boost aggregate demand in the EMU and foster convergence of the peripheral to the core countries, a 'Flexible Euro' strategy is recommended. Since it would come with a discretionary monetary policy, on the one hand it would help in sustaining the activity level, and on the other hand it would permit the downward flexibility of the real wage rate, which will then remain as a viable policy instrument.

References

Akerlof G., W. Dickens and G. Perry, 'The Macroeconomics of Low Inflation', *Brookings Papers on Economic Activity*, 1 (1996).

Alesina A. and V. Grilli, 'On the Feasibility of a One-Speed or Multispeed European Monetary Union', *Economics and Politics*, 5 (1993) 145–65.

Barro R. and D. Gordon, 'Rules, Discretion and Reputation in a Model of Monetary Policy', *Journal of Monetary Economics*, XII, 1 (1983) 101–21.

Bayoumi T. and B. Eichengreen, 'Shocking Aspects of European Monetary Unification', in F. Torres and F. Giavazzi (eds), *Adjustment and Growth in the European Monetary Union* (Cambridge: Cambridge University Press, 1993).

Bleaney M., 'Does Long-run Purchasing Power Parity Hold within the European Monetary System?', *Journal of Economic Studies*, IX, 3 (1992) 66–72.

CEPR, *Flexible Integration. Towards a More Effective and Democratic Europe* (London: Centre for Economic Policy Research, 1995).

Chen Z. and A. Giovannini, 'The Determinants of Realignment Expectations Under the EMS: Some Empirical Regularities', in C. Johnson and S. Collignon (eds), *The Monetary Economics of Europe. Causes of the EMS Crisis* (London: Pinter, 1994).

De Grauwe P., *The Economics of Monetary Integration* (Oxford: Oxford University Press, 1994).

De Grauwe P., 'Inflation Convergence during the Transition to EMU', in P. De Grauwe, S. Micossi, and G. Tullio (eds), *Inflation and Wage Behaviour in Europe* (Oxford: Clarendon Press, 1996a).

De Grauwe P., *International Money. Postwar Trends and Theories* (Oxford: Oxford University Press, 1996b).

De La Croix D. and M. Lubrano, 'Are Interest Rates Responsible for Unemployment in the Eighties? A Bayesian Analysis of Cointegrated Relationship with a Regime Shift', *Advances in Econometrics*, 11 (1996), JAI Press.

Dornbusch R., 'The Effectiveness of Exchange-Rate Changes', *Oxford Review of Economic Policy*, XII (1996) 27–38.

Drazen A. and P. R. Masson, 'Credibility of Policies versus Credibility of Policymakers', *Quarterly Journal of Economics*, CIX (1994) 735–54.

European Economy, *The Economic and Financial Situation in Germany*, Report n.2, (1994).

Farina F., 'From the EMS to the EMU: The Role of Policy Coordination', in M. Baldassarri and R. Mundell (eds), *Building the New Europe* (London: Macmillan, 1993).

Fitoussi J. P. and E. S. Phelps, *The Slump in Europe: Reconstructing Open Economy Theory* (Oxford: Basil Blackwell, 1988).

Frankel J., S. Phillips and M. Chinn, 'Financial and Currency Integration in the European Monetary System: the Statistical Record', in F. Torres and F. Giavazzi (eds), *Adjustment and Growth in the European Monetary Union* (Cambridge: Cambridge University Press, 1993).

Fratianni M. and J. von Hagen, *The European Monetary System and European Monetary Union* (Boulder: Westview Press, 1992).

Giavazzi F. and A. Giovannini, *Limiting Exchange Rate Flexibility: The European Monetary System* (Cambridge, MA: MIT Press, 1989).

Giavazzi F. and L. Spaventa, 'The New EMS', in P. De Grauwe and L. Papademos (eds), *The European Monetary System in the 1990's* (Brussels: Centre for European Policy Studies, 1990) ch. 4.

Krugman P., 'Target Zones and Exchange Rate Dynamics', *Quarterly Journal of Economics*, CVI (1991) 669–82.

Krugman P., 'Lessons of Massachusetts for EMU', in F. Torres and F. Giavazzi (eds), *Adjustment and Growth in the European Monetary Union* (Cambridge: Cambridge University Press, 1993).

Lockwood B., M. Miller and L. Zhang, 'Central Banks and Reputation: some Transatlantic Contrasts', in Canzonieri *et al.* (eds), *The New Transatlantic Economy* (Cambridge: Cambridge University Press, 1996).

Mastropasqua C., S. Micossi and R. Rinaldi, 'Interventions, Sterilization and Monetary Policy in European Monetary System Countries, 1979–87', in F. Giavazzi, S. Micossi and M. Miller, *The European Monetary System* (Cambridge: Cambridge University Press, 1988) ch. 10.

Mundell R. A., 'Currency Areas, Common Currencies, and EMU', *American Economic Review*, LXXXVII (1997) 214–16.

Obstfeld M., 'The Logic of Currency Crises', in B. Eichengreen, J. Frieden and J. von Hagen (eds), *Monetary and Fiscal Policy in an Integrated Europe* (New York: Springer Verlag, 1995).

Persson T. and G. Tabellini, 'Designing Institutions for Monetary Stability', *Carnegie-Rochester Conference Series on Public Policy*, XXXIX (1993) 53–84.

Rogoff K., 'The Optimal Degree of Commitment to an Intermediate Monetary Target', *Quarterly Journal of Economics*, C (1985) 1169–90.

Rose A. and L. Svensson, 'European Exchange Rate Credibility before the Fall', *European Economic Review*, XXXVIII, 6 (1994) 151–79.

Spaventa L., 'From the European Monetary System to an European Monetary Union: An Uneasy Transition', *Economie Appliquée*, XLIV (1991) 5–27.

Notes

* University of Siena, Italy.
1. For an estimate of the real appreciation experienced by the currencies of the high-inflation peripheral EMS countries, see Bleaney (1992).
2. The sustainability of the peripheral countries' diverging price trends with respect to Germany and of their negative impact on the objective of full nominal convergence has been stressed in De Grauwe (1994, pp. 154–5).
3. Cf. Bayoumi and Eichengreen (1993).
4. During the 1970s, German manufacturing productivity augmented at high rates, while high quality levels were maintained; afterwards, a declining productivity growth and rising wages have eroded cost competitiveness, so that the trade balance has become more dependent on non-price competitiveness. See European Economy, (1994 ch. 4.)
5. In the literature there is a large consensus that it was German monetary policy that influenced the money stock in the other EMS member countries. Against this view of an hegemonic position of the DM inside the ERM, see Fratianni and von Hagen (1992).
6. This strategy shows up very neatly thinking of the long run decline of the US real exchange rate. Germany struggled to avoid the inflationary effect of productivity growth rates higher than those of the US, by implementing sterilization policies leading to the DM real appreciation.
7. The expected change in the exchange rate can be split into two components: the expected rate of currency depreciation within the band (D) and the expected rate of realignment of the central parity (C), and the time-varying credibility corresponds to the second term:

$$({}_tE_{t+1} - E_t)/E_t = ({}_tD_{t+1} - D_t)/D_t + ({}_tC_{t+1} - C_t)/C_t$$

   In the measurement of exchange rate credibility, one must take into account, in addition to the expected realignment, the expected change within the band. Since the hypothesis of 'full credibility' of the Krugman Target Zone model (cf. Krugman, 1991) does not apply to the EMS, the relationship between the exchange rate and the interest differential is positive (the opposite of the Krugman model). When the exchange rate reaches the upper limit of the band, speculators are not confident that the authorities will intervene to appreciate the domestic currency, and start buying the foreign currency forecasting a depreciation, thus accelerating the realignment of the domestic currency. This may be the reason why subtracting the estimate of the expected change of the exchange rate within the band from the interest differential, in order to measure the expected realignment, gives approximately equivalent results as the simple measure of the exchange rate credibility through interest differentials (cf. Rose and Svensson, 1994).
8. Farina (1993) analyses the role played by capital controls in France and Italy.
9. Cf. Giavazzi and Giovannini (1989, ch. 7).
10. Cf. Frankel, Phillips and Chinn (1993, pp. 273–9).
11. The 'uncovered' interest rate parity can accomodate a 'currency risk premium': $i = i^* + ({}_tE_{t+1} - E_t)/E_t - \xi$, where ξ expresses the 'currency risk premium'. The expected exchange rate will then exceed the forward exchange rate by the current rate multiplied by the absolute value of the risk premium: ${}_tE_{t+1} = F_t + E_t \, \xi$.

12. Cf. Frankel, Phillips and Chinn (1993, p. 281).
13. Cf. CEPR (1995, pp. 169–71).
14. Cf. Barro and Gordon (1983).
15. 'A modification in the process by which exchange rate expectations are determined can be interpreted as a 'change of regime' (...). Once exchange rate controls have been eliminated, authorities seem to preceive that realignments have become virtually impossible.' (cf. Giavazzi and Spaventa, 1990, p. 123).
16. Many models analysing the EMS disinflation process are based on this assumption. The following example regards the 'natural' output instead of the 'natural' unemployment rate. 'This wedge between the market-generated, natural level of output (...) and the target level (...) can be justified by the existence of various distortions in the labour market, such as income taxation and labour unions. These distortions keep unemployment and output below the levels that would be achieved in an undistorted economy. Thus, the policymakers have an incentive to circumvent these distortions by generating unexpected inflation, which increases the level of economic activity' (cf. Alesina and Grilli, 1993, p. 147). See also De Grauwe (1996a, p. 198).
17. Formally, $\pi^e = E(\pi/\Omega - 1) = \pi + \phi E(\phi) = 0$, where the inflation rate is based on all information $\Omega - 1$ available in the previous period and ϕ represents white noise.
18. 'I thus conclude that an important part of the story told by the models is true: the commitment to the exchange rate mechanism did affect the objective functions of governments and central banks and hence their behaviour and their reactions. The sufficiency of that commitment for disinflation is far more elusive and dubious, as it is predicted on the immediate effects of credibility on forward looking agents stipulating their contracts in equilibrium models' (cf. Spaventa, 1991, pp. 13–14).
19. 'The NWR [nominal wage rigidity] is a good deal lower in the EU than in the US. Estimates of the parameter (...) in the EU are only about one-eighth of the US value in the short run. (...) On Rogoff's reasoning this should lead to a greater conservative bias in America – because the government there needs to offset a perceived greater temptation to spring monetary surprises' (cf. Lockwood, Miller and Zhang, 1996, pp. 252, 255).
20. 'If ... the authorities follow the "rules of the game", they will have to deflate total spending to restore external equilibrum. The increasing unemployment resulting from this policy choice, however, is perceived as suboptimal by policy-makers, who care about unemployment .... The commitment to fixed exchange rate quickly loses credibility.' (cf. De Grauwe, 1996b, p. 153).
21. This interpretation is advocated by Drazen and Masson (1994), by arguing that their tests exclude that the unemployment rate and the interest differential were jointly endogenous.
22. 'The most important finding is that expected parity changes vary over time, and appear to be significantly related to a number of variables. The variables that have consistently high explanatory power are the length of time since last realignment (measuring the reputation of the central bank) and the deviation of exchange rates from central parity.' (cf. Chen and Giovannini, 1994, p. 129).

23. De La Croix and Lubrano (1996) have demonstrated that in most European countries real interest rates and employment are cointegrated, the former causing the latter. Fitoussi and Phelps (1988), relate the slow growth of the European economies in the 1980s to a causal link going from the raising in interest rates to lower asset prices, to a decreasing aggregate demand and higher unemployment.
24. Cf. De Grauwe (1994, pp. 121–2.)
25. The question of coping with the divergence of a specific currency inside the parity grid has never been tackled, as the 'divergence indicator', aimed at selecting the currency which would have performed the adjustment after a large deviation from the central parity, has never been used.
26. Whether a zone of fixed exchange rates has to be labelled as a 'true' or a 'pseudo' currency area depends on the balance of payments determining or not monetary policy. See Mundell (1997).
27. The view based on the fundamentals can be traced back to Krugman (1991); the view related to self-fulfilling speculation has been modelled by Obstfeld (1995).
28. Cf. Mastropasqua, Micossi, and Rinaldi (1988, pp. 269–82) and De Grauwe (1994, pp. 108–11).
29. Cf. Fitoussi and Phelps (1988).
30. See De Grauwe (1994), pp. 38–9. The negative slope of the CA line depends on the fall in the domestic output which is needed for the equality to hold when p_D increases, as p_A augments less proportionately than p_D.
31. Cf. Krugman (1993, pp. 243–55).
32. Several proposals have been put forward in order to make the ECB credible and accountable. See, for instance, Persson and Tabellini (1993, pp. 56–62).
33. Akerlof, Dickens and Perry (1996) have argued that 'zero inflation', by impairing real wage flexibility, can resurrect the long-term trade-off between inflation and unemployment.
34. To give an example, for the recovery in aggregate demand which took place in Italy in the aftermath of the ERM collapse it was decisive that, along with the reinstatement of nominal wage flexibility, the nominal devaluation process brought about a huge rise in exports (cf. Dornbusch, 1996, p. 32).

2
Dynamic Structural Changes in Selected European Countries, with a Comparison with Japan and the United States

*Bernhard Böhm and Lionello F. Punzo**

We analyse a set of data on the development of three European countries, Japan, and the US over the last two decades, proposing a characterization of certain phenomena which are taken to represent structural changes. To interpret such 'dynamic discontinuities' we employ a descriptive framework derived from dynamical systems theory. Our method departs from traditional and modern growth theories as we use a more disaggregated description of the economy and focus on the interplay of distinct, typically fluctuating, paths instead of assuming the existence of long-run steady states and looking, accordingly, for them. This dynamic framework is developed in Section 2.2 against the background of established growth theory. Then, it is used in the subsequent sections for the presentation of stylized facts of the structural dynamics observed in the countries mentioned, and in its interpretation in terms of growth cycles with bifurcation events.

2.1 Introduction

It is a general perception, by now, that there are substantial economic and social differences between the countries of the European Community, which the process of continental unification does not seem able to overcome. This has prompted several researchers to look back as far as the Second World War, at the whole history of such economies, to find the roots of these seemingly diverging dynamics. Such studies have emphasized structural and/or institutional aspects as key explanatory factors. This paper focuses on the characteristics of development across countries and within countries across industries, in order to chart growth regimes and regime shifts. This exercise takes in a wealth of dynamic variety which appears to be the key issue that the programme for European cohesion will have to face.

Analysed in this paper is a set of data on the development over the last two decades of three European countries, together with Japan and the US, proposing a characterization highlighting certain phenomena which represent structural changes. The evolution of the economies under scrutiny exhibits certain 'dynamic discontinuities'. To interpret them, we employ a descriptive framework derived from the mathematical theory of dynamical systems and the related bifurcation approach. The method for attacking the issues involved departs from traditional and modern growth theories in two respects. On the one hand, a more disaggregated description of the economy is used. On the other hand, the interplay of distinct paths which are typically fluctuating is focused, instead of assuming the existence of long-run steady states which would be homogeneous throughout the whole structure of the selected economy. Such lack of dynamic homogeneity is in fact so pervasive, that it has recently surfaced even in the aggregative growth literature (for example, Bernard and Jones, 1996). The framework presented here and its results may offer an alternative viewpoint to address the issue of the convergence among the European countries (further explored in Punzo, 1997).

Methodologically, the exercise proposed hereafter (and in previous publications) can be seen as the first phase in the development of Qualitative Econometrics as suggested by Day (1993). This is a modelling approach that emphasizes the emulation of qualitative properties of given historic data sets, rather than quantitative estimation and prediction. However, the time perspective is different, the very long run of Day complementing (or contrasting with) the medium run lookout presented here.

2.2 Background

Just like in certain well-known static models, an economy is described as a set of producing sectors or industries. Its time evolution is followed by focusing on the dynamic relationship between capital accumulation, including technological change, and productivity gains. Employment dynamics, which is an ever increasingly important item in the assessment of the performance of world (and European) economies, lies behind the scenes, and thus this study gives only a partial account of the historical evidence on structural dynamics.

One way to present the *heuristic* model implicit in this approach is comparing it with available alternatives. Simply to fix ideas, one may lump the latter into two distinct traditions. In the Neo (and New) Classical theories of growth, production functions are assumed to be known, factors are measured in their physical quantities, capital (defined by a variety of measures, as fixed and human) enters as the stock(s) available at a given date. Posited production functions relate, at each point of time, output levels, to factors endowments and technology. In other words, there is an explicit relation between stocks and the flows they are assumed to generate. A dynamic equilibrium relation between investment and net savings is derived from such relationship, which then becomes the crucial condition to obtain the Solow-type of dynamics and related developments (including a variety of endogenous growth adaptations).

Instead, presented here are experiments with a framework without explicitly stated production functions. This is tried for several reasons. First, the notion of a capital stock is rather shaky on an operational basis, as it is an estimate whose value depends crucially on a number of questionable assumptions. (For a discussion, see, for example, Scott, 1989.) Second, the framework being sectorally disaggregated would require the presence of several production functions (sectorally specified), thus creating statistical and conceptual problems that practitioners of Input-Output analysis, among others, know very well. The notion of a capital stock as an argument in a production function seems to perform better, if at all, in the aggregative parable of growth as long-run dynamics than in an account of shorter term cross-sector diversified dynamics. The latter must accommodate time variability that is hardly compatible with the stability of production relations. Allowing for the possibility of 'innovations' in production seems hardly consistent with the notion of stable production functions, a static notion that can only be justified in an unchanging economic environment.

Within the tradition that is referred to here as 'alternative', there are still two possibilities available, showing that it does not span a coherent paradigm. One view sees technical progress as a fundamentally embodied phenomenon, which has been incorporated into capital stocks of the most recent vintages, and thus it maintains that investment is its (privileged) vehicle. The faster the productivity growth, the faster is the process of capital accumulation. This view claims to be dynamical because it does not posit any relationship between levels of variables (productivity and investment) but is instead formulated in terms of growth rates: at least in one version, it 'regresses' the growth rate of net output on the growth rate of investment as gross capital formation. This idea has received many formulations, one being the 'technical progress function' by Kaldor (1957), and it was cleared up analytically in Kaldor and Mirrlees (1961).

Lack of explicitly stated production functions is a feature also of the neo-Schumpeterian view, which questions the very existence (or relevance) of a functional (causal) association between investment and productivity patterns. The dynamics of productivity is explained entirely by the pace of innovations, for example new forms of organization of production and distribution and/or new products which increase the gap between material input costs and sale prices (that is, value added). Investment, hence, would not really 'explain' either the time profile of economic performance or that of technological advance. Neo-Schumpeterian models are best formulated in terms of the variables of employment and productivity measured by value added. However, full employment is neither a result nor an assumption in these models. In contrast with the growth theories of the other tradition, the possibility arises of fluctuations which would be reflected crucially by the dynamics of labour employment.

To sum up, the present analytical framework is based upon model variables (gross capital formation, value added and employment), which do appear in the literature but are treated differently. They are sectorally disaggregated and then are manipulated so as to obtain, from levels, growth rates. The parallel dynamics of industrial sectors in an economy are modelled as a set of fluctuations in growth rates. Sets of (pairs of) growth rates are used here to characterize the *structural cycles* of the European economies (and in Japan and the US) over two decades.

2.3 A dynamic framework

Implicitly, this discussion considers an economy as a multi-component, complex dynamical system. Such complexity reflects the feature of structural diversity within an economy, as well as across economies.

The selected data, as mentioned above, are time series of *value added* (*VA*), *gross physical capital formation* (*I*) – both taken at constant prices – and *employment* (*E*). In this chapter, data for three European economies (Italy, Germany, France) and for Japan and the US are considered. By dividing *VA* and *I* by *E*, time series are converted into intensive forms. In the following the growth rates of 'value added per person employed' *v* and of 'investment per person employed' *i*, as the state variables of the systems investigated are considered. Data sets are taken in a disaggregation into economic sectors, and whenever available the OECD classification of productive sectors is followed.[1] Therefore the basic statistical and conceptual unit is a productive sector.

Let v_j notate the growth rate of value added per person employed in sector j *at some date* (which is omitted for the moment), or

$$v_j = d\log(VA_j/E_j)/dt \tag{1}$$

and, likewise, let i_j notate the growth rate of gross physical capital formation per person employed in sector j

$$i_j = d\log(I_j/E_j)/dt \tag{2}$$

The economy is a set of distinct but functionally interdependent sectoral dynamical (sub-)systems whose time behaviours are represented by pairs of growth rates. They are wired together in an architecture that is, in principle, of the parallel type. A pair of values as in equations (1) and (2) for any of the component sectors will give two coordinates in a plane which will be called the *Framework Space* (*FS*) after a certain logical operation has transformed it into something richer than a geometrical device.

Such a plane is, first, endowed with two coordinate axes, called the innovation and accumulation axes, respectively, in the conventional order. The former is associated to the growth rate of the value added per person employed, which is the selected indicator for productivity growth. The other axis records the investment pace by plotting the economy's *dated* $i_{j,\tau}$ values. The abscissa axis is the 'innovation axis' as is associated with the neo-Schumpeterian interpretation of productivity dynamics. The 'accumulation axis', which monitors the process of change in investment intensity, would then be privileged by conventional (mostly aggregate) theories of growth and technological progress. In this frame-work, however, the two axes need to be plotted one against the other.

The path of a whole system or of a given sector can thus be traced as a sequence of dated states, or pairs of coordinate values geometrically shown in *FS*. States are dated according to a certain 'clock', a device to define the relevant time horizon. It is straightforward to consider the time intervals used to construct the original data set as giving the natural periodization. Accordingly, the states of a system would be recorded following a sort of natural clock which, however, does not necessarily provide a clock useful for all investigative purposes. In fact, relevant economic phenomena exhibit considerable volatility over time, which makes it hard to distinguish between systematic and erratic behaviours, especially if one takes into account that the observations are aggregates of economic agents' behaviours. For such cases, a sort of temporal aggregation can be used as a simple statistical device.

The criteria to carry this out may vary with the phenomena under investigation and one's own viewpoint. One may, thus, orientate the determination of system time intervals on for example the business cycle, measured by the time span between peak or troughs values of the GDP growth rate. Often, external or supplementary information can be used to determine a time breakdown based upon the rhythms of exogenous and/ or domestic shocks. These could be interpreted as macroeconomic clocks employed to generate a periodization uniform across sectoral dynamics. The opposite is in that a general cycle period may differ sensibly from the timing of individual sectoral cycles (which would provide specific or endogenous clocks). For certain investigations, the properties of sectoral fluctuations must be retained, and in principle they will give rise to different periodizations ('clocks').

At any rate, once the clock has been chosen, a state represents the growth path of the chosen system at a given date. In comparison to the two established (growth and neo-Schumpeterian) approaches, one of the novelties here is that a path is observed through two variables. In addition, the overall evolution of a sector is reconstructed as a set of growth paths, akin to a *segmented trend*,[2] which may (and often does) exhibit oscillations with a variety of patterns.

Obviously, this geometric representation in *FS* is based upon concepts of the mathematical theory of dynamical systems. A *given sequence of dated states* spans a *trajectory* as a single instance of the phase portrait in the sector's own phase diagram. As any of the empirically given pair of growth rates is seen to move about in the state space, sectors are similar to *generic* dynamical systems in the two-dimensional (v, i) plane. The actual history of an individual sector gives us only one time series of states (a single trajectory); this implies that it is difficult (if not impossible) to recover explicitly the *mathematical* dynamical system, or dynamic equation(s) with appropriate restrictions, which generate such trajectory. However, one such system does exist conceptually, and it might take one of two classical formulations. Setting the vector $y_j = (v_j, i_j)^T$, in continuous time formulation we get

$$\dot{y}_j = \Psi(y_j) \tag{3}$$

with $\dot{y}_{j,\tau} \equiv dy_j/dt$, at date τ, or, for the growth rate i alone,

$$\dot{i}_j = \Psi_1(i_j, v_j) \tag{4}$$

and similarly for the corresponding v variable. Otherwise, the formulation can be in discrete time with, say, a two-dimensional system of first-order difference equations:

$$y_{j,t+1} = \Phi(y_{j,t}) \tag{5}$$

It is reasonable to expect, however, that such a system be implicitly defined only locally, around an observed path (itself an oscillating sequence of shorter run growth paths).

Treating the economy as a bunch of interdependent sectoral dynamical systems, we have two equations in discrete (continuous) time for each of its n components: for example

$$y_{j,t+1} = \Phi_j(y_{1,t}, y_{2,t}, \dots, y_{n,t}) \tag{6}$$

of which equation (5) above is the special case whereby sectors are independent of each other, as a result of dynamic decoupling[3] (hence, only the sector's own state variables appear there).

It has been noticed already that the one-sector model in equations (3) or (5) faces a twofold difficulty. One is related with the mathematical formulation: by choosing discrete time dynamics as it might seem more appropriate, we are already in the realm of chaotic dynamics, given that in principle the system in equation (5) is nonlinear. The other difficulty is related with the insufficient statistics to identify the explicit form of the system (that is the pair of Ψ_1, Ψ_2, or Φ_1, Φ_2 functions). Both problems are obviously greatly amplified once a feature of reality is allowed for, that is the dynamic interdependence among sectors as posited in the system in equation (6). In fact, in either case, *n parallel but coupled* two-dimensional dynamical systems (the n sectors) are dealt with. Even if it is assumed that each of them is relatively simple, the overall or global interlocked dynamics can be anything one may imagine. An 'economy' is the *complex dynamical system* that was alluded to at the beginning of the section.

Modelling equation (6) explicitly requires a strategy that can now only be partially and intuitively articulated, and the following is rather sketchy on this and related mathematical issues. One may hope that, *for real economies*, interdependence takes up some simpler form (with asymmetries introducing hierarchical orders, hence decomposing equation (6) into smaller, or in principle computationally simpler) as subsystems of nonlinear equations. The complementary move is to introduce a set of hypotheses which would generate dynamic behaviours *compatible* with the actual dynamics of the cloud of sectors. The latter approach is based on an understanding of the implicit dynamical system in equation (6) as a *reduced form* of some, yet unspecified, structural model.

Alternatively, one can proceed heuristically as follows. If equations (3) or (4) set out the global model of a sector's behaviour, one can segment it into a set of local models that give dynamics under particular conditions, that is for certain values of the two coordinates only. The intuition is that, locally, one can represent a sector's behaviour with a description that in principle is simpler than the overall dynamic model. The local model is meant to explain the dynamics from one path to a 'nearby' path of the same family, or dynamical class. A *regime* is a set of growth paths that are generated by the same standard model with parameters, for restricted sets of values for the latter. Thus, in the *FS* six such regimes plus one special regime, the *Harrodian generalized path*, which corresponds to bifurcation values of the parameter(s), will be distinguished. All paths exhibiting the steady state-typical property of time-constant ratios of investment to value added are on a Harrodian generalized path. It plays the role here of a generalized equilibrium set, to be compared with the isolated equilibrium state postulated by standard growth theories. These include as a special case those steady state paths of constant levels of capital and production discussed in conventional growth theories, which are all mapped into the origin. The more general set where investment and value added are growing at the same rate (that is the 45° line) constitutes its natural extension: it is convenient to speak of a corridor around it, the *Harrodian corridor*, allowing for some *small* dispersion of statistical data. This again complies with the standard estimation practice for steady state, or equilibrium states in empirical applications of theoretical models of growth.

The *Harrodian corridor*, together with the other semi-axes, is now used to induce a particular partition of the coordinate plane into dynamical *regimes*. In the *innovation regime* (Regime I), corresponding to the area *below* the Harrodian corridor in the first quadrant, all paths show positive productivity growth rates exceeding positive investment growth rates. The set *above* the corridor, where productivity falls behind investment growth, is the regime that can be associated with conventional growth theories which rely upon production functions and/or referring to capital-driven growth paths (Regime VI). With the quadrants numbered clockwise, beginning with the innovation Regime – and observing that the positive and the negative quadrants are further subdivided by the *Harrodian corridor* – a classification is obtained: no. II is associated with 'restructuring phases' showing negative investment growth rates but positive productivity growth, while the remaining three are mirror images of those just described. It is only when the coordinate plane is endowed with this induced partition that it makes sense to call it *framework space*.

2.4   Country movies and stylized facts of structural dynamics

The term *economy* may refer to a local district, a group of firms or an economic and/or administrative region, or a macro-region such as north-centre Italy and the Mezzogiorno, or Bavaria, or finally some of the new regional aggregates which are being created by the process of continental integration. An economy may thus coincide with an aggregate (one-sector) system or be made up of a set of sectors, depending on the level of descriptive disaggregation selected. As employed in this paper, it identifies whole countries: Italy, France, Germany, Japan, the United States. Individual sectors that are located in a defined economy are treated as component systems, locations in different economies making them different. The ultimate, binding constraint to the detailed treatment of economies is in the available data, the way in which they are collected and the level of aggregation in which they are finally released. Ideally, systems should be as close as possible to microeconomic decision units. The foregoing results only show the promises of better but also, and more importantly, differently structured data. From a set of stylized facts one can infer the relative empirical relevance of certain theoretically defined dynamic behaviours represented in the *FS*.

Hence, there is a distinct *FS* for each identified *economy*. Visualizing its history requires the making of as many pictures ('shots') as there are 'dates' in the chosen clock, their sequence being called a movie. In each picture, the simultaneous states of several *sectors* are superimposed giving a cloud of growth paths. Looking at one sector at a time, a single picture suffices to represent its evolution and exhibits a cloud of paths followed by that sector over different dates. In this case the picture resembles closely a realization of its phase portrait.

Changes of regime imply structural changes, and therefore the dynamics of sectors and/or economies, taking them across regimes, is basically an instance of structural dynamics, represented with the level of precision allowed by a low-dimensional dynamic model. Stylized facts refer to such structural dynamics and do not retain all the details of the finer description typical of the business cycle analysis.

The movies of five countries are reproduced in the appendix. Each movie is a set of five sequential shots or pictures in the respective *FS*, plus one picture that represents the long-run average path in the two growth rates. The latter is reproduced for comparison with the viewpoint of the conventional growth approach. A single clock has been applied homogeneously across all European countries; it is derived from the timing of the business cycles in the countries' GDP growth rates (peak to peak). This unique clock cannot capture some important features of the observed fluctuations, e.g. the different phasing of Europe with respect to the US and Japan (for them a specific periodization has been used), but this is not the focus of this analysis. In any case, a date is a full cycle; hence, in each shot, the growth dynamics in terms of net rates in the two chosen variables is averaged over the set of years spanning the corresponding business cycle. Likewise, for ease of comparison, a fixed focus approach has been adopted: in other words, all graphs have the same maximum and minimum values, so that clouds of sectoral paths can be directly compared across time and/or across countries.

It can be seen that equilibrium behaviours, defined as growth paths that persist for longer than one period or 'date', and steady state paths (that is, those lying along the 45 degree line) are generally 'rare' and, moreover, even when they represent the behaviour of a sector over some date, they are soon abandoned. This is not entirely true of Japan, and for this reason it seems better to separate the comments on this country's dynamics from the others.

Over the time-span covered by our graphs, Italy and France are sharing the many difficulties of devising and shaping up their participation in the process of European unification. Japan is exiting the era of fast growth and has to cope with the problems of building up and then adjusting to a new role as an internationally integrated economy. It is interesting that countries are being taken with quite different initial conditions.

One can see that, between 1970 and the early 1990s, there is not a single sector in the three European countries selected which does not cross from path to path. In other words, traverse dynamics showing the instability of individual paths is a generic behaviour both across sectors and across countries. The actual histories of the sectors, moreover, appear to be made up of sets of traverses taking them from path to path, but also from regime to regime. For the three European countries under investigation, the 1970s and 1980s are years of high instability. Its intensity is not the same, though: Italy seems the least stable; France is somewhere in between, at the other extreme lies Germany.

A marked tendency to instability seems to be characteristic of the history of Italy in particular. Although this may also reflect some distortion in the data, it would seem to be evidence of the drive towards increasing flexibility in response to increased economic environmental uncertainty, that the Italian literature has seen in the strategies of the industrial sectors. The alternating low and high levels of investment perhaps are due to the incapability of facing structural problems (linked with technological lags, geographic dualism, and other structural problems), and the general inadequacy of the various economic policies implemented.

Italy, like France, had a fast accumulation-driven development in the 1960s and the experience of great social unrest at the end of that decade, signalling a change of the political and economic atmosphere. The 1960s were a time of rapid output expansion at low labour cost and often obsolete technologies, fuelling rapid accumulation. This path came to an end due to causes internal to the countries and to the accumulated effects of the past history, thus totally endogenously. For both countries, the sequence of labour union strikes showed the need to look for a new model of development.

Comparing France's and Italy's movies, one notices that in 1970–73, France's sectoral behaviours seem to be more dispersed, and along a different direction. Italian sectors reacted to the new relative factor prices with a comparatively higher, and sectorally more homogeneous, recourse to acceleration of innovative behaviours. If development at the very end of the 1960s has seen the restructuring of traditional sectors in the industrial core of the country, with fast productivity gains, this process seems not to have spent yet all of its impetus.

The dynamics of the French economy, on the contrary, appears to be markedly diversified across sectors, although almost all sectoral paths are in the first quadrant (with a majority of them actually in Regime VI of fast accumulation). Such behaviour can perhaps be explained (in accord with the existing literature) by recalling the devaluation of the French Franc at the end of 1969, which created sheltered conditions for French firms.

Such sheltering conditions last for a while in France, even when Italy begins to perceive the need for restructuring, as it happens already in the following period, 1973–79. For the French it is the time to invest with the favour of generous investment subsidies, in certain industries at least; Italian sectors, making a bare living under the shelter of an exchange rate policy of the French style, begin to feel the shortcomings of the excessive investment levels realized in the earlier period. This induces paths falling into Regime I and slowly trending down towards Regime II, quite a few sectors landing there fairly soon. Accommodating macro-policies have as unique effect (in both countries) to postpone or to slow down a needed re-adjustment. All in all, however, they seem to reflect a European approach to cope with the new resource prices (as opposed, for instance, to the Japanese).

Adjustment comes, for it had to come one day, in the first half of the 1980s. Both countries have to restructure; there is, however, a process of diversification in the reactions to environmental conditions between so-called traditional and modern sectors. In Italy, dramatic restructuring affects all key sectors of the economy, with dramatic labour shedding (partially absorbed by an expanding tertiary or service sector, with little investment). Here, all evidence shows that data disaggregated by firm size would be much more informative. Different strategies by big and small firms *vis-à-vis* investment and innovation lie behind the drive for sectoral specialization. The traditional sector (the stronghold of SMEs) had shown from the end of the 1960s great capacity to reorganize and to do well in an internationally very competitive market. Firms-level evidence points out that again this is the case in these years. SMEs, with their inventive rearrangements (in industrial districts, network firms, and so on) are the candidates to play the role of backbone of the Italian economy and of its rescuer of last resort. In France, the slowing down of the investment pace is somewhat more diversified across sectors.

From 1984 to 1988, in both countries there seems to be an apparent return to an accumulation-driven growth model, all sectors returning to the first. A new phase of accumulation seems to be under way. At the tail end of the time-span, the period 1988–92, both economies re-enter a phase of restructuring, possibly related to the creation of the Common European Market.

While during the 1970s Italy, on average, is going through a process of accelerating investment, with restructuring and innovation introduction where productivity gains are quickly harvested, Germany begins the decade with a process of restructuring already on the way. This continues, particularly in manufacturing, as it is triggered by labour market rigidities and income distribution dynamics, and is favouring labour share to the detriment of profits. The first oil shock was accommodated better than in the nearby countries (Japan and the United States, as well, for that matter) by refuelling the economy with the public deficit. They sustained the pace of accumulation in certain sectors, especially those more directly affected by government expenditure. It is the following oil shock (in contrast to what happens to the other European countries) that brings about a dramatic change in the dynamic scene, causing a substantial and widespread reduction in both the productivity and the accumulation paces across the sectors. While there is a beginning of the process of labour shedding, investment in physical equipment and capital formation comes almost to a halt, with some investment being diverted to R&D (at least according to external information available in the literature). This reallocation of investment outlays from the traditional capital goods to R&D expenditure and other likewise intangible assets seems to be a common trend that begins to manifest itself in all European countries, except the UK, and perhaps including Japan. It is one of the ways (perhaps a diffused one) of realizing industrial restructuring.[4] In the next period, the overall sectoral behaviour shows a resumed path of fast accumulation, with predominant dynamics in Regime VI. This lasts well into the final period of this investigation, that is from 1988 to 1992, a period in which on the contrary the other two European countries had already fallen in the incumbent crisis of the early 1990s. This can be largely attributed to the positive external shock of the German reunification, with its high investment and consumption demand.

The overall predominance of dynamics in the regime of accumulation-driven growth, which is a relative characteristic of Germany *vis-à-vis* France and Italy, emerges also from the inspection of the graphs of the USA. In other words, the pattern of structural fluctuations is more similar between Germany and the USA than between the former and the other two European countries. The United States begins the 1970s still on a sectorally widespread path of fast accumulation, and this continues almost through the end of the 1970s, although at a lower average speed and at the cost of productivity slowdown. The period across the two decades, which includes the second oil shock, sees a set of policy measures that, in relative terms, compared with other countries, managed to cushion investment and to prevent a similarly dramatic and widespread fall (although the effect was not as strong as it turned out to be in Japan). The sectoral cloud spreads out over various regimes in the next and in the final period, reflecting indirectly the sectoral reallocation of resources linked with the restructuring of traditionally important production sectors.

2.5   A telling story

From this slice of the European growth experience, one may conclude that the relative weight of innovative behaviours has been on the whole moderate, and certainly only cyclical. The search for greater flexibility, which has been said to have generated development without accumulation, does not seem to have been the driving force behind adjustments to inflation in the 1970s or to the slumps in activity levels at the beginning of the 1980s. In the European countries (if they conform to the partial picture we give here, that looks only at some of them in the core of the union), these resulted basically in changes in the pace of accumulation, hence in acceleration and deceleration of investment dynamics. The US altogether exhibits a different picture, more stable and centred on accumulation-driven behaviours.

These bold generalizations need certainly to be qualified in the case of Japan. Its history could be better narrated by what its dynamics does not show (as compared with the others), than by what it does show. Japan has a system of seasonal concerted wage (*shunto*); a tradition of structural or real policies, instead of simply fiscal or monetary, which is comparable with the experience of Italy and France; it has a tradition of bargaining economic dirigism which is also typically French; finally, like other European countries, it has a large economic presence of the state in the economy. *Vis-à-vis* all this, in its graphs there is a high proportion of sectors showing a tendency to equilibrium as a time-persistent dynamical behaviour ('each stays on its path'). Some of these sectors, among them some of the internationally competitive sectors, evolve along the Harrodian corridor (as close as they could be) for long stretches of their histories.

The three stylized macro facts that appear in the relevant literature[5] are reproduced in the sectoral behaviours in our graphs: (i) after the high growth period of the 1960s, a marked and generalized slowdown follows; (ii) there is a decreasing correlation of investment paths across sectors; (iii) there is a fall of growth rates in the 1980s, compared with the exceptional performance of the 1960s.

Immediately, this confirms the thesis according to which the country enters the 1970s already in the middle of a major structural adjustment (induced by the loss of propulsive force from the domestic market),[6] but it manages to surf fairly smoothly over the troubled years of the 1970s and 1980s. Thus, Japan's sectorally dominant behaviour lies in the first quadrant, between the innovation and the accumulation regimes, actually with a tendential predominance of the latter. There is a very limited and short-lived episode of restructuring by way of Regime II, with labour shedding (which is dominant in the European countries, instead). This is experienced only by some sectors, which, however, are neither prominent nor those in particular classified as traditional. This fact is quite interesting when compared with the experience of Italy, where traditional sectors had, and still have, to go through repeated restructuring to survive. The corresponding Japanese sectors seem to enjoy a quieter life, because Italian traditional sectors work for the international market, while in Japan they lost their international competitiveness at the beginning of the 1970s, so that they work more for the domestic market and are beneficiaries of structural policies for declining industries. However, the new role of driving forces for the country's expansion led by exports, that will be played by sectors such as general machinery, automobile and electronics, is clearly prepared by their innovative behaviours in the

1970s. The reshaping of the whole production structure of the Japanese economy taking place at that time is clear in the picture of 1969–72, just before the first oil shock.

In all countries sectors exhibit 'structural cycles' or generical fluctuations in regime behaviours; however, for a typical Japanese sector the sequence, the number of Regime switches and their timing are generally different when compared with their European counterparts. Japan's restructuring basically takes place in the 1970s (in particular, it is accomplished after the first oil shock), compared with adjustments in Europe that come later. The suggestion here is that, for domestic and policy reasons, Japan has been forced to adjust immediately to the new relative prices for raw materials. This implied, first, searching for new technologies (hence restructuring in the first Regime) and then, in the 1980s, the realization of massive substitution investment (at a lower level of macroeconomic performance). General reaction in the European countries has, at first, taken the form of an assorted variety of short-term adjustments induced by macro-policies (perhaps in the belief that the shocks, being external, were only temporary). Only the second oil shock made everybody realize that something had changed at the level of the fundamentals.

One can appreciate how the capability to respond with structural adjustments[7] was far stronger in Japan and was surely enhanced by the simultaneous implementation of direct (real or structural) policy measures. On the whole, one derives the impression of an orderly and relatively stable structure of Japan, with a development model based upon investment expansion under balanced conditions commonly shared by all sectors. For this, no unique explanation exists; a mixture of policy considerations, cultural values strongly shared by the whole country and economic factors all had a role to play.

2.6   Some tentative conclusions

To conclude this comparison of five countries,[8] the following stylized facts of structural dynamics are tentatively proposed.

(i) Innovation and capital accumulation are not alternative growth behaviours. On the contrary, they belong to alternating regimes in basically irregular sectoral fluctuations.

(ii) Structural change, defined here as a change in the growth model for a country, has been the all-pervasive phenomenon throughout the period under observation, seeing repeated regime shifts in a large proportion of sectors and of economies investigated.

(iii) Its phasing was different across countries, which can be partially attributed to political business cycles and other related phenomena (for example implementation of specific economic and industrial policies).

(iv) Thus, sectoral structural fluctuations as well seem to follow different patterns in Europe and the United States compared with Japan. This reflects weight re-allocation within the country's economy.

(v) The other side of the same coin is that steady state paths are rarely observed and generally they are short-lived. If, however, we compare the long-run representation with the average performances over the whole time-span, portraits of different countries tend to look similar and this seems to support the hypothesis of a steady state prevailing in the long run. On the other hand, this framework suggests that long-run equilibrium theories basically disregard important segments of the histories of observed economies. They rely on the optical deformation generated by comparing isolated pictures of a system taken at some time distance but leaving out the history to which they belong.

A history based upon a short(er) term perspective reveals interesting features that reflect the fluctuating nature of economic dynamics and the ever changing structures that support it.

APPENDIX

The data base

Data for Germany, France, and the United States are taken from the OECD publication, *National Accounts*, vol. II (various issues),

- value added by kind of activity (Table 12),
- gross fixed capital formation by kind of activity of owner (Table 3),
- employment by kind of activity (Table 15).
- For Germany all value added and investment data at constant prices have been converted into 1991 prices; for US they have been converted into 1985 prices, and for France into 1980 prices.

Data for Italy have been constructed from two sources. For the period from 1970 to 1980 they are from the ISTAT publication *Annuario di Contabilità Nazionale*, Tomo 2, tav 1.7 etc. and converted into constant prices for 1980. For data from 1980 to 1992 they are from the ISTAT data bank as published. Tests for the period 1980–83 for both data sets have shown that the calculated growth rates are not affected by the systemic change in Italian national accounts.

The data for Japan are from regular publications by EPA, Economic Planning Agency.

Table A2.1 Coding of sectors

Sector	OECD (Germany, France, US)	ISTAT (Italy)	EPA (Japan)
Agriculture, hunting, forestry and fishing	1	01	02
Mining and quarrying	2	–	03
Manufacturing	3		IND
Food, beverages and tobacco	31	36	04
Textiles, clothing and leather industries	32	42	TEX
Wood, and wood products, including furniture	33		
Paper, and paper products, printing and publishing	34	47	06
Chemicals and chemical petroleum, coal, rubber and plastic products	35	17	07
Non-metallic mineral products except products of petroleum and coal	36	15	09
Basic metal industries	37	13	10
Fabricated metal products, machinery and equipment	38	24.28	MACH
Metal products, except machinery and transport equipment			11
Office and data processing machines, precision and optical instruments			PREC
Electrical goods			ELTR
Transport equipment		28	AUT
Other manufacturing industries	39	50	16
Electricity, gas and water	4	06	08.18
Construction	5	53	17
Wholesale and retail trade, restaurants and hotels	6	58	19
Transport, storage and communication	7	60	22
Finance, insurance, real estate and business services	8	69	20
Community, social and personal services	9	74	21
Producers of government services	9	86	23

55

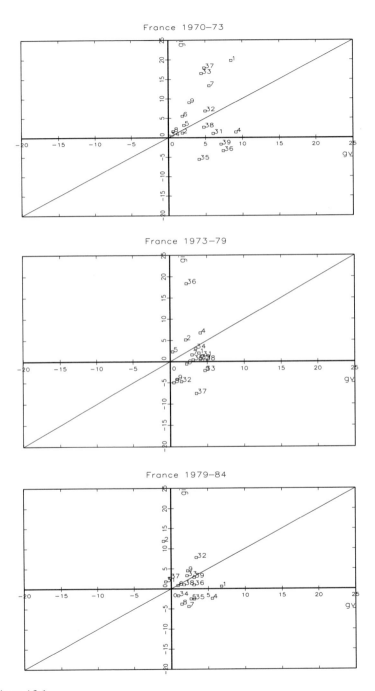

Figure A2.1

56

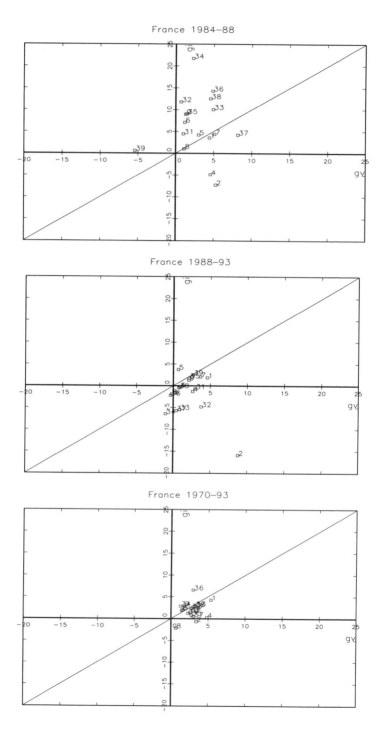

France 1984–88

France 1988–93

France 1970–93

57

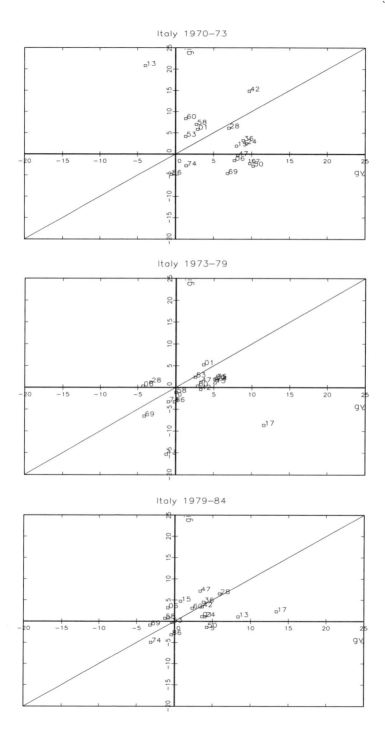

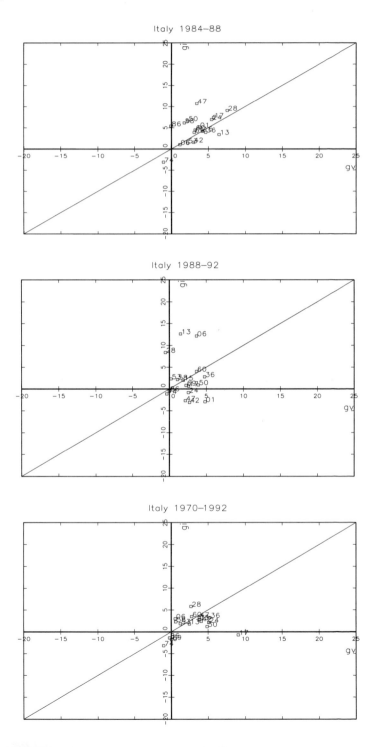

Italy 1984–88

Italy 1988–92

Italy 1970–1992

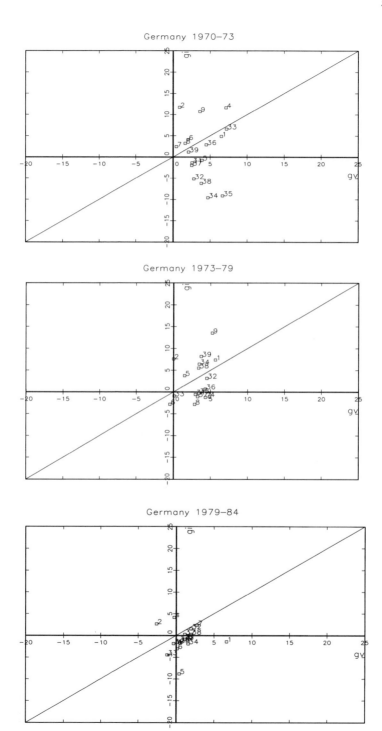

Germany 1970–73

Germany 1973–79

Germany 1979–84

60

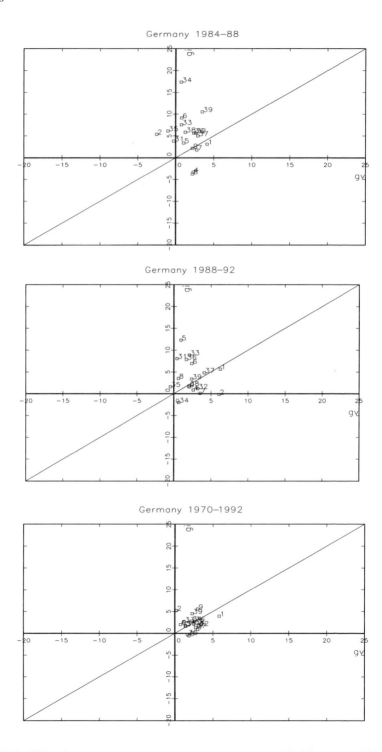

61

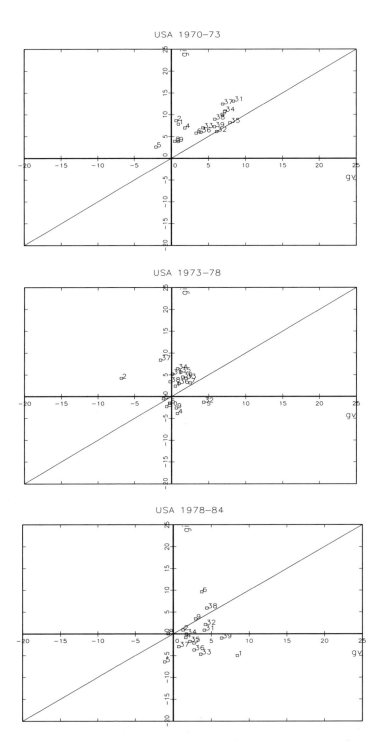

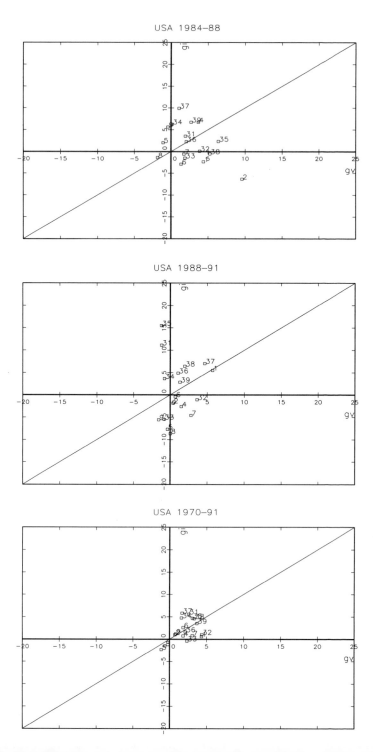

Japan 1969-72

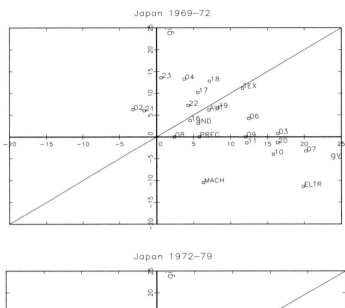

Japan 1972-79

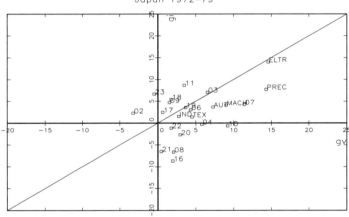

Japan 1979-85

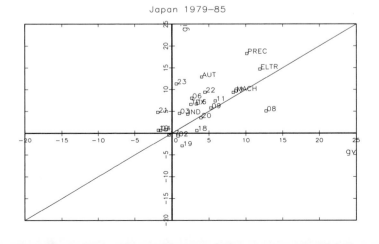

64

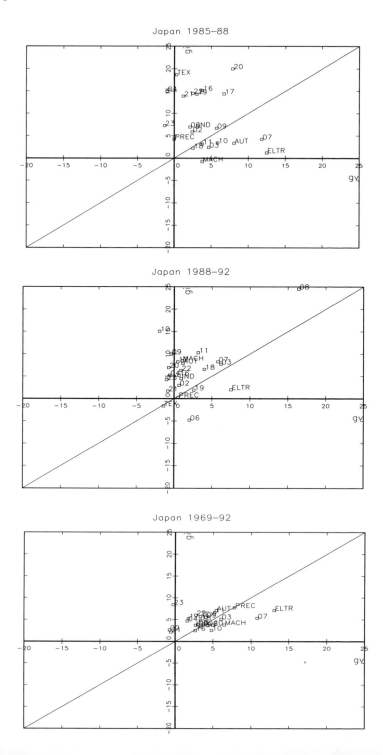

Dynamic Structural Changes 65

References

Amendola M. and J. L. Gaffard, *The Innovative Choice* (Oxford: Blackwell, 1988).

Bernard A. B. and C. I. Jones, 'Comparing Apples to Oranges: Productivity Convergence and Measurement Across Industries and Countries', *American Economic Review* (Dec. 1996).

Böhm B. and L. F. Punzo, 'Detecting Structural Change: A Scheme for the Comparison of Austria and Italy in the Seventies and Eighties', in O. Clauser, P. Kalmbach, G. Pegoretti and L. Segnana (eds), *Technological Innovation, Competitiveness, and Economic Growth* (Berlin: Duncker & Humboldt, 1992).

Böhm B. and L. F. Punzo, 'Dynamics of Industrial Sectors and Structural Change in the Austrian and Italian Economies, 1970–1989', in B. Böhm and L. F. Punzo (eds), *Economic Performance. A Look at Austria and Italy* (Heidelberg: Physica Verlag, 1994).

Böhm B. and L. F. Punzo, 'Structural Change in the Context of Uneven Regional Development. The Path of Italian Dualistic Economy Revisited with a New Dynamical Approach', paper presented at the XI International Conference on Input-Output Techniques (New Delhi, 1995).

Day R., 'Nonlinear Dynamics and Evolutionary Economics' in R. Day and P. Chen (eds), *Nonlinear Dynamics and Evolutionary Economics* (New York: Oxford University Press, 1993).

Day R., *Complex Economic Dynamics* (Cambridge, MA: MIT Press, 1994).

Durlauf S. N. and P. A. Johnson, 'Multiple Regimes and Cross-Country Growth Behaviour', *Journal of Applied Econometrics*, X (1995) 365–84.

Goodwin R. M., 'Static and Dynamic Linear General Equilibrium Models', in *Input-Output Relations* (Netherlands Economic Institute, 1953). Reprinted in R. M. Goodwin, *Essays in Linear Economic Structures* (London: Macmillan, 1983).

Goodwin R. M., *Nonlinear Economic Dynamics* (London: Macmillan, 1982).

Goodwin R. M. and L. F. Punzo, *The Dynamics of a Capitalist Economy. A Multi-Sectoral Approach* (Cambridge: Polity Press and Boulder, CO: Westview Press, 1987).

Hicks J., *Capital and Time* (Oxford: Oxford University Press, 1973).

Horiuchi T., 'Japan's Fast Investment Growth with Special Reference to Investment and Technical Development Adjustment', *Economic and Business Review* (1991).

Kaldor N., 'A Model of Economic Growth', *Economic Journal* (1957).

Kaldor N. and J. Mirrlees, 'A New Model of Economic Growth', *Review of Economic Studies* (1961).

Komiya R., M. Okuno and K. Suzumura (eds), *Industrial Policy in Japan* (Tokyo: Academic Press, 1988).

Moriguchi C., 'The Japanese Economy: the Capacity to Transform and Restructure', *Japanese Economic Studies*, XVII, n. 3 (1990).

Moriguchi C., 'Japan's Macroeconomic Policy and Japan-US Economic Relations during the Eighties', in M. Dutta (ed.), *Economics, Econometrics, and the Link: Essays in Honour of Lawrence R. Klein* (Amsterdam: Elsevier Science, 1995).

OECD, *Industrial Policies in OECD countries, Annual Review* (Paris: OECD, 1990).

Punzo L. F., 'Some Complex Dynamics for a Multisectoral Economy', in J. L. Gaffard and L. F. Punzo (eds), L'économie hors de l'equilibre, *Revue Economique* special issue, XLVI (1995) n. 6.

Punzo L. F., 'Cyclos Estructurales y Convergencia durante los procesos de integracion economica', *Revista de Economia*, Banco Central de Uruguay (1997).

Scott M. F., *A New View of Economic Growth* (Oxford: Clarendon Press, 1989).
Yoshikawa H., *Macroeconomics and the Japanese Economy* (Oxford: Clarendon Press, 1995).

Notes

*   TU Vienna, Austria and University of Siena, Italy.
1. This corresponds to the SNA system of classification (cf. Appendix).
2. This has recently become popular even in the tradition of endogenous and exogenous aggregative theories; see. e.g., Durlauf and Johnson (1995).
3. A notion introduced by R. M. Goodwin (1953) in his contribution, and later investigated in, e.g., Goodwin and Punzo (1987).
4. See OECD (1990).
5. See, e.g., the recent Yoshikawa (1995).
6. See Yoshikawa (1995). Comparing it with the European graphs above, one has, however, the impression that these countries had already entered into a new phase, even before the first oil shock. Hence, Yoshikawa's thesis is applicable to all of them, if applicable to Japan. Perhaps we should try to explain the oil shock as a reaction to the state of the Western (and Japan's) economies by the producing countries, rather than the other way round! An economic theory of the shock is more needed than the theory of adjustment to the shock!
7. As pointed out by Horiuchi (1991), Moriguchi (1990, 1995).
8. Sectoral histories have partly been mixed up with the comment of the country movies and, in this presentation, need not be repeated individually.

3
Emergence and Development of the Service Economy in the European Union

*Jacques De Bandt**

With regard to the importance of services in both GDP and employment, the European Union countries have clearly entered into the service economy. Many economists, still sticking to the 'industrial paradigm' and thus to the idea that only 'manufacturing matters', consider service growth as being very negative: their productivity surpluses are zero or small, they are inflationary, and they lead to stagnation. Before entering into this debate, it is necessary to know more about the real content of the emergent service economy. Taking into account the heterogeneity of tertiary activities, an attempt is made to clarify, on the basis of recent statistics, where growth and performances are located. This highlights the central position of banking and business service activities.

3.1 The emergence of a service economy?

In developed economies and thus in the European Union, tertiary activities have been on the increase for a very long period and now represent the largest proportion – two thirds or more – of both employment and GDP. Primary activities having come down to less than 5 per cent, further increases of tertiary activities in the recent period (since the 1980s) have taken place at the expense of secondary activities. The share of these secondary activities, including of course the manufacturing sector, is progressively decreasing, both in terms of GDP and of employment. With the important exception of Germany, whose manufacturing sector still represents a larger share of the total, the manufacturing sector is now typically of the order of 20 per cent, both in terms of employment and GDP.

This clearly seems to mean that the economies of developed countries in general, and of the European Union in particular, are 'service economies': they are not entering into the service economy, they are installed in it. When a particular category of activities represents 65 per cent, and up to 75 per cent in some countries, can one seriously doubt that we are really and deeply embedded in the service economy? But is it really so? If so, what does it mean? If not, why?

Most people – whoever they are: economists and other scientists, politicians and people of the public administration and public opinion – are not really aware either of the quantitative importance of service activities or of the fact that we are deeply engaged in something we can call a 'service economy'. True, things have been changing in this respect, very recently. But until very recently – until the opening of the Uruguay Round, organized at least partly for the negotiation of service trade issues – services did not really matter or were not seen as important.

This is obviously a question of representation: our economies do not seem to exist *per se*, but we seem to decide, collectively, on the basis of our representation, on how the world is, what it looks like or what it should look like. Since the beginning of the industrial revolution, it has been industry and, more so, manufacturing that matters. It is no longer agriculture that counts, except for the industrial parts (agricultural equipment and food industries) of the agro-system; neither is it services, which are not and cannot be rationalized or industrialized.

This kind of representation of the 'industrial economy' (of an economy which can only be 'industrial') is best illustrated by A. Smith, showing how Quesnay was wrong and (doing exactly as Quesnay had been doing for manufacturing) eliminating *ex abrupto* service activities as being non-productive. An 'industrial paradigm' has thus been developed as the basis for the whole body of economics. This all means that, both from the standpoint of theory and from the standpoint of society at large, service activities are of minor interest only.

It is shown elsewhere (De Bandt, 1998) that, as a basis for the study of service business realities, this 'industrial paradigm' can only lead to severe misunderstandings. For example, on the basis of his 'industrial representation' of the world, Baumol (1989) defines and measures activities in such a way that he can safely observe that the US economy has not entered into an information economy. But let us try to look at the facts, in order to answer our question about the 'service economy'.

3.2 The quantitative importance of tertiary activities

Of course, the answer to this question depends on the criteria used for defining a service economy. The first possibility, in line with what is said above, is to measure activities in quantitative terms.

It can be shown quite easily, for example on the basis of the World Tables, that both the service part of GDP per head and the share of services in GDP systematically increases with GNP per head. There is, on the basis of such statistics, no doubt that, according to the Fisher-Clark model, the tertiary sector is systematically growing with the level of development (as measured by GNP per head). Table 3.1 indicates the increases in the share of services in terms of total value added and in the labour force.

One interesting point is that, at the lower end the share of services is much higher in terms of value added than in terms of employment, while at the higher end, they tend to be equal (the more so if one takes account of the five year difference between the figures).

If we suppose that the figures are comparable, relative productivity levels[1] in the service sector would be as indicated in Table 3.2.

Table 3.1   Share of services in GDP and employment according to income levels

	Value added (1995):%	Labour force (1990):%
China	31	11
Low-income countries (without China)	41	16
Lower middle-income countries	49	37
Upper middle-income countries	53	52
High-income countries	66	64
United States	72	69

Table 3.2   Relative productivity levels in the service sector according to income levels

	Relative productivity levels
China	2.81[2]
Low-income countries (without China)	2.56
Lower middle-income countries	1.32
Upper middle-income countries	1.02
High-income countries	1.03
United States	1.04

Table 3.3   Shares of tertiary activities in GDP and total employment, in European Union countries

Countries	1985			1995[3]		
	V.A.[4]	Employment	Wage-earners	V.A.	Employment	Wage-earners
Austria	57.5	54.8	58.5	63.7	61.8	64.2
Belgium	62.0	68.1	67.1	65.8	71.0	70.2
Denmark	68.8	65.0	68.0	70.3	68.3	67.4
Finland	57.5	56.2	60.5	62.8	63.9	67.4
France	60.9	62.0	65.3	67.4	70.3	72.4
Germany	57.4	58.6	56.3	62.2	61.6	61.4
West Germany	55.0	54.7	55.2	62.2	61.6	61.6
Greece	53.5	43.7	58.0	62.0	56.4	68.5
Ireland	56.1	56.4	62.2	56.0	60.2	65.8
Italy	58.9	58.0	58.5	64.3	63.4	63.7
Luxembourg	76.6	62.4	63.1	76.4	70.1	70.7
Netherlands	58.5	72.7	68.7	65.0	71.1	66.7
Portugal	(57.2)	(42.7)	(51.9)	63.4	53.3	57.3
Spain	60.8	53.2	56.1	64.4	61.8	62.7
Sweden	57.5	66.5	68.3	62.6	69.8	71.2
UK	61.2	n. a.	67.5	71.1	71.0	67.5

As indicated above, in the European Union, service activities are indeed dominant in quantitative terms, at least for some criteria: production, value added, employment, and – even if this is not true for some other criteria – energy consumption, investment and international trade.

The latest OECD figures (OECD, 1998) are for the countries of the European Union, in terms of percentages of GDP and of total employment as in Table 3.3.

What conclusions can be drawn from this table? First, in the past ten years, shares of GDP have increased in all but two countries (Ireland and Luxembourg) in which these shares have remained constant. Shares have increased by some 5–7 per cent in most cases, going up from figures in the order of 55–65 per cent to figures in the order of 60–70 per cent, over the period.

Second, if one eliminates the two extreme cases (the same as above), all shares are typically, in 1995, between 62 and 71 per cent. By and large, two-thirds of the GDP are produced in tertiary activities.

Third, shares of total employment have increased equally systematically (except for the Netherlands), but somewhat less: they have generally increased by some 3 percentage points, going up typically from figures of the order of 53–68 per cent to figures in the order of 56–71 per cent.

Fourth, on the whole, tertiary activities tend to weigh somewhat more in terms of GDP than in terms of employment. But, according to the different countries, tertiary activities weigh somewhat more either in terms of GDP (Austria, Denmark, Germany, Greece, Italy, Luxembourg, Portugal, Spain) or in terms of employment (Belgium, Finland, France, Ireland, Netherlands, Sweden). True, at this global (heterogeneous) level, differences are small and not necessarily meaningful.

Finally, in most cases, the percentages are quite similar in terms of both total employment and wage earners, even while the percentages tend to be somewhat higher in terms of wage earners. But here again, it is necessary to refer to the very heterogeneous character of tertiary activities (mixing, for example, small retail stores and large administrations).

3.3   The impact of prices

Of course some people feel that these figures, which are current price figures and thus by definition include actual relative prices, give a wrong picture of the relative importance of services. Because prices are supposed to be necessarily higher in the case of services than in the case of goods, wages being higher the higher the levels of development and income are.

Summers (1985) has tried to show that, by eliminating the price differences using PPP rates, the relation between the share of services in GDP and GNP per head disappears. His calculation in respect of the changes (for 1975) with regard to shares of services in GDP, in European Union member countries are set out in Table 3.4.

Table 3.4   Relative shares of GDP with regard to nominal and PPP exchange rates

Countries	Real GDP per head US = 100[5]	Share of GDP	'Real' share of GDP
Ireland	42.5	41.2	40.6
Italy	53.8	38.2	36.9
Spain	55.9	30.6	31.4
UK	63.9	47.8	46.6
Austria	69.6	34.2	32.2
Netherlands	75.2	39.9	29.9
Belgium	81.9	39.2	31.3
Luxembourg	82.0	37.6	33.2
Denmark	82.4	45.1	39.7
Germany	83.0	39.8	32.3

These figures show important changes, the changes being – generally – the more important the higher the level of income of the countries concerned.

I have criticized these figures elsewhere (De Bandt, 1989, 1996). They are, from my standpoint, completely false, being based, for the sake of calculations, on unacceptable hypotheses (homogeneity of products, absence of any productivity difference in a number of sectors in which outputs are approximated by inputs). Moreover, they raise serious questions about the validity of the PPP exchange rates emerging from such calculations.[6]

Of course, if one compares – over time or between countries – shares of GDP of tertiary activities in constant prices, things are quite different. Compared with the figures given in Table 3.3, the shares of tertiary activities as indicated in Table 3.5, have increased less and are thus lower in 1995.

In all but one country (Portugal), shares are significantly lower in constant prices. It can of course easily be seen that the differences tend to be the smaller the nearer the base year. In one extreme example, that of the Netherlands, in which case the constant prices are those of the preceding year, there is of course no difference. The opposite case, that of

Table 3.5   Shares of tertiary activities in both current and constant prices,[7] in 1995[8]

Countries	Value added (current prices)	Value added (constant prices)	Difference
Austria (1983)	63.7	60.4	–3.3
Belgium (1990)	65.8	64.8	–1.0
Denmark (1980)	70.3	67.1	–3.2
Finland (1990)	62.8	59.5	–3.3
France (1980)	67.4	61.7	–5.7
Germany (1991)	62.2	61.2	–1.0
West Germany (1991)	62.0	61.6	–0.4
Greece (1970)	62.0	60.6	–1.4
Ireland (1990)	56.0	53.3	–2.7
Italy (1990)	64.3	63.0	–1.3
Luxembourg	76.4	n. a.	
Netherlands	65.0	64.8	–0.2
Portugal (1990)	63.4	65.3	1.9
Spain (1991)	64.4	60.6	–3.8
Sweden (1991)	62.6	60.4	–2.2
UK (1990)	71.1	n. a.	

France, is one in which both the base year is remote (1980) and the difference in the calculated shares is very large.

But how does one decide which base year is correct, on the basis of which the weighting system is adopted with reference to observed relative prices?

Of course, one could also raise the question of why price differences should be eliminated at all. There are many different aspects here, which have to be examined separately.

The first aspect has to do with the whole 'cost disease' or inflationary aspects of services. If productivity growth in services is zero or low, which is supposed to be the case, wages in service activities can follow the overall evolution of wages only by increasing relative prices. They are seen as being typically the types of activities which have lower than average productivity surpluses, but are compensating by increasing their relative prices (by taking away all or part of the surpluses of the client sectors). It can even be shown that in some of these activities, prices are increasing more than proportionately compared to the inferiority of their productivity growth. Of course, in order to show this, we have to accept the way products and productivities are usually measured in the services sector (see below). Those activities are thus seen as being *per se* inflationary, reducing the potentials for accumulation processes in other activities.

Hence the theory that price evolutions or differences are unjustified rents and have thus to be eliminated from any serious evaluation of the products of such activities. But, apart from the fact that prices can be different for many reasons, while many services belong to the non-tradables (even if this category is progressively dwindling), it is the client/consumer who decides what it is worth paying with regard to his needs and utility, and payments received are real income like all others.

3.4 Measurement problems

The second, complementary, aspect has to do with measurement problems. In the case of the PPP figures above, the hypothesis was that products are homogeneous all over the place. This means, *de facto*, that to the extent that qualitative differences have an impact on prices, quality differences are seen only as price differences and are washed away by the elimination of price differences.

It is known, of course, that service or at least non-material or informational service activities are, in their essence, purely qualitative. But what if the measurement device is eliminating the qualitative dimension?

There is a very general problem with output statistics in non-material service activities. This problem is usually recognized in the United States,[9] but not so in Europe, where price and output statistics are mostly said to be correct, or nearly so. Yet this is not the case, for very understandable reasons.

The consensus of statisticians, as reflected in the OECD manual, is of course that, in order to measure output in constant prices, one should use double deflation; however, because double deflation is impossible owing to the absence of reliable price indexes, approximations have to be used, which are referring one way or another to inputs and their prices. But measuring output somehow on the basis of inputs is indeed nonsense. By definition these reflect inputs, and thus activities or efforts or whatever, but not output. The simple reason is that for many services there is no technical unit of the product and thus no unit price. There is thus no possibility of having reliable price indexes.

Without going further into these problems related to the measurement of output of service activities and particularly of informational or non-material service activities, I want to stress three rather general conclusions. First, there is no solution to these measurement problems: as long as economists, on the basis of their representation of the world, corresponding to the 'industrial paradigm', pretend to handle informational or non-material service activities as if these were comparable with or similar to industrial or material activities, they are doomed to come up with conclusions which only reflect their representation of what they consider to be productive activities. Productivity growth in informational service activities is low because productivity is defined and measured in such a way as to come up with such a conclusion.

Second, to the extent that the way we measure products over time is eliminating the qualitative components of the evolution of the product, this component is divided between the price and the quantity components: it is divided, not only arbitrarily or randomly, but, owing to the way output is approximated with reference to inputs, systematically to the prejudice of the output component and to the benefit of the price component.This is at least one possible explanation of the so-called inflationary character of services.

Third, as long as we are not able to measure output in constant prices appropriately, there are no obvious acceptable reasons for using arbitrary figures, as most people do, and we should stick to current prices. There is one decisive argument for using current prices: the fact that the client/consumer accepts to pay those prices, without any other reference than user value and utility.

3.5 Looking within the heterogeneous tertiary category

If this is the case, the tendency is clear: tertiary activities are continually increasing, both absolutely and relatively. But it is necessary to look further for more detailed evolutions.

As indicated, the tertiary sector is a very heterogeneous category. Such grouping is mainly negative: tertiary activities are essentially activities which are neither primary nor secondary activities, for which we have rather clear definitions. A first important distinction is between three main tertiary categories, which are, if not completely different, at least substantially so. They may share some common characteristics, but their objectives, logic and ways of functioning are in their essence quite different. These three categories are:

- non-market services: for which even if some price has to be paid, there is no reference to market prices;
- trade activities: consisting essentially in buying in order to resell with a mark-up;
- service activities: consisting, according to the generally accepted definition of T. P. Hill in changing the state of a person or a good.

These are indeed completely different types of activities. The difficulty is that these categories may be overlapping or that some of those activities may be moving from one category to another. There are several reasons for this.

First, many non-market activities are typically service activities, but they function on a completely different basis. The boundaries between market and non-market are not given by the definition or the nature of the activities involved, and may thus be changing through time and space. The same health or educational activities, for example, can belong to either categories, depending on the countries or the period concerned. This is true for many activities. The recent period has shown that things can be changing quite rapidly.

Second, in most or at least many trade activities, some service relation component is likely to be needed and can be seen as making the difference. But besides the fact that such service relation seems progressively to be required in all (including industrial) activities, a clear distinction should be made between user-friendly relations, corresponding to the traditional sense of the word 'service' (to smile, be friendly, at the disposal of), and customized or co-production activities built on the integration of the client/consumer in the production process. In this sense, trade activities are not, in their essence, service activities, even if more or less important service components (for example insurance or after-sale services) can be added to them.

Third, some activities can be seen as mixing these categories, more or less significantly: when a public laboratory is doing research for a private firm; when, at the low quality end of the spectrum, restaurants are more trade than service oriented.

3.6   Structural changes and relative productivities

What does the picture look like if we make those distinctions? On the basis of the same OECD statistics, but only for a smaller number of countries (which have more complete statistics), it is possible to show that the really dynamic component are services as such (see Table 3.6).

What do the figures in Table 3.6 show?

First, these figures show that, on the whole, the shares of both the trade and the non-market activities have remained more or less stable (around 30 per cent of GDP), or have slightly decreased, at least in some countries. There are some changes, country by country, but these are only of minor importance.

Second, the rise of tertiary activities is mainly due to increasing service activities. The service activities proper are clearly responsible for most of

Table 3.6   Comparative shares of services, trade and non-market activities, in seven European Union countries

Countries	Tertiary activities		Trade		Non-market		Services	
	V.A.	Empl.	V.A.	Empl.	V.A.	Empl	V.A.	Empl.
Austria 1985	57.5	54.7	13.3	14.7	15.4	16.6	28.8	23.4
Austria 1995	63.7	61.8	13.1	15.6	16.0	18.4	34.6	27.8
Belgium 1985	62.0	68.1	13.3	16.4	14.4	23.1	34.3	28.6
Belgium 1995	65.8	71.0	14.4	16.0	13.3	21.5	38.1	33.5
Denmark 1985	68.8	65.0	14.2	11.2	22.8	30.7	37.0	41.9
Denmark 1995	70.3	68.3	11.9	11.1	23.1	31.9	36.3	25.3
Finland 1985	57.5	56.2	11.4	13.4	19.1	22.7	27.0	20.1
Finland 1995	62.8	63.9	9.4	12.9	21.3	28.4	32.1	22.6
France 1985	60.9	62.0	12.2	14.1	16.9	24.7	31.8	23.2
France 1996	67.4	70.2	12.0	14.1	17.5	28.2	37.9	27.9
Netherlands 1985	58.5	66.7	10.8	15.0	11.6	16.0	36.1	35.7
Netherlands 1995	64.9	71.1	11.1	16.8	10.2	13.3	43.6	41.0
Sweden 1985	57.4	66.5	10.0	12.4	22.0	33.9	25.4	20.2
Sweden 1995	62.6	69.8	9.6	12.6	20.1	32.5	32.9	24.7

the increase (or even more than the increase) in the shares of tertiary activities in GDP.

Third, more typically, the important phenomenon is that service activities have come to represent systematically more than 50 per cent of value added in tertiary activities. This was not systematically the case in 1985: with the exception of Belgium and the Netherlands, where services were already significantly more important than the other two activities taken together, in 1985,[10] they were only slightly more important in France, and equally in Austria or less in Denmark, Finland, Sweden. In 1995, in all countries, service activities represent a larger share of GDP than trade and non-market activities combined. In the extreme case of the Netherlands, services represent twice the share of trade and non-market activities in GDP.

Fourth, the shift is even more important in employment terms. Even if service activities still do not represent 50 per cent of employment in tertiary activities, the shares of employment in service activities proper have been changing dramatically, from 1985 to 1995: Austria, + 4.4%; Belgium, + 4.9%; France, + 4.7%; Denmark, + 2.2%; Finland, + 2.5%; Netherlands, + 5.3%; Sweden, + 4.5%.

Finally, with regard to employment, there is a clear contrast between countries (such as Austria, France, Finland) in which the share of employment in non-market activities has continued to significantly increase, and other countries (such as Belgium, Denmark, Netherlands and Sweden) in which this share has been reduced.[11]

These structural changes are also reflected in the relative productivities of these three main categories of tertiary activities (see Table 3.7).

Table 3.7 shows quite contrasted situations. First, on the whole, relative productivities in tertiary activities are rather close to one, that is to the average for all activities. This is quite normal, taking account of the quantitative importance of tertiary activities both in GDP and in total employment. Until quite recently (in the mid 1980s), relative productivities in tertiary activities were somewhat above the average in developed countries.[12] This is the case for Austria and Denmark, still in 1995, in Table 3.7. For the other countries, relative productivities are now systematically below 1 (the average). In the case of Belgium, the Netherlands and Sweden, relative productivities are now significantly below 1. This is due to the trade activities and, more so, to the non-market activities.

Second, as concerns trade activities, with the (unexplained) exception of Denmark, relative productivities are below the average and generally decreasing over the ten-year period. This would seem to be

Table 3.7   Relative productivities in trade, non-market and service activities, in seven European Union countries

Countries	Relative productivities in							
	Tertiary activities		*Trade*		*Non-market*		*Services*	
	1985	1995	1985	1995	1985	1995	1985	1995
Austria	1.05	1.03	0.90	0.83	0.93	0.87	1.23	1.24
Belgium	0.91	0.92	0.81	0.90	0.62	0.62	1.19	1.13
Denmark	1.06	1.03	1.27	1.07	0.74	0.72	1.38	1.43
Finland	1.02	0.98	0.85	0.73	0.84	0.76	1.34	1.42
France	0.98	0.96	0.86	0.85	0.68	0.62	1.37	1.36
Netherlands	0.88	0.91	0.72	0.66	0.73	0.77	1.01	1.06
Sweden	0.86	0.90	0.81	0.76	0.65	0.62	1.26	1.33

due to increased entries and competition, in most developed countries.

Third, and to a certain extent more typical, are the non-market activities. Relative productivities are systematically at rather low levels: typically of the order of between two thirds and three quarters of the average (if one eliminates the extreme case of Austria, which is at a somewhat higher level). In all countries (but one), relative productivities are on the decrease over the period. This general situation of non-market activities should be stressed. Apart from some measurement problems,[13] this means that, overall, relative levels of income in such activities are below average, while skill differences do not seem to account for this.

Fourth, in contrast with these figures, relative productivities are systematically and significantly above 1 in the service activities, and are in most cases on the rise. This means that, relatively, the productive contributions of these service activities are above average.

Finally, part of the explanation for these differences in relative productivities between the different activities may be due to differences in skill levels. But in all cases there exists a quite large spectrum of skill levels, depending on the different activities involved. At such rather global levels, at which the above analysis is made, the differences are rather minimal. But it remains true that, according to these relative productivities, service activities are rather on the side of the higher skilled, more productive activities.

There is a well-known paradox here. Service activities which are generally non-productive or only minimally so, or in any case have only low productivity growth, are here shown to have above-average

productive contributions. How can the same activities have simultaneously lower-than-average productivity growth and higher than average
relative productivities? The explanation is very simple. In order to
compare products and productivities, one needs to refer to relative prices,
and, as has been shown, the choice of relative prices is completely
arbitrary. In the above paradox, low productivity growth is referring to
relative prices in some more or less remote base year, while relative
productivities are referring to actual relative prices.

3.7   More detailed service categories

Services themselves are still a rather heterogeneous category, including
both rather traditional low-skilled service activities (communication
activities and the commercialization of traditional household activities)
and some more recent, highly skilled informational service activities. Of
course the distinction is not that simple: some communication activities
are not traditional, while some financial activities are.

According to OECD statistics (see Table 3.8), broad distinctions can be
made between: (i) transport and communication; (ii) banking and
business services; (iii) community, social and personal services. Hotels

Table 3.8   Shares of service activities in GDP and employment

Countries	Services		Transport Communication		Banking Business		Community, social, personal/Hotels, Restaurants.	
	V.A.	Empl.	V.A.	Empl.	V.A.	Empl.	V.A.	Empl.
Austria 1985	28.8	23.4	6.0	6.5	16.3	7.8	6.4	9.1
Austria 1995	34.6	27.8	6.2	6.5	20.5	10.3	7.8	10.7
Belgium 1985	34.3	28.6	8.0	6.7	5.5	3.9	20.8	18.1
Belgium 1995	38.1	33.5	8.2	6.4	5.2	3.8	24.8	23.3
Denmark 1985	31.8	23.1	8.3	6.9	17.3	8.8	6.3	7.3
Denmark 1995	36.3	25.3	9.1	6.9	19.1	10.2	7.1	8.3
Finland 1985	27.0	20.1	8.0	7.1	14.8	6.9	4.1	6.0
Finland 1995	32.1	22.6	8.8	7.6	18.9	9.1	4.5	6.0
France 1995	31.8	23.2	6.2	5.8	18.3	8.7	7.2	8.6
France 1996	37.9	27.9	5.6	5.8	23.1	11.3	9.1	10.7
Netherlands 1985	36.1	35.7	6.0	6.7	17.3	10.1	12.8	18.9
Netherlands 1995	43.6	41.0	6.6	6.7	23.4	13.8	13.6	20.5
Sweden 1985	25.4	20.2	5.4	6.6	16.9	7.3	3.1	6.2
Sweden 1995	32.9	24.7	5.9	6.7	23.2	10.2	3.7	7.9

and restaurants, which in the OECD statistics are included in trade activities, have been added here.

In Table 3.8, it will be seen that situations are quite contrasted.

In the first two columns, taking the same figures as above, the systematic increase of shares of service activities both in terms of GDP and employment are highlighted. In 1995, service activities represent between 32.9 per cent (Sweden) and 43.6 per cent (Netherlands). A line can be drawn between on the one hand, the Scandinavian countries, where service activities represent typically about one third of GDP,[14] and the other countries, where services represent between 35 and 40 per cent (up to 43.6 per cent in the Netherlands). The same can of course be observed as concerns employment, but at a somewhat lower level. Shares of total employment vary between one quarter and one third, with Finland somewhat below and the Netherlands significantly above.

The shares of transport and communication together are rather stable and strongly converging in terms of GDP (between around 6 and 9 per cent) and still more so in terms of employment (between 5.8 and 7.6 per cent).

Most of the increases have taken place in the banking and business service sectors: shares of both GDP and employment have been increasing significantly over the ten-year period. If one excludes the particular case of Belgium (which seems difficult to understand), those activities represent more than 19 per cent of GDP, and up to 23 per cent in three countries (France, Netherlands and Sweden),[15] and more than 9 per cent of total employment, in 1995.

The last category (community, social and personal services), which corresponds mainly to the more traditional service activities to people, has also been increasing more or less systematically. But this category, which is also more heterogeneous, represents varying shares according to the various countries studied. These service activities are more dependent on culture, ways of life, society.

Taking account of the differences between those sub-categories, it may be worthwhile to look further into relative productivities (see Table 3.9).

The figures in Table 3.9 clearly show the very contrasted situations of the two categories of service activities, as suggested above.

First, the transport and communication activities are not very meaningful: this is likely to be because this category is mixing both different types of transport activities and telecommunication activities. These activities should be separated.

When more detailed figures are available, they tend to show that transport activities (but for air transport) have lower-than-average relative

Table 3.9   Relative productivities of service sub-categories

Countries	Relative productivities in				
	Services	Transport communications	Banking business	Community social personal	Hotels restaurants
Austria 1985	1.23	0.92	2.09	1.00	0.55
Austria 1995	1.24	0.87	1.99	1.07	0.52
Belgium 1985	1.19	1.19	1.41	1.20	0.90
Belgium 1995	1.13	1.28	1.36	1.06	1.03
Denmark 1985	1.38	1.20	1.96	0.90	0.74
Denmark 1995	1.43	1.31	1.87	0.93	0.65
Finland 1985	1.34	1.13	2.14	0.65	0.73
Finland 1995	1.42	1.15	2.08	0.85	0.63
France 1985	1.37	1.07	2.10	0.86	0.79
France 1996	1.36	0.97	2.04	0.86	0.83
Netherlands 1985	1.01	0.90	1.71	0.68	0.68
Netherlands 1995	1.60	0.99	1.70	0.66	0.68
Sweden 1985	1.26	0.82	2.32	0.43	0.65
Sweden 1995	1.33	0.88	2.27	0.42	0.59

productivities, while, telecommunication activities have higher-than-average relative productivities.

Second, relative productivities are sky high in banking and business services. If again we eliminate the case of Belgium (where relative productivities are at 1.36), relative productivities are between 1.7 (Netherlands) and 2.3 (Sweden). This is clearly the highly skilled, highly productive, highly performing sector: thanks to high relative productivities, their shares are systematically on the rise, both in terms of GDP and employment.

Third, compared with this, the more traditional sector, grouping 'community, social and personal' services, shows lower than average and in some countries very low relative productivities, down to abnormally low levels in a country like Sweden.

Fourth, still lower (but for some exceptions) are the relative productivities of hotels and restaurants: with the exception of Belgium, relative productivities are already low in France (0.8), but lower than two-thirds of the average in all the other countries. This would tend to reflect what has been called the development of 'McDo' jobs.

3.8   The central role of banking and business services

Very central appear to be banking and business service activities. Taking into account that relative productivities in the manufacturing sector as a whole are usually found to be very near 1 (at least until the end of the 1960s and probably somewhat later than that, the manufacturing sector was determining the average, allowing, however, for differences between sectors), these banking and business activities, with their relative productivities at about double the average level, and representing more than 20 per cent of total GDP in several countries, are necessarily playing a central role in the dynamics of the productive system.

But our analysis stops here. This performing sector is still quite large and still quite heterogeneous. It includes substantially different activities: within the banking and financial sector, both financial services and speculation or rent-seeking activities; within business services, both informatics or consulting, but also on the one hand leasing activities and on the other hand cleaning activities. All these activities can be seen to have significantly different relative productivities in those countries for which more detailed figures are available.

It should be possible to pursue the analysis in more detail, because within all the above categories there is a large diversity of situations: with more disaggregation, the more variables and ratios are differentiating. But in order to pursue this analysis, it would be necessary to obtain more detailed information, and more precise information than national accounts.

The analysis in those countries where more detailed statistics are indeed available suggests two major tendencies. The first is the increasingly clear dividing line between traditional low-skilled services on the one hand and highly skilled informational service activities on the other. The second is the difficulty, or even impossibility, to disentangle, within the bright performances of the last activities, that part which is 'real' productive contribution and that part which is rent or abnormal profit.

Conclusion

This analysis enables us to clearly see what is at stake when speaking of the dynamics of service activities. Not all tertiary activities, not even all service activities are growing. The combination of two criteria, both relative growth and relative productivity, allows us to identify a set of highly performing activities which are essentially accompanying the activity of firms: they have outstanding relative productivities and contribute to a growing share of GDP. This is far from any 'cost-disease' theory, but it is still not possible to identify the exact contribution of those service activities to overall growth. The trouble is that some of these performing activities are also more rent-seeking than productive activities.

References

Baumol W. J., S. A. B. Blackman and E. N. Wolff, *Productivity and American Leadership: the Long View* (Cambridge:, MIT Press, 1989).
Buigues P., F. Ilzkovitz, J. F. Lebrun and A. Sapir, 'Market Services and European Integration', *European Economy: Social Europe*, III (1993).
Clark C. *The Conditions of Economic Progress* (London: Macmillan, 1957).
De Bandt J., 'Can We Measure Productivity in Servicies Activities', in A. Bressand and K. Nicolaïdis (eds), *Strategic Trends in Services: an Inquiry into the Global Service Economy*, A Services World Forum Project (New York: Harper and Row, 1989).
De Bandt J., *Service aux Entreprises: Informations, Produits, Richesses* (Paris: Economica, 1995).
De Bandt J., 'Business Services: Markets and Transactions', *Review of Industrial Organization*, XI (1996) n. 1.
De Bandt J., 'Is there a Relation between Knowledge Production and Productivity?', paper presented at the 2nd International Conference on Technology Policy and Innovation, Lisbon, 3–5 Aug. 1998.
Fisher A. G. B., *The Clash of Progress and Security* (London: Kelley, 1935).
Illeris, S., *The Service Economy: a Geographical Approach* (Chichester: Wiley, 1996).
OECD, *Services: Statistics on Value Added and Employment, 1997 Edition* (Paris: OECD, 1998).
OECD, *Services: Measuring Real annual Value Added* (Paris: OECD, 1996).
Quesnay F., *Le Tableau Économique* (Versailles, 1758–59).
Smith A., *An Inquiry into the Nature and Causes of the Wealth of Nations* (Everyman's Library, 1950).
Summers R., 'Service in the International Economy', in R. Inman (ed.) *Managing in Service Economy: Prospects and Problems* (Cambridge: Cambridge University Press, 1985).

Notes

*   CNRS, Valbonne, France.
1.   Relative productivity (De Bandt, 1996) is defined as the usual productivity measure: value added/employment, each term being related to its total: total value added or GDP and total employment or labour force. The definition is thus: VA in sector i. related to total VA in all sectors, divided by employment in sector i. related to total employment.
2.   Interestingly, in the case of China, where the level of relative productivity is very high, as in most poor countries, the level of relative productivity is still higher in the industrial sector, which is not the case in most of the other poor countries. On the basis of the same figures as above (with the same five year difference), relative productivity in the industrial sector would be 3.2 in the case of China, and two on average for all low-income countries (excluding China and India). Of course the consequence of this is that relative productivities are extremely low in the agricultural sector (0.28 in the case of China and 0.49 in the case of the other low-income countries). This corresponds to the theory I have been building for many years, saying that in underdeveloped countries tertiary activities are appropriating any surplus produced in any other activity, thus preventing any accumulation processes in

the other activities, and that for industrialization to succed the necessary conditions must exist for the self-appropriation of surpluses, as reflected in the relative productivity. This is apparently what happens in China.

3. In the case of France (1996), and in the case of Spain and Portugal (1993).
4. Value added figures are at current prices (or current factor costs).
5. This first column is also based on purchasing power parities, meaning that, compared to official statistics, the corrections are increasingly downwards starting from Austria.
6. These PPP rates have the enormous advantage of showing a (politically correct) representation of the world in which, compared to the United States, both the other developed countries are significantly less rich and the poorest countries are significantly less poor. But what do these figures show when the hypotheses are both that all service (health, education, transport) are qualitatively identical and that replacing output by inputs comes down to implying that, for an identical product(for example, a transport over 100 km), output is higher when productivity is lower?
7. The dates within brackets indicate the base year.
8. As in table 3.3, 1996 for France, 1993 for Spain and Portugal.
9. According to *Business Week*, (15 Sept, 1997), Alan Greenspan said in an interview that 'the non-farm productivity data are nonsense'.
10. This may due to a problem of classification. Belgium is characterized, on a comparative basis, by an extraordinary large share of 'Community, social and personal services' which include, apart from services to households, series of service activities which may be more of the non-market type. The same is true for the Netherlands, but to a lesser extent. But this is only hypothesis.
11. Non-market activities represented up to about or even more than one-third of total employment in Denmark (30.7%) and Sweden (33.9%) in 1985.
12. According to the World Tables.
13. By definition, non-market activities are different and somewhat difficult to integrate in national accounting procedures. Their product is usually measured, some way or another, on the basis of wages which are paid. There are of course no profits, but there are also some problems with the way investment or depreciation are taken into account.
14. The hypothesis being that, in the case of Sweden and maybe the other Scandinavian countries, a propotion of those activities which are market service activities in other countries is in the non-market sector.
15. The shares are still higher in the UK: 26.2 of GDP and 16.5 of Employment, in 1995.

PART II
Government, Governance

4
Lean Government: Goals and Problems

Oliver Fabel and Bruno Miconi*

This study identifies the different roads towards currently existing reform proposals for the provision of government services and isolates the essence of 'lean government' policies. Focusing on both the political sphere and theories of bureaucratic organization, it issues a clear warning concerning the effects of implementing only partial reforms. This is confirmed by investigating a simple model designed to capture the possible impacts of 'flattening' the decision hierarchy. The results are applied to discuss the consequences of European bureaucratic integration.

4.1 Introduction

In contrast to other popular wisdom which cannot be confirmed by thorough scientific research, the view of an ever growing government is supported by a vast number of empirical studies. It even appears robust given the variety of possible measures of governmental size.[1] Thus, Gemmell (1993) focuses on governmental expenditure as a percentage of total GDP (both in current and deflated dollars), Henrekson and Lybeck (1988) and Saunders (1993) account for the percentage of total outlays, Berry and Lowery (1987) distinguish the cost of government, and the scope of government purchases and transfers as compared to GDP, Meyer (1985) analyses employment figures and the number of bureaucratic entities, Moths and Wulf-Mathies (1973) investigate personnel costs, Nutter (1978) calculates the fraction of total expenditures, defence expenditures, and transfer expenditure as of national income, and Peters (1978) defines measures as total expenditure, defence expenditure, social service costs, and transport costs as a percentage of GNP, of primary sector income, and of primary plus secondary sector income. Furthermore, such indices are applied to various countries – both developed and developing. Although every study certainly adds specific structural knowledge, they are united in supporting a general warning. Acknowledging some fluctuations in the value of the growth rates, governments all over the world have persistently expanded their influence on national economies. However, while the empirical phenomenon which sparked off the current investigation is easily defined, solutions to the multitude of problems arising when discussing governmental or bureaucratic reform appear much less obvious. This particularly applies to any attempt to define the term 'lean government' and the search for suitable means to achieve it.

Whereas bureaucracies are a pervasive phenomenon of every organization, this term is usually strictly connected with the idea of government. Currently, there appears to exist a strong contrast between the ever growing importance of the government in the concrete functioning of national states and an anti-government movement in economics, philosophy, and politics.[2] In particular, government is accused of dealing with matters which should not be in its realm. However, the public choice approach in economics ignores the existence of the national state and its influence on the behaviour of the national governments[3] as an important feature of the real world. At the political and philosophical level the existence of the market is simply posed as if in a 'vacuum', disregarding the complexity of the institutional rules – hence, bureaucracies which the market itself requires for its very existence. However, even with a more balanced view of the development of governmental intervention, there seems to be ample scope for at least restraining its role. Such an aim is therefore on the agenda of many politicians and has become one of the most popular slogans of the 1990s. Moreover, the increased mobility of people also allows for comparisons of the bureaucratic organizations of the different national states. Thus, some homogenization of organizational forms is taking place across countries. This particularly applies if these try to form a more cohesive group under some supranational political and economic organization. The development of organizational economics has then added a further influence. Recent applied research not only studies the differentiation of institutional organizations, but also usually offers some particular model as the standard to which the different institutional organizations – and, hence, bureaucracies – should converge. In the real world there rather appears to exist a movement of amalgamation of the different bureaucratic machines due to the existing supranational entities, however.

At least in the short term, this seems to add new rules and regulations for the citizens of each national state – affecting their life in the web of institutions surrounding them – rather than to simplify matters. Moreover, new fields of interventions increasingly appear on the scene. Thus, discussions on the scope of government are (re-)initiated with respect to environmental problems, gender issues, or the direction of AIDS-research, for example. Possible solutions always imply institutional adjustments – hence, some form of organizational change. In approaching a 'lean government', choices must therefore be made between different modes of bureaucratic organization, rather than between the simple existence of a bureaucracy and its abolishment. The current analysis thus intends (i) to clarify the possible aims to be reached in terms of the market or the state, (ii) to distinguish the different approaches towards the common aim of establishing a 'lean government' , and (iii) to investigate the options to implement this goal. Clearly, lean government policies imply a new attitude of its bureaucratic organization. Thus, it is necessary to disentangle the inspiring principles and the suggested methods of the different approaches. Generally, this requires a deep analysis in each country and at the European level as a whole in terms of their structural characteristics.[4] Yet, as the respective rules and institutions belong to every aspect of an organized human life, the bureaucratic aspects of them also more generally appear to depend on the non-familiarity of their use in everyday life.

4.2 Guidelines for a bureaucratic reform

4.2.1 Final and intermediate services

Consider bureaucratic services. Like every other type of services, final services to the customer and intermediate services internal to the bureaucratic organization itself can be distinguished. With regard to the first kind of service, a lean government should obviously follow the principle of being 'user–friendly' for the customer. When facing the ordinary citizen, the bureaucratic machine should – in every aspect of its relation with him or her – try to follow simple homogeneous rules which are easily understood, remembered, or worked out. Clearly, this image is taken from the language of software. The comparison is compelling, since software programs do much the same. Their success or failure ultimately hinges on the way how a person can achieve task completion. This particularly applies when the operation to be developed with the computer is new and/or rarely occurs involving the same person.

The lines of reforms with respect to internal service provision should then be inspired by the principles developed in organizational economics.[5] The two kinds of services cannot be considered independently, however. Very often, the internal rules of a bureaucracy influence the demands towards their final beneficiaries. In particular, many rules towards the public are already fixed more for the comfort of the bureaucratic machine rather than with a view for rendering a service to the final consumer, or lending towards an orderly administration of the general system. Even from the internal point of view, rules may often be obsolete. They are simply followed as a bureaucratic ritual, reminding of religious habits and behaviour. Furthermore, the rules should be fixed as much as possible accounting for their general interdependence. The solution of a particular problem in some part of the organization of the public system frequently implies the occurrence of another – maybe even more complicated – problem in some other part of the general, public or private system. The partial equilibrium approach of public choice and organizational economics cannot capture the full array of effects. It focuses only on improvements of the small part of the system to which they are directed. Organizational analyses are also very sensitive to the value of the parameters employed. As exposed in detail below, for instance, it is interesting that for certain values of parameters – which cannot be excluded as unreasonable – the often proposed 'flattening' of the bureaucratic hierarchy will not minimize its scale.

4.2.2   A simple organizational scheme

Problems of organizational interactions could be placed under the scheme 'time – information – control – result' . The client – another organization or a final customer – is involved in some time-consuming activity in order to receive a certain service. The time consumed by the client translates into information to be processed by the bureau which then – following an activity of control – decides on the result. A scheme considering the basic categories of time and information should be suggestive of a change of view in the analysis of the bureaucratic organization. It appears useful to substitute the idea of a bureaucracy as a mechanical machine with one more apt to an age in which the characteristic feature is the information content of an organization. The image of the software soul of a computer can well influence the design of a more agile and thin governmental activity. It suggests a bureaucracy with an almost absolute emphasis on impartiality – replacing cost benefit analyses by a 'user friendly' and productivistic approach[6] as an analytic tool. Moreover, it stresses the entrepreneurial capacity of the bureau to process information properly as well as the wider role of expertise concerning the signalling content received. Consequently, the influence of law as a signal received and obeyed in terms of bureaucratic behaviour is diminished. Rather than providing an identical impartial service to everyone at the same price, differentiated tariffs induce a market-like co-ordination of the partial activity which the customer directly chooses.

This approach to a lean government requires a well documented series of productivity and quality indices. Such indices are particularly difficult to be constructed in the realm of bureaucratic and governmental activities.[7] Very basically, this reflects exactly the same reasons which also induce the existence of opportunism and imperfect information. However, lack of competitive pressure in many public activities – which is at the heart of the respective organizational literature – significantly adds to the general problem. Therefore, the design of such indices appears to require some ingenuity in order to avoid results which are just the opposite of the imposed goals. In the public sector the problem is enhanced by the particular final service to be provided. For example, certifications of non-mafia activities would be easily given to everybody, if that would be counted positively in the productivity index of such an office. However, if the office would be asked to account only for individuals not even having slight affiliation with a mafia organization, the number of people receiving such a certification would be extremely small and the time of reaching a result inappropriately long. In this respect, the concept of 'effectiveness' used in the administrative sciences could again prove to be useful in defining such indices. It places a constraint on the absolute value to be reached which is outside economic efficiency considerations.

4.2.3 Politicians, bureaucrats, and citizens

Even if a bureaucratic reform could be successfully shaped along the way suggested above, further problems arise due to the functioning of the public system. There are obvious differences between the interactions of politicians, bureaucrats, and citizens of a state compared to the owners, managers, and shareholders of a private enterprise. Accepting that the second triad – under some very important provisos – operates efficiently, is almost irrelevant when designing efficiency-enhancing reforms of the public system. First, the control schemes between the two organizations are quite different. An element of control of a private corporation occurs every day in the stock exchange. In contrast, elections reoccur only every few years. Also, private budgets and public budgets vary enormously. In fact, the very idea of budgeting public organizations clearly follows the economic rather than the formalistic legal approach. The aims of the two organizations vary from mainly uni-dimensional profit maximization in the case of a private corporation, to being certainly multidimensional in the case of a governmental office. For example, the redistribution motive can never simply be achieved by redistributing initial income. The competitive environment in which private corporations exist allows people to enter and exit, as consumers or as shareholders, an idea perfectly foreign to the concept of citizenship.

Also, the present experience implies that the final products would still be of different shapes and personalities. For example, public employees should be more involved in planning and shaping directions rather than executing them. The executive part should then be left to different, possibly private organizations. Nevertheless, in order to carry out their tasks, public employees would require capacities of planning and controlling which come under the umbrella of private information in the executive part of the business.

Furthermore, the vast contracting-out of activities could – in a world of imperfect information – easily produce a monopolistic external private power. Otherwise there would have to be in place an ultimate capacity to conclude complete contracts on the side of the public contractor. This, however, is denied by the organizational economics approach. The different characteristics of national states would still be present in the final result. Different institutions and the scope of governmental involvement in the functioning of the socioeconomic system will remain present, not to mention other levels of governmental organizations also to be added.

Thus, the suggested road to bureaucratic reform must consider the chance of success and failure. On first sight, each one of the interest groups will possess reasons for supporting a reform. Politicians could see their role directed more to the strategic steering of the country. Bureaucrats could earn a more respected role in society and satisfaction in their jobs. Citizens could find their sovereignty strengthened. However, matters are obviously more complicated. Therefore, a bureaucratic reform towards a lean government would abolish an enormous amount of rules, regulations, and laws. Most of these are internal to the bureaucratic machine, rather than directed towards the public. Thus, pursuing this goal would be difficult and unprofitable. However, in pre-election periods, politicians increase their re-election prospects by offering direct benefits for voters. Bureaucrats can simply hide their power behind the multiplicity of existing rules. Even citizens and separate corporate groups will occasionally find it advantageous to be protected by non-efficient rules and laws. Furthermore, in designing a supranational bureaucracy, national states could intervene in an attempt to win control over the new bureaucracy. Ideas of a lean government thus have to be developed as a complete strategy, to be supported by a well prepared plan. In contrast, the current popular discussion rather appears to present simple suggestions – either as academic exercises or token examples of organization. Even taking the optimistic view that piecemeal activities often succeed, their implementation may be associated with an enormous waste of resources along the way.

4.2.4 Inside bureaucracy

Given the difficulty of even labelling what exactly constitutes a reform towards a lean government, it does not come as a surprise that views vary greatly on whether the bureaucratic system as such entails efficiency-enhancing virtues or rather constitutes a synonym for existing inefficiencies. Thus, the scientific treatment of the bureaucratic phenomenon begins with Weber's (1976) postulate of its superior efficiency in organizing economic activities.[8] According to this classic and historic analysis the bureaucratic organization primarily reflects the gains from specialization which can be achieved by defining separate sub-tasks in the pursuit of an overall goal. The hierarchical positions are filled with individuals who derive their authority from their superior knowledge and ability in exercising the tasks. In turn, decision routines tie the authority to control and to rule on a certain subject directly to the hierarchical position. Requirements to collect files documenting the decision process establish an information system that constitutes the historic memory of the organization and, thus, ensures continuity. At the same time, this information is used to control the organization's members.

While this classic text is still at the very heart of bureaucratic analysis, the roots of more recent approaches appear to fall within one of two distinct streams of literature on the treatment of institutions like bureaux, both clearly distinguished from market analysis. Hence, critical with respect to the Weberian model of a co-operatively rational bureaucracy, March and Simon (1958) and Simon (1976) reinvestigate its efficiency-enhancing virtue. Breaking up complicated optimization problems into several computable sub-problems is seen to overcome the 'bounded rationality' of the organization's individual members. Nevertheless, the decisions frequently fall short of achieving the full optimum. Decision-makers 'satisfy' rather than optimize. In contrast, the second line of literature emphasizes the rational content of organizations. In the administrative sociological studies field, Thompson (1967) thus notices that this organization of the decision process is mainly intended to eliminate 'environmental uncertainty'. The successful bureaucracy acts perfectly autonomously. In consequence, Terreberry (1968) observes a diminishing influence of the bureaucratic organization as the environment is becoming more complex, other players in the market – such as labour and capital – become increasingly organized, and, thus, the bureaucracy is developing more reliance on outside actors.

These two opposing views are mirrored by the respective development in economic theory which begins with Coase's (1937) postulate of a positive efficiency principle. Specialization can clearly not constitute the reason for formal organization as specialized tasks may well be traded by way of markets.[9] However, both market and internalized transactions exhibit specific transaction costs. Therefore, in a competitive environment the marginal cost of internalizing one additional transaction must equal the respective marginal cost of operating through the market. Moreover, according to Williamson (1983), also explicitly acknowledging the role of 'bounded rationality' as a decentralization motive, these costs are transaction-specific. This then explains the varying degrees of formal organization in the economic world.[10] However, rigid hierarchical organizations are also seen to lose influence – the multidivisional structure of large firms constituting the most recent organizational innovation of prime importance. Dissatisfaction with this abstract and empirically non-verifiable analysis[11] then again induced approaches emphasizing the efficiency losses due to the individual rationality of its members. Merton (1957) and Crozier (1964) warned that blind adherence to procedural rules suffices to justify actions within the hierarchical organization. Ultimately, this yields a tendency to ignore the clients' interests. The same impersonal rules which ensure efficiency in the Weberian model also generate perfect knowledge concerning the limits of acceptable effort.

Consequently, opportunistic bureaucrats will only provide the minimum acceptable effort level. Since the bureaucratic system is in fact mainly designed to satisfy the human desire to exercise control and gain power over other individuals, there appears to exist no limit for bureaucratic growth – sheer size being the single most important characteristic of this organizational form.[12] Additional support for the hypothesis of the bureaucratic organization's inherent inefficiency can be found in Baumol (1962) and Marris (1963), who investigate the role of rent-seeking activities by the management of large enterprises motivated by a personal desire for growth.[13] Leibenstein (1966, 1978a) coins the term 'x-inefficiency' to refer to the resulting efficiency loss in the pursuit of the organization's overall goal.[14] This argument is taken up by

Niskanen (1968, 1975), Davis *et al.* (1974) and Cullis and Jones (1993) and applied to the public administration. It can be shown that budget constraints imposed by a democratic public are not sufficient to prevent an inefficiently large bureaucracy.[15]

Similarly, studies which focus on internal incentive mechanisms are also split between either highlighting efficiency-enhancing or postulating an efficiency-reducing effect of hierarchical structures. Hence, Stiglitz (1975) and Lazear and Rosen (1981) analyse hierarchical promotion ladders as an incentive device designed to cope with 'adverse selection' and 'moral hazard' problems – associated with the individual's ability to hide its skill level and effort supply, respectively. However, Green and Stokey (1983) reveal the possible existence of efficiency losses compared with direct incentive schemes. Direct performance indices not only allow the fine-tuning of incentives; the risk-shifting properties of such schemes may dominate those associated with relative performance measurement. Thus, it remains questionable whether incentive arguments can actually explain efficient multilayer hierarchies other than merely distinguishing the level of the 'principal' from that of the 'agent' . In this respect, Alchian and Demsetz (1972) only demonstrate the necessity of establishing top-level management as a residual-claimant. Also, a decentralization motive alone – associated with the necessity to extract additional information from agents, or to select among agents with private knowledge concerning their specialized skills as in De Groot (1987), Bolton and Farrell (1990), or Rotemberg (1991), respectively – generally does not induce multi-layer authority structures.[16] Finally, Mirrlees (1976) shows that communication losses[17] can at best generate rather weak diminishing returns to increasing control levels. In particular, the existence of an optimal size cannot be shown. Implicitly this is confirmed by Calvo and Wellisz (1978, 1979) who are unable to simultaneously determine both the optimal number of bureaucrats and the optimal number of hierarchical levels.[18]

4.3 A simple model of bureaucracy

4.3.1 Motivation of the particular model structure

Contrasting with the rather vivid public discussion which only too often claims to identify the sources of bureaucratic inefficiencies, the preceding sections have thus made very clear that the issue of reforming this system involves several highly complex issues. In particular, reform proposals raise questions of the measurability of the (in)efficiencies, the concrete form of deregulation associated with 'user-friendliness' , and the implied choice of the basic bureaucratic model to which such reforms are to be applied. However, even accepting the neo-classical hypothesis of inherent inefficiencies due to opportunistic behaviour, the analysis – then investigating different second-best solutions – typically does not yield clear-cut results with respect to the effects of implementing certain reform proposals. This may be exemplified by the following very simple and highly stylized model.[19] It is particularly designed to address the issue of 'flat' *v* 'tall' hierarchies. Shortening decision chains – thus, 'flattening' the hierarchy – in order to achieve better service for the clients and simultaneously decreasing the organizations' size constitutes a prominent and reoccurring theme in the public lean government discussion. Hence, Garston (1993, pp. 228–9) predicts that the current pressure placed upon bureaucratic organizations will yield a 'trend toward more compressed structures (fewer levels)'. However, such reforms may increase the size of the bureaucracy and decrease the quality of service. This possibility generally exists if the organizational change is carried out in an isolated manner without simultaneously changing the incentive-scheme as well.

The analysis focuses on the dual problem of adding a new top-level decision-making unit to an already existing bureaucracy. Clearly following the neo-classical criticism, it highlights the dependence of overall size on the individual members' desire to be promoted rather than satisfying the needs of their clients. Its relevance for evaluating the danger of developing 'Eurocracy' in the process of European unification is therefore particularly obvious. European administrative integration introduces an additional top layer of decision-making – the European level – which at the same time offers new chances for promotion. Given this interpretation, the model thus assumes full integration of the European bureaucracy in the decision-making process. Although this may actually be too optimistic with respect to political development, it clearly constitutes the 'worst case' from the viewpoint of the critics of European integration.[20] Moreover, Andersen and Eliassen (1991) have observed significant increases in European Community lobbying reflecting of European institutions' developing influence.[21] Further, although according to Bach (1992) the European level itself does not constitute a rigid hierarchical bureaucracy, it suffices that it acts as a superior level of decision-making. At the same time, the analysis also possesses a more general virtue in modelling a hierarchical control process which does not entail a perfect separation of tasks. Following the discussion above, it distinguishes service from pure control positions. In public administrations, bureaucrats at a higher level frequently have the authority to directly overrule lower level decisions on clients' cases. In this case, however, altering the length of the decision chain may exhibit rather varying influences on the quality of the decisions and the overall administrative size.

4.3.2 The set of formal assumptions

In the following let k, $k = 1, \ldots, K$, denote hierarchical layers. Restricting the attention to a minimal bureaucracy implies that $K = 2$ and $K = 3$, before and after the addition of a new top-layer, respectively. Given the German political system, the three layers may then obviously be interpreted as 'state', 'federal', and 'European' levels of decision-making. Clients wish to generate a desirable action by the organization by entering cases at its bottom level ($k = 1$). If the respective bureaucrats agree, the client's welfare is served and no further decisions are needed. However, negative decisions of the first layer may be appealed and taken to the second level, at which they may be revised. This implies that the desired action is now initiated. Given the existence of a third layer, the procedure may be repeated, if the second-level bureaucrats have also decided to turn down the client. Top-level decisions are always final. The organization's files document which decisions are 'original' to a particular bureaucrat. This is associated with an individual member's first issuing of a new ruling on the case. Thus, bottom–level decisions and – in the three-layer system – revisions of such acts constitute 'original' decisions which are in danger of being revized. The organization is 'fair' in a sense that each bureaucrat will hold responsibility only for 'original' acts.

Positions within the organization's hierarchy can only be filled by promotions. All individuals initially enter the system at its bottom level. Such promotions take place simultaneously for all positions. The time-span between promotion rounds is denoted 'one service year'. Let j, $j = 1, \ldots, J$, refer to the tenure of a bureaucrat in terms of 'service years'. Clearly, feasibility requires that maximum tenure J cannot fall short of K, accounting for the possibility of a three-layer hierarchy. For simplicity, it will then be assumed that $J = 3$. In deciding on promotions, all potential candidates are first ranked according to their success rate. This rate is calculated as the fraction of this bureaucrat's 'original decisions' which have not been revised by superior levels. Then, those with the highest success rates will be promoted first and reach the next higher level in the bureaucracy until all vacancies are filled. The wage differentials associated with ascending within the system are assumed to be sufficiently large such as to ensure that all candidates will attempt to maximize their success rates. Moreover, the population of the hierarchical layers and the number of cases entering the appeal process are taken to be sufficiently large. Thus, the average success rate constitutes the best approximation of an individual member's expected success rate. All potential candidates for promotion are assumed to possess identical abilities in analysing cases and knowledge concerning the organization's formal decision-making process. Hence, they will choose an identical type of reasoning when documenting their decisions. Quite clearly, these assumptions generate a highly competitive environment for the bureaucrats. Although very probably too optimistic accounting for real-world bureaucracies,[22] they shall serve to isolate the pure effects of hierarchical control and promotion ladders within the present framework.

In deciding on cases bureaucrats can choose to follow or emphasize the routines and formal procedural rules well established within the bureaucracy. This type of decision-making will lead to an average appeal rate $n_k(T)$ of level-k decisions by the clients. On the other hand, the bureaucrat can attempt to fully evaluate the benefits of the decision to the client – even if deviating from traditional ruling on similar subjects. In this case, the appeal rate will be denoted $n_k(E)$. In the light of the discussion above, it will obviously be assumed $n_k(T) > n_k(E)$, for all k. Referring to the process of European bureaucratic integration again, the comparative advantage of E-type decisions may reflect either improved co-ordination in the provision of a public good,[23] or the benefits of allowing the client to participate in the Common Market by not exercising a national regulation.[24] However, success rates also depend on the probability to experience revisions, if the decision is appealed. This will reflect the superior level bureaucrats' preferences for a particular decision type. For simplicity, this relationship is taken to be linear. The probability of revising a type-X decision, $X = E, T$, of level k by bureaucrats of level $k + 1$ is denoted

$$p_{k+1}(X) = 1 - \alpha - \beta[N_{k+1}(X)]/[N_{k+1}] \tag{1}$$

with $\alpha > 0$, $\beta > 0$, and $0 < \gamma := \alpha + \beta < 1$. It should be noted that equation (1) also introduces a risk of revision irrespective of the decision type as bureaucrats are also prone to making errors. The risk of revision due to their superiors' preferences is then seen to depend on the fraction of $N_{k+1}(X)$ of such higher level bureaucrats favouring the same decision-type among the total N_{k+1} members of this hierarchical layer. Thus, the model focuses on an organization's individual members' incentives to adopt an innovative ruling on cases (type E) when balancing the external probability of appeal against the internal probability of revision.[25]

Some rather technical assumptions must be added. First, the promotion incentives obviously cannot motivate bureaucrats of tenure 3. With respect to this group it is therefore assumed that they will not differ from the rest of their colleagues on the same hierarchical layer. This may reflect the human desire to be respected by colleagues as they have nothing else to gain. Second, all cases entered at the bottom level actually reach the top-layer within one service-year. Finally, in order to preclude a solution in which bureaucrats maximize their success rate by always agreeing with their clients and never turning down cases, assume that a sufficiently large number of revisions occur randomly.

4.3.3 The induced decision quality

In calculating the organization's members' success rates it is interesting and important to note that the proportion of cases which are turned down by the bottom-layer bureaucrats among all cases entered is completely irrelevant. Thus, let M denote the total number of cases filed by the clients and $n_0(X)$ – with $X = E, T$, again – the proportion of cases initially turned down. Then, it suffices that the total number of cases entering the appeal process – $N(X) = n_0(X)M$ – is sufficiently large in order to calculate success rates solely reflecting the internal revision process. The individual members are only evaluated taking account for those decisions which enter the appeal process at all and, thus, capture the attention of their superiors. Hence, the clients' degree of satisfaction or discontent with first-layer decisions which it may be thought should actually constitute a prime indicator of bottom-level service quality, only very imperfectly enters the calculation of success rates. It is merely reflected by the probability of clients appealing initial negative decisions.

Table 4.1 contains the success rates for bottom-level decisions in the initial two-layer hierarchy. It immediately becomes clear that, if the top-level bureaucrats favour type-E decisions themselves, bottom-level decisions will also be of this type. This follows from:

$$(1 - \gamma)/(1 - \alpha) < 1 < n_1(T)/n_1(E) \tag{2}$$

For historically well-established bureaucracies, this case appears to be unlikely, however. Thus, assuming that top-level superiors prefer type-T

Table 4.1 Success rates in a two-layer hierarchy

	Top level (k = 2)	Type E	Type T
Bottom level (k = 1)	Type E	$1 - n_1(E)(1 - \gamma)$	$1 - n_1(E)(1 - \alpha)$
	Type T	$1 - n_1(T)(1 - \alpha)$	$1 - n_1(T)(1 - \gamma)$

Table 4.2   Success rates in a three-layer hierarchy

	Top level (k = 3)	Type E	Type T
Second level (k = 2)	Type E	$1 - n_2(E)(1 - \gamma)$	$1 - n_2(E)(1 - \alpha)$
	Type T	$1 - n_2(T)(1 - \alpha)$	$1 - n_2(T)(1 - \gamma)$

Top level Type E and second-level type E

Bottom level (k = 1)	Type E	$1 - n_1(E)[1 - \gamma(1 - (1 - \gamma)n_2(E))]$
	Type T	$1 - n_1(T)[1 - \alpha(1 - (1 - \alpha)n_2(T))]$

Top level Type E and second-level type T

Not feasible!

Top level Type T and second-level type E

Bottom level (k = 1)	Type E	$1 - n_1(E)[1 - \gamma(1 - (1 - \alpha)n_2(E))]$
	Type T	$1 - n_1(T)[1 - \alpha(1 - (1 - \gamma)n_2(T))]$

Top level Type T and second-level type T

Bottom level (k = 1)	Type E	$1 - n_1(E)[1 - \alpha(1 - (1 - \alpha)n_2(E))]$
	Type T	$1 - n_1(T)[1 - \gamma(1 - (1 - \gamma)n_2(T))]$

decisions, bottom-level bureaucrats will be induced to exert decisions of:[26]

$$\text{Type } T, \text{ if } (1 - \gamma)/(1 - \alpha) - n_1(T)/n_1(E) > 0$$
$$\text{Type } E, \text{ if } (1 - \gamma)/(1 - \alpha) - n_1(T)/n_1(E) \leq 0 \tag{3}$$

Adding a new top-level of decision-making, it may well be true that its respective – 'European' – bureaucrats favour type-E rulings. In this case Table 4.2 can easily be seen to confirm that second-level and bottom-level bureaucrats will also strictly prefer this type. Hence, innovative top-level bureaucrats can always induce innovative decisions throughout the whole bureaucracy.

However, even if the top-level is more restricted in imposing new views on dealing with clients' cases – thus, rather accepting type-*T* decisions as valid – its mere presence induces additional incentives to adopt type-*E* rulings for the lower levels. This is trivially so for the now-second level bureaucrats who did not face any risk of appeal and revision before. The argument is more elaborate though. If the second-layer bureaucrats choose type-*E* decisions, the organization's bottom-level members will make an identical choice – irrespective of the type of top-level decision-making. Furthermore, consider the final case of Table 4.2 characterized by top- and second-level bureaucrats' preference for type-*T* decisions. Bottom-level bureaucrats will now choose:

$$
\begin{aligned}
&Type\ T,\ if\ [1 - \alpha(1 - (1 - \alpha)n_2(E))]/[1 - \gamma(1 - (1 - \gamma)n_2(T))] \\
&\qquad\qquad\qquad -n_1(T)/n_1(E) > 0 \\
&Type\ E,\ if\ [1 - \alpha(1 - (1 - \alpha)n_2(E))]/[1 - \gamma(1 - (1 - \gamma)n_2(T))] \\
&\qquad\qquad\qquad -n_1(T)/n_1(E) \leq 0
\end{aligned}
\tag{4}
$$

It is easily checked that

$$
[1 - \alpha/(1 - \gamma) > [1 - \alpha(1 - (1 - \alpha)n_2(E))]/[1 - \gamma(1 - (1 - \gamma)n_2(T))] \tag{5}
$$

Therefore, equation (4) constitutes a weaker constraint than equation (3) with respect to the incentives to adopt innovative type-*E* rulings. Consequently, bottom-level bureaucrats will now choose type-*E* decisions in cases which would be characterized by a *T*-preference in the two-layer hierarchy.

4.3.4 Bureaucracy size

In analysing the induced size of the bureaucracy, the attention is confined to a stable hierarchy which entails no changes in the absolute and relative numbers of bureaucrats employed over time. It appears plausible to assume that the number of bureaucrats necessary on each layer is proportional to the number of cases reaching this decision level. For simplicity, the respective factor of proportionality is taken to equal unity for all levels in the following. Let N_k and $N_{k,j}$ refer to the total number of level-*k* bureaucrats and the number of bureaucrats in tenure year *j* on level *k*, respectively. The two-layer hierarchy can then generally be characterized by the relationships

$$
n_0 n_1 M = N_2 = N_{2,2} + N_{2,3} = q_1^{2,L} N_{1,1} + q_1^{2L} N_{1,1} + q_1^{2L} N_{1,1}(1 - q_1^{2L}) \tag{6}
$$

$$
M = N_1 = N_{1,1} + N_{1,2} + N_{1,3} = N_{1,1} + N_{1,1}(1 - q_1^{2L}) + N_{1,1}(1 - q_1^{2L})^2 \tag{7}
$$

In equations (6) and (7), q_1^{2L} denotes the promotion-rate. Solving for this rate yields a quadratic equation. However, the fact that $0 \leq q_1^{2L} \leq 1$ allows to identify the negative root as the solution

Table 4.3   Fraction of cases reaching next higher level

Two-layer hierarchy	
Top-bottom type combination	*Proportion of cases reaching top level*
$E - E$	$n_0(E)n_1(E)$
$T - E$	$n_0(E)n_1(E)$
$T - T$	$n_0(T)n_1(E)$

Three-layer hierarchy		
Top-second-level-bottom type combination	*Proportion of cases reaching*	
	Second level	*Top level*
$E - E - E$	$n_0(E)n_1(E)$	$n_0(E)n_1(E)n_2(E)$
$T - E - E$	$n_0(E)n_1(E)$	$n_0(E)n_1(E)n_2(E)$
$T - T - E$	$n_0(E)n_1(E)$	$n_0(E)n_1(E)n_2(Av.)^*$
$T - T - T$	$n_0(T)n_1(T)$	$n_0(T)n_1(T)n_0(T)$

* Note: $n_2(Av.) := (1 - \gamma) n_2(T) + \gamma n_2(E)$.

$$q_1^{2L} = \frac{3}{2} - \left[\frac{9}{4} - (3n_0n_1)/(1 + n_0n_1)\right]^{\frac{1}{2}} \tag{8}$$

Thus, $q_1^{2L} \in [0, \frac{3}{2} - (\frac{3}{4})^{\frac{1}{2}}]$. Consulting Table 4.3 the case-specific appeal rates n_0 and n_1 can then be inserted in order to calculate the exact promotion probability. Clearly, bottom-level T-type decisions yield a larger number of cases to be treated by the top level. This implies a larger total number of bureaucrats. Moreover, it also generates a greater number of bureaucrats newly hired in each period and a corresponding increase in the promotion rate.

Similarly, the three-layer hierarchy can be described by

$$n_0n_1n_2M = N_3 = N_{3,3} = q_1^{3L}N_{2,2} = q_1^{3L}q_2^{3L}N_{1,1} \tag{9}$$

$$n_0n_1M = N_2 = N_{2,2} + N_{2,3} = q_1^{3L}N_{1,1} + q_1^{3L}N_{1,1}(1 - q_2^{3L}) + q_1^{3L}N_{1,1}(1 - q_1^{3L}) \tag{10}$$

$$M = N_1 = N_{1,1} + N_{1,2} + N_{1,3} = N_{1,1} + N_{1,1}(1 - q_1^{3L}) + N_{1,1}(1 - q_1^{3L})^2 \tag{11}$$

The relationship between the probabilities of ascent from the second to the top and from the first to the second level is obtained as:

$$q_2^{3L} = n_2(3 - q_1^{3L})/(1 + n_2) \tag{12}$$

Table 4.4   Numerical example

Assumed values: $n_0(E) = n_1(E) = n_0(E) = ¼$; $n_0(T) = n_1(T) = n_0(T) = ½$; $\gamma = ½$; $M = 1000$.

Two-layer hierarchy			
Top-bottom type combination	N_2	$N_{1,1}$	q_1^{2L}
$E - E$	62.5	345.167	0.060
$T - E$	62.5	345.167	0.060
$T - T$	250	416.667	0.215

Three-layer hierarchy					
Top-second-level-bottom type-combination	N_2	N_3	$N_{1,1}$	q_1^{3L}	q_2^{2L}
$E - E - E$	62.5	15.625	359.375	0.074	0.585
$T - E - E$	62.5	15.625	359.375	0.074	0.585
$T - T - E$	62.5	23.438	361.979	0.081	0.796
$T - T - T$	250	125	458.333	0.303	0.899

Solving then yields

$$q_1^{3L} = \tfrac{3}{2} - [\tfrac{9}{4} - 3(n_0 n_1 + n_0 n_1 n_2)/(1 + n_0 n_1 + n_0 n_1 n_2)]^{1/2} \tag{13}$$

Inserting the respective fractions of cases reaching the different layers from Table 4.3 again reveals that overall size, the number of newly hired bureaucrats $N_{1,1}$ in each period, and both promotion rates increase with the hierarchies propensity to generate T-type decisions.

Comparing the two-layer with the three-layer hierarchy it also becomes evident that – conditional on the appeal and revision rates – the latter may actually employ a smaller number of bureaucrats. This solely hinges on the fact that it can induce E-type decisions when conditions prevail, under which the former does not. Interestingly, the promotion rates – now generally within the (0,1)-interval – will still be larger in the three-layer hierarchy. This is also confirmed by the numerical example reported in Table 4.4. Although the present model is certainly exemplifying rather than possessing great general virtue, it thus highlights the differences in size which can be attained by the two organizational, respectively incentive structures under consideration.

4.4   Conclusion

Despite – or perhaps owing to – its very simple structure, the model set out above succeeds in issuing a clear warning concerning the possible effects of implementing an isolated reform to cut the number of hierarchical layers. Furthermore, it appears to allow some discussion concerning the potential consequences of European bureaucratic integration. On first sight providing merely a motivating example of application above, the Maastricht Treaty in fact contains a summary of the European nations' attitudes towards restraining bureaucratic growth – at least as far as the European administration itself is concerned. These manifest in its so-called 'subsidiarity' and 'mutual recognition' principles. Following the discussion of Section 2.2, these rules for organizing the New Europe's public administration can probably be best understood as reflecting the results of a first round in the national states' battle for bureaucratic control. Thus, they certainly warrant a more thorough consideration than has so far been exercised.

To begin with, recall that innovative European ruling or simply lengthening the decision chain may result in a better service for the clients in all member states and, at the same time, decrease the overall size of the administration. Of course, conditional on the parameter constellation, it cannot be ruled out that this development may also merely add a new layer of top and top-salaried bureaucrats without exerting any effect on the quality of service. Yet, this 'worst case' must be weighed against the fact that the political decision to establish a European administration has been made and will definitely not be revised. Thus, the actual choice only concerns the question whether or not it should be fully integrated. The analysis clearly suggests that potential benefits can only be captured by full integration – thus, contrasting sharply with popular wisdom. In fact, the European bureaucracy should for the benefit of all be encouraged to exploit all gaps still left open after the Maastricht Treaty. Thus, quite in contrast to Starbatty (1993) and many other sceptics emphasizing the European administration's extreme problems in finding definitions and rules for the heterogeneous society of nations, strict adherence to the 'subsidiarity principle' spelled out in the Treaty can certainly only generate the 'worst case'.

Admittedly, however, Maastricht's second principle of 'mutual recognition' may possess an efficiency-enhancing virtue. Clients who are actually free to choose to which national bureaucracy to appeal will generate a competitive environment. This may then induce additional internal efficiency gains.[27] In this respect, Casella (1992) and Feinstein (1992) already agree in warning that economic convergence need not necessarily imply an increased institutional stability, if the preferences for public goods are sufficiently heterogeneous.[28] Neven (1992) doubts that 'mutual recognition' will actually exert sufficient pressure for the existing national bureaucracies, and Christensen (1989) again stresses the probable strong resistance of the bureaucrats themselves, if they are to face drastic changes in their work environment.

Recalling the structure of the present model, however, an important argument must be added. Once the process of bureaucratic integration is completed, there will obviously exist strong incentives to adopt traditional (*T*-type) rulings again in order to increase promotion chances and the size of the now-European hierarchy. Thus, the benefits of bureaucratic integration may in fact be of a short-term nature and certainly do not constitute a general cure.

References

Alchian A. A. and H. Demsetz, 'Production, Information Costs, and Economic Organization', *American Economic Review*, LXII (1972) 777–95.

Andersen S. S. and K. A. Eliassen, 'European Community Lobbying', *European Journal of Political Research*, XX (1991) 173–87.

Aron D. J., 'Firm Organization and the Economic Approach to Personnel Management', *American Economic Review*, LXXX (1990) 23–7.

Bach M., 'Eine leise Revolution durch Verwaltungsverfahren', *Zeitschrift für Soziologie*, XXI (1992) 16–30.

Baumol W. J., 'On the Theory of Expansion of the Firm', *American Economic Review*, LII (1962) 1078–87.

Berry W. D. and D. Lowery, *Understanding United States Government Growth* (New York: Praeger, 1987).

Besley T. and S. Coate, 'Public Provision of Private Goods and the Redistribution of Income', *American Economic Review*, LXXXI (1991) 979–84.

Bolton P. and J. Farrell, 'Decentralization, Duplication, and Delay', *Journal of Political Economy*, XCVIII (1990) 803–26.

Borland J. and X. Yang, 'Specialization and a New Approach to Economic Organization and Growth', *American Economic Review*, LXXXII (1992) 386–91.

Buchanan J. M., *Better than Plowing* (Chicago, IL: Chicago University Press, 1986).

Buiter W. H. and K. M. Kletzer, 'Fiscal Policy Coordination as Fiscal Federalism', *European Economic Review*, XXXVI (1992) 647–53.

Bureau D. and P. Champsaur, 'Fiscal Federalism and European Economic Unification', *American Economic Review*, LXXXII (1992) 88–92.

Button K. J. and T. G. Weyman-Jones, 'Ownership Structure, Institutional Organization and Measured X-Efficiency', *American Economic Review*, LXXXII (1992) 439–45.

Calvo G. and S. Wellisz, 'Supervision, Loss of Control, and the Optimum Size of the Firm', *Journal of Political Economy*, LXXXVI (1978) 943–52.

Calvo G. and S. Wellisz, 'Hierarchy, Ability, and Income Distribution', *Journal of Political Economy*, LXXXVII (1979) 991–1010.

Cantner U. and T. Kuhn, *Technischer Fortschritt in Bürokratien*, Discussion Paper no. 61 (Augsburg: Universität Augsburg, Institut für Volkswirtschaftslehre, 1991).

Carstensen V. *Hierarchien: Status und Entlohnung*, Discussion Paper no. 163 (Universität Hannover, Institut für Quantitative Wirtschaftsforschung, 1991).

Cartelier L., 'L'état et le Marché: quelques Éléments de Problématique', in *ADIS: L'État et le Marché* (Paris: Economica, 1994).

Casella A., 'On Markets and Clubs: Economic and Political Integration of Regions with Unequal Productivity', *American Economic Review*, LXXXII (1992) 115–21.

Casella A. and B. Frey, 'Federalism and Clubs – Towards an Economic Theory of Overlapping Political Jurisdictions', *European Economic Review*, XXXVI (1992) 639–46.

Christensen J. G., 'Regulation, Deregulation and Public Bureaucracy', *European Journal of Political Research*, XVII (1989) 223–39.

Coase R. H., 'The Nature of the Firm', *Economica*, IV (1937) 386–405.

Coase R. H., 'The Institutional Structure of Production', *American Economic Review*, LXXXII (1992) 713–19.

Coombes D., *Politics and Bureaucracy in the European Community* (London: P.E.P, 1970).

Crozier M., *The Bureaucratic Phenomenon* (Chicago, IL: University of Chicago Press, 1964).

Cullis J. G. and P. R. Jones, 'The Economics of Bureaucracy', in N. Gemmell (ed.), *The Growth of the Public Sector* (Aldershot: Edward Elgar, 1993) 86–102.

Davis O. A., M. A. H. Dempster and A. Wildavsky, 'Towards a Predictive Theory of Government Expenditure: US Domestic Appropriations', *British Journal of Political Science*, IV (1974) 419–52.

De Alessi L., 'Property Rights, Transaction Costs and X-Inefficiency', *American Economic Review*, LXXIII (1983) 64–81.

Dearden J., B. W. Ickes and L. Samuelson, 'To Innovate or Not To Innovate: Incentives and Innovation in Hierarchies', *American Economic Review*, LXXX (1990) 1105–24.

De Groot H., *Decentralization Decisions in Bureaucracies as a Principal-Agent Problem*, Discussion Paper no. 8706/P (Rotterdam Erasmus University Rotterdam, Institute for Economic Research, 1987).

Downs A., 'Non-Market Decision Making – A Theory of Bureaucracy', *American Economic Review*, LV (1965) 439–46.

Etzioni-Halevy E., 'Has the New Right Curbed Growth of Bureaucracy?', *Journal of Political and Military Sociology*, XXXIII (1985) 283–96.

Fabel O., 'Richterhierarchien und die Verbreitung der ökonomischen Analyse des Rechts', *Zeitschrift für Wirtschafts- und Sozialwissenschaften*, CXVI (1996) 1–13.

Feinstein J. S., 'Public-Good Provision and Political Stability in Europe', *American Economic Review*, LXXXII (1992) 323–9.

Frydman R., 'Les Identités du Marché', in *ADIS: L'État et le Marché* (Paris: Economica, 1994) ch. 2.

Garston N., 'Paradigms, Insights, and Problems', in N. Garston (ed.), *Bureaucracy – Three Paradigms* (Recent Economic Thought Series) (Boston, Dordrecht, and London: Kluwer, 1993).

Gemmell N., 'The Public Sector: Definition and Measurement Issues', in N. Gemmell (ed.), *The Growth of the Public Sector* (Aldershot: Edward Elgar, 1993) pp. 1–14.

Gradstein M., 'Rent-Seeking and the Provision of Public Goods', *Economic Journal*, CIII (1993) 1236–43.

Green J. and N. L. Stokey, 'A Comparison of Tournaments and Contracts', *Journal of Political Economy*, XCI (1983) 349–64.

Henrekson M. and J. A. Lybeck, 'Editors' Introduction and Summary', in J. A. Lybeck and M. Henrekson (eds), *Explaining the Growth of Government* (Amsterdam: Elsevier, North-Holland, 1988) pp. 3–19.

Horn H., H. Lang and S. Lundgren, 'Competition, Long-Run Contracts and Internal Inefficiencies in Firms', *European Economic Review*, XXXVIII (1994) 213–33.

Lazear E. P. and S. Rosen, 'Rank-Order Tournaments as Optimum Labor Contracts', *Journal of Political Economy*, LXXXIX (1981) 841–64.

Leibenstein H., 'Allocative Efficiency vs. 'X-Inefficiency' ', *American Economic Review*, LVI (1966) 392–415.

Leibenstein H., 'On the Basic Proposition of X-Inefficiency Theory', *American Economic Review*, LXVIII (1978a) 328–32.

Leibenstein H., 'X-Inefficiency Xists – Reply to Xorcist', *American Economic Review*, LXVIII (1978b) 203-11.

Levine A. (ed.), *The State and its Critics* (Aldershot: Edward Elgar, 1992).

March J. G. and H. A. Simon, *Organizations* (New York: Wiley, 1958).

Marris R., 'A Model of the Managerial Enterprise', *Quarterly Journal of Economics*, LXXVII (1963) 185–209.

Mayntz R., 'Max Webers Idealtypus der Bürokratie und die Organisationssoziologie', *Kölner Zeitschrift für Soziologie und Sozialpsychologie*, XVII (1965) 493–502.

Merton R. K., *Social Theory and Social Structure* (Glencoe, IL.: Free Press, 1957).

Meyer M. W., *Limits to Bureaucratic Growth* (Berlin: Walter De Gruyter, 1985).

Miconi B., *Three Themes in Institutions and Public Economics*, EU CompEcs Working Paper n. 2 (Siena: Università di Siena, Dipartimento di Economia Politica, 1995).

Milgrom P. R. and J. Roberts, 'The Efficiency of Equity in Organizational Decision Processes', *American Economic Review*, LXXX (1990) 154–9.

Mirrlees J. A., 'The Optimal Structure of Incentives and Authority within an Organization', *Bell Journal of Economics*, VII (1976) 105–31.

Molle W., *The Economics of European Integration* (Aldershot: Dartmouth, 1990).

Moths E. and M. Wulf-Mathies, *Des Bürgers teure Diener* (Karlsruhe: C. F. Müller, 1973).

Müller A., *Entscheidungsprozesse in öffentlichen Verwaltungen und Privaten Unternehmen* (Frankfurt a.M: R. G. Fischer, 1984).

Müller W., 'Die Relativierung des Bürokratischen Modells und die Situative Organization', *Kölner Zeitschrift für Soziologie und Sozialpsychologie*, XXV (1973) 719–49.

Neven D. J., 'Regulatory Reform in the European Community', *American Economic Review*, LXXXII (1992) 98–103.

Niskanen W. A., 'Non-Market Decision Making: The Peculiar Economics of Bureaucracy', *American Economic Review*, LVIII (1968) 293–305.

Niskanen W. A., 'Bureaucrats and Politicians', *Journal of Law and Economics*, XVIII (special issue, 1975) 617–43.

Nozick R., *Anarchy, State and Utopia* (New York: Basic Books, 1974).

Nutter G. W., *Growth of Government in the West* (Washington, DC: American Enterprise Institute for Public Policy Research, 1978).

Pempel T. J. and M. Muramatsu, *The Japanese Bureaucracy and Economic Development – Structuring a Proactive Civil Service*, EDI Working Paper no. 26 (Washington, DC: The International Bank for Reconstruction and Development – The World Bank,1993).

Peters B. G, *The Politics of Bureaucracy* (New York: Longman, 1978).

Petretto A. and G. Pisauro, 'La Riforma della Pubblica Amministrazione sotto il Profilo dell'Analisi Economica: I Controlli e la Ristrutturazione degli Uffici', *Politica Economica*, XI (1995) 13–59.

Roppel U., *Ökonomische Theorie der Bürokratie* (Freiburg i. Brsg: Haufe, 1979).

Rotemberg J. J., 'A Theory of Inefficient Intra-Firm Transactions', *American Economic Review*, LXXXI (1991) 191–209.

Sapir A., 'Regional Integration in Europe', *Economic Journal*, CII (1992) 1491–1506.

Saunders P., 'Recent Trends in the Size and Growth of Government in OECD Countries', in N. Gemmell (ed.), *The Growth of the Public Sector* (Aldershot: Edward Elgar, 1993) pp. 17–33.

Simon H. A., *Administrative Behavior*, 2nd edn (New York: Free Press, 1976).

Smith A. and A. J. Venables, 'Completing the Internal Market in the European Community', *European Economic Review*, XXXII (1988) 1501–25.

Starbatty J., *Was und wie bestimmt Brüssel tatsächlich? Wege gegen bürokratische Ausuferung*, Discussion Paper no. 27 (Tübingen: Universität Tübingen Wirtschaftswissenschaftliches Seminar, 1993).

Stigler G. J., 'The Xistence of X-Efficiency', *American Economic Review*, LXVI (1976) 213–16.

Stiglitz J. E., 'Incentives, Risk, and Information: Notes towards a Theory of Hierarchy', *Bell Journal of Economics*, VI (1975) 552–79.

Stiglitz J. E., *Wither Socialism?* (Cambridge, MA: MIT Press, 1994).

Terreberry S., 'The Evolution of Organizational Environments', *Administrative Science Quarterly*, XII (1968) 590–613.

Thompson J. D., *Organizations in Action* (New York, Toronto, and London: McGraw-Hill, 1967).

Weber M., *Wirtschaft und Gesellschaft – Grundriß der verstehenden Soziologie*. 5th rev. edn (Tübingen: Mohr, 1976).

Westrum R. and K. Samaha, *Complex Organizations: Growth, Struggle, and Change* (Englewood Cliffs, NJ: Prentice-Hall, 1984).

Williamson O. E., 'Hierarchical Control and Optimum Firm Size', *Journal of Political Economy*, LXXV (1967) 123–38.

Williamson O. E., *Markets and Hierarchies* (New York: Macmillan, 1983).

Wilson J. Q., *Bureaucracy – What Government Agencies Do and Why They Do It* (New York: Basic Books, 1989).

Notes

* Universität Konstanz, Germany, and Università di Siena, Italy.
1. See Gemmel (1993) on the underpinnings of various measures of governmental growth.
2. Prominent examples include Buchanan (1986), Nozick (1974), and the collection of essays in Levine (1992), respectively.
3. See Cartelier (1994), Frydman (1994), and Miconi (1995).
4. Etzioni-Halevy (1985).
5. A prime example of such an approach can be found in Petretto and Pisauro (1995).
6. Stiglitz (1994, ch. 13).
7. A thorough modern treatment of efficiency measurement can be found in Petretto and Pisauro (1995).
8. Due to lack of available space this survey can only point at the theoretic developments – emphasizing their impact on economic modelling. More details on the respective discussions within the sociological literature can be found in Coombes (1970, ch. 5), Meyer (1985, ch. 2), Müller (1973), Müller

(1984, ch.1), and Westrum and Samaha (1984, ch.1), for example. As the present survey, Roppel (1979, ch. 1) highlights the respective developments in economic theory, but places particular emphasis on reviewing approaches in political economy.

9. See also Coase's (1992) account of how dissatisfaction with classic economic theory motivated his research.

10. A more recent study by Borland and Yang (1992) associates increasing transaction costs with increased specialization, however – thus, reintroducing the classical hypothesis of a relationship between specialization and formal organization.

11. Mayntz (1965).

12. Downs (1965). In this spirit, Coombes (1970, p. 119) therefore concludes that, if the EU 'Commission has ... performed ... effectively, then it has not been a bureaucracy ....'

13. Milgrom and Roberts (1990) thus emphasize that 'equity' in the payment schedule can limit such activities.

14. In contrast, Stigler (1976) maintains that 'x-inefficiency' merely constitutes a special case of 'allocative efficiency'. Yet, compare Leibenstein (1978b). Also, see De Alessi (1983) for an evaluation and Button and Weyman-Jones (1992) for an attempt to discriminate empirically.

15. Hence, following Wilson (1989), a growing number of studies on the effects of rent-seeking behavior in the provision of public goods emphasizes privatization policies. Compare Gradstein (1993), for example. In contrast, Besley and Coate (1991) stress the redistributive virtue of publicly providing comsumption goods.

16. Following Aron (1990), establishing a control level may serve to signal a commitment to monitoring, however.

17. Williamson (1967).

18. Carstensen's (1991) analysis of the distribution of wages and the number of hierarchical layers thus necessarily requires an individual preference for 'status' again.

19. More precisely, the present account only constitutes a brief example. Yet, given somewhat more restrictive assumptions concerning the promotion mechanism, the results can be generalized. See Fabel (1996).

20. Compare Starbatty (1993).

21. See Molle (1990, ch. 4) for information on the organization of the European institutions and Starbatty (1993) on the current state of bureaucratic integration.

22. According to Pempel and Muramatsu (1993) the superior efficiency of the Japanese bureaucracy – compared with its western counterparts – must to a large extent be attributed to its ability of attracting high-quality personnel and its competitive interior incentive-system.

23. Compare Casella and Frey (1992). However, Etzioni-Halevy (1985) warns that the citizens' support for reforms in the provision of public goods may be particularly weak as the induced redistributive effects appear to favour middle-income and low middle-income groups. See Bureau and Champsaur (1992) for an investigation of the respective impacts of the EU structural programs.

24. This argument has attracted a rather vivid discussion (cf. Sapir (1992) and Casella (1992)). Smith and Venables (1998) provide a computable equilibrium approach particularly focusing on the benefits of integrating national markets.

25. Whereas Cantner and Kuhn (1991) conclude that a bureaucracy will always exploit all gains from technical innovations in order to increase the resources available for bureaucratic expansion, the present study thus follows Dearden, et al. 1990 in emphasizing the internal incentive-structure.
26. The '$\leq$' – sign only reflects a slight inherent preference for type-E decisions which is of no consequence for the results obtained below.
27. Compare Horn et al. (1994) for the respective argument as it applies to firms.
28. Also, Buiter and Kletzer (1992) stress that some sort of formal coordination will always be required as there exist regional public goods.

5
Long-Term Care Insurance, Savings, and Strategic Bequests

*Oliver Fabel and Daniela Georgus**

This study reviews the theoretical arguments put forth to explain market failure in the provision of private long-term care (LTC) insurance and describes the relevant stylized facts as they apply to Germany. It then develops a simple principal-agent model of intra-family strategic bequest/care exchanges. Within this framework the risk-relief effect associated with mandatory LTC-insurance – as introduced in Germany in 1995 – is seen to induce a decrease in the private savings of parents. Very likely total accumulated wealth, including insurance claims, is also depressed. At the same time, strategic bequest/care exchanges will be observed less frequently over all consumer groups and the level of expected bequests tends to be decreased as well. Interestingly however, care for parents who are LTC patients will become more common.

5.1 Introduction

Actuarially unfair premium payments clearly constitute a prime reason why individuals choose not to purchase adequate insurance against the long-term care (LTC) risk. Therefore, given reasonable data, Friedman and Manheim (1988) demonstrated that in many cases the individually optimal accumulation decisions may in fact preclude LTC-insurance. However, the question remains why the necessary premium payments fail to approach actuarial fairness. In this respect, Gaulke (1992), Segerer (1992), and Cutler (1993) stress insurers' difficulties in premium calculation owing to the lack of information concerning the current and future costs of care. However, this argument certainly applies to the introductory phase of every new insurance product dealing with lifetime risks. Thus, Schubert (1990) rather emphasizes the consumers' information deficit with regard to their general health insurance's provision in case of permanent illness and/or concerning the probabilities of becoming an LTC patient. The premium for additional LTC-insurance may then be subjectively perceived as excessively high. However, as noted by Buchholz and Wiegard (1992), there are clear commercial incentives which should encourage insurers to inform consumers in such cases. Moreover, consumer myopism contrasts strongly with the widespread trade in life insurance.[1] However, asymmetric information structures and the possibility of strategic misrepresentation of private information may give rise to persistent market failures. Although the pure incidence of becoming an LTC patient certainly does not impose an informational problem for the insurance firms,[2] Buchholz and Wiegard (1992) and Scanlon (1992) propose that there exists considerable moral hazard as far as the actual cost of care is concerned. In particular, the patient's options to choose between care services provided by either family members or professionals give rise to significant cost differences. Scanlon (1992) adds that the mere availability of family care constitutes private information of the patient and, thus, induces an additional adverse selection problem. Consequently, optimal contracts will generally provide less than perfect LTC-insurance. In the extreme such insurance contracts may then not be traded at all.

Contrasting with market imperfection approaches, Pauly (1989, 1990) pursues a rather different line of argument. The observed lack of private LTC-insurance demand is directly associated with the existing institutional environment. In particular, the benefit rules embodied in the US medicaid/medicare system are seen to reduce the individuals' incentives to insure against LTC risks. They provide LTC cost coverage only upon first completely exhausting the patients' private wealth – including insurance claims. The costs of LTC regularly exceed the available non-insurance wealth of the individual. Hence, the marginal utility of purchasing private LTC-insurance equals zero as the benefits received would only replace possible medicaid coverage. This yields a 'rational non-purchase motive' . A considerable number of authors – including Buchholz and Wiegard (1992), Breyer (1992), and Strüwe and Zweifel (1994), for example – have since noted that the same argument also applies to the German 'Sozialhilfe' (Social Aid) scheme. This tax-financed system guarantees a subsistence income for all citizens irrespective of social security membership. Its intentionally subsidiary character implies that all private wealth must be depleted before becoming eligible for Social Aid benefits. Thus, it developed to provide the single most important source of LTC cost funding in Germany in recent decades.

Consequently, Germany's new LTC-insurance legislation was publicly motivated by the widespread reliance on Social Aid by LTC patients. Most importantly, it established a new pay-as-you-go financed social LTC-insurance from January 1995. Following the arguments above – and, thus, rather ironically – the lack of private insurance coverage may be attributed to the government's failure to set correct incentives within the system. As demonstrated by Breyer (1992), the elderly will clearly benefit from pay-as-you-go. On first sight, the advantages of the young appear much less obvious. However, Pauly (1989) and Strüwe and Zweifel (1994) – drawing on the strategic bequest theory – suggest that a 'rational non-purchase' motive may also result from the intra-family principal-agent problem. Parents who prefer care by family members[3] over treatment by professionals must ensure that their children cannot *ex post* easily turn their responsibilities over to nursing homes. This can be achieved by purchasing none or only partial LTC-insurance *ex ante*. Richter and Ritzberger (1995) then further prove that the optimal timing of the rewards for family care implies bequeathing remaining wealth. By the same argument the newly introduced social LTC-insurance clearly exhibits a protective character as far as such bequests are concerned. Given the currently rather exploding volume of expected bequests in Germany, the newly introduced social LTC-insurance can thus also be interpreted as a mandatory 'bequest insurance' serving the particular interests of the children.

This paper is positive in nature, however. Distinguishing the institutional environments without and with social LTC-insurance, it contrasts the respective induced accumulation, bequest, and family care behaviour. Upon first providing a very brief description of the relevant stylized facts, it will develop a rather simple principal-agent model of strategic bequests which can be used to compare the individually optimal behaviours. The results – whose details need some qualifications, however – demonstrate a general tendency to decrease non-insurance savings and total wealth accumulation. Similarly, the bequest levels will be depressed also. Interestingly, introducing the LTC-insurance will yield less overall care of children for their parents. At the same time, however, it will increase the attention devoted to parents in need of LTC.

5.2 The stylized facts of LTC provisions in Germany

The fact that less than 2 per cent of the US elderly population possesses private LTC-insurance coverage constitutes the point of departure for

Pauly's (1989, 1990) original studies. However, as can be verified from Scanlon (1992) and Gabanyi (1993) similar observations can be obtained for most industrialized countries. Consequently, the need for government intervention has also been articulated for some time and in varying national policy environments. Again for the US, Jacobs and Weissert (1985) already note that LTC costs range between $12,000 and $50,000 annually. Thus, they typically exceed the average income of the patients, of which 90 per cent are elderly.[4] The particular German situation briefly portrayed in the following may thus in fact be rather representative. According to PKV (1993) only less than 0.2 per cent of the German population had purchased private LTC-insurance immediately prior to the introduction of the mandatory insurance legislation. This contrasts strongly with the widespread use of private health insurance to supplement social health insurance benefits. In this respect, it should be noted that such health insurance contracts only supply a very limited amount of additional LTC cost coverage. It is restricted to purely medical bills and available only upon long-lasting membership.[5] In fact, German insurers, largely responding to government pressure,[6] only began to offer LTC-insurance from 1985.

As indicated in Table 5.1, the LTC risk can be characterized as a typical old-age risk. Rather extreme losses match with relatively low probabilities of infliction. Thus, the LTC risk should be well insurable. Nevertheless, the overwhelming bulk of the respective financial burden was shifted towards the Social Aid system. Thus, although only 18 per cent of the Social Aid recipients applied for LTC cost coverage,[7] Deininger (1993) estimates that roughly 35 per cent of the DM 15 billion Social Aid budget was spent on LTC cost subsidies in 1992 – 31 per cent for nursing home bills alone.[8] Moreover, over the past three decades these subsidies were increasing at an average annual rate of 12 per cent. This is clearly because, according to Krug and Reh (1992), 67 per cent of institutionalized LTC patients relied completely on Social Aid payments due to insufficient income and already exhausted private wealth. The average per-person subsidy for nursing home patients reached DM 2022 in 1990. Table 5.2 indicates the respective distribution of Social Aid subsidies.

The introduction of the mandatory LTC-insurance in Germany clearly reflects the government's intention to provide an alternative financial source. Whether it has succeeded in doing so on a large scale may be doubted, however. Since January 1995, all individuals legally required to participate in the social pay-as-you-go financed health insurance contribute an additional 1 per cent of gross income to the newly founded social LTC-insurance – also operating as pay-as-you-go. As usual in

Table 5.1   The LTC risk in Germany

Cases	Persons permanently needing:		
	Household assistance and medical care (1990–91)	Only household assistance (1990–91)	Nursing home care (1990)
Millions	1.12	2.09	0.36
% of population	1.40	2.70	0.60

Age composition of LTC-patients (% of patients in 1990–91)					
Age group	0–15	16–39	40–64	65–79	80 and above
In private homes	6	9	14	28	43
Institutionalized	1		11	25	63

LTC-patients as percentage of their age-group in the population (1990–91)					
Age group	0–15	16–39	40–64	65–79	80 and above
In private homes	0.5	0.4	0.6	3.5	16.4
Institutionalized	(insignificant)		0.2	1.2	9.2

Distribution of monthly LTC costs in nursing homes (1990)						
DM-range	0–1, 500	1500 – 2000	2000 – 2500	2500 3000	3000– 3500	3500– 4000	Above 4000
% of patients	1	8	17	35	21	10	8

Note: Figures for age composition of LTC patients and percentage of LTC-patients per age group in private homes apply to former West Germany only.
Sources: Infratest (1993), Krug and Reh (1992), own calculations based on additional statistics by Statistisches Bundesamt (1992).

Germany the contribution was divided into equal 50 per cent contribution shares between employers and employees. From its start, the rate was scheduled to rise to 1.7 per cent by July 1996. This mirrored the fact that the scheme at first only covered outpatient costs. Nursing home cost coverage was introduced in July 1996. All other individuals are mandated to purchase private LTC-insurance with (at least) equal coverage. In this respect, it should be noted that the legally necessitated social health insurance membership excludes mainly self-employed and high-income employees. Thus, individuals who before were likely to contribute considerable private wealth in order to cover LTC costs are not required to participate in the new public scheme. By the same argument, the lower income groups now actually participating were previously characterized

Table 5.2 Social Aid subsidies for nursing home services and characteristics of private home LTC in Germany

LTC cost subsidies per institutionalized patient derived from Social Aid (1990)				
DM-range	0–1000	1000–2000	2000–3000	Above 3000
% of patients	13	42	31	14

Suppliers and recipients of LTC in private homes (1991)			
Supplier is:	All recipients: %	Recipient is: Aged 65–79 %	Above 80 %
Husband/wife	37	61	17
Parent	14	0	0
Child or child's husband/wife	38	32	67
Other relative	7	6	9
Friend/neighbour	4	2	7

Supplier is:	All recipients: %	Recipient is: Husband/wife %	Parent %	Child %
Female	83	65	≅ 100	92
Male	17	35	≅ 0	8

Sources: Krug and Reh (1992), Infratest (1993), own calculations.

by a higher average level of necessary LTC cost subsidies. Moreover, due to lower tax rates they had also contributed less to finance Social Aid than those who are now turning to private insurers. While this institutional change therefore appears to favour the rich rather than the poor, pay-as-you-go financing itself must further generally be viewed as inadequate given the ageing of the German population.[9]

The social LTC-insurance's benefits distinguish private from nursing home care. With respect to the former, three degrees of need for care are defined medically. They yield a choice between maximum monthly benefits in kind valued DM 750, DM 1800, and DM 2800 and monetary payments of DM 400, DM 800, and DM 1300, respectively. For extreme cases an absolute maximum of DM 3750 applies. The scheme will also pay the contributions for the social pension insurance for those who provide the private home care and, thus, cannot take up full employment. In this respect, it is worth noting that for 79 per cent of those primarily responsible for the provision of LTC, this constitutes a full-time job.[10] From Table 5.2 it can also be seen that the overwhelming majority of the suppliers of LTC are women and in most cases have a direct relationship with the patient. As patients age – hence, according to Table 5.1, the probability of infliction becomes more significant – responsibility for care further gradually shifts from husbands/wives to children. Nursing home costs will be refunded up to DM 3300, the average payment originally required not to exceed DM 2500. However, these figures only apply to medical treatment. The so-called 'hotel costs' – which are officially estimated to constitute 30 per cent of the total costs on average[11] – should be paid by the patients. According to Rüdiger and Seiler (1992), it can thus be doubted whether the social LTC-insurance actually provides an improvement for hospitalized patients. This can also be confirmed by checking against the data provided by Krug and Reh (1992): 47 per cent of LTC patients formerly receiving Social Aid benefits possessed less than DM 1000 accountable private income, while the average 'hotel costs' were already estimated to amount to DM 846.

Thus, the attention should generally shift towards emphasizing the implicit effects of the institutional change. In this respect, the increased importance of obtaining 'bequest insurance' is quite easily verified. Wahl (1994) points out that the current parent generation in former West Germany is the first postwar generation which has been able to accumulate over its full life span. Obviously, the volume of the currently expected bequests can only be estimated, but is certainly rather significant. Thus, IWG (1990) reports estimates of DM 80 billion for 1989, a value which needed upward correction only a few years later. Over the decade 1990–2000 IWG (1994) now estimates total bequests of DM 1 trillion, increasing from DM 100 billions in 1993 to DM 135 billions in 2000. Similarly, the Bundesbank (1993) expects annual bequests ranging from DM 100 to DM 200 billion. According to Heise (1993), there will be roughly five million deaths in the 1990s to be associated with 25 million bequests. The average individual bequest can therefore be approximated to amount to DM 200 000 for 1989, increasing to DM 270 000 in 2000. Information on a possibly existing strategic saving/bequest motive cannot be provided as easily. A survey by Noelle-Neumann (1993) reveals rather split evidence. Among all respondents, 42 per cent expected that the new LTC-insurance will lead to more institutionalization, while 35 per cent did not expect change. At the same time, 61 per cent (17 per cent) of the respondents aged 60 and above claimed private home care (nursing home care) to be superior, however.

5.3   Basic assumptions and notations

The model introduced in the following distinguishes a principal – referred to as the 'parent' – and an agent, the 'child' . The parent's certain lifetime consists of two periods – 'youth' and 'retirement' – identified by subscript $t = 1,2$. First-period utility is solely derived from consumption c_1, while second-period utility depends on consumption c_2 and the level of attention or care a received from the child. The parent bears the risk of becoming an LTC patient only in the second period, with p, $0 < p < 1$, denoting the probability of incurring the adverse health shock. Let superscript j, $j = h, i$, identify the two possible health states 'healthy' and 'permanently ill' during retirement, respectively. The parent's expected lifetime utility is then further specified as

$$EU = \ln(c_1) + \rho\big[(1 - p) + \{\ln(c_2^h) + v^P\ln(a^h)\} + p\{\ln(c_2^i) + v^P\ln(a^i)\}\big] \quad (1)$$

with $\rho = 1$ denoting the subjective discount factor and $v^P > 0$. This particularly simple form of expected lifetime utility serves to emphasize that the current study intentionally restricts the effect of becoming an LTC patient to realizing a purely pecuniary shock. Thus,

$$c_1 = W^P - s - \frac{p}{R}\theta K \qquad (2)$$

$$c_2^h = X + Rs - b^h \qquad (3)$$

Given equation (1), the incidence of becoming an LTC patient exhibits no impact on either the marginal utility of consumption, nor the marginal utility of attention received from the child. However, if reaching state i during retirement, the parent must bear medical costs $K > 0$. These can be covered by savings s out of labour income and inherited wealth $W^P > 0$ received in the first period and old-age pension benefits $X > 0$. Furthermore, the parent may be able to turn to an LTC-insurance which pays benefits conditional on becoming an LTC patient. If it exists, this insurance will be assumed to be actuarially fair. Note that this does not necessarily imply a particular financing method, however. The assumption only rules out additional adverse income effects associated with resorting to pay-as-you-go under population ageing. Thus, it actually generates a more optimistic setting with respect to the wealth accumulation process.[12] Parents who wish to obtain benefits $\theta K, \theta \in [0,1]$, in retirement state i, must therefore provide premium payments $\frac{p}{R}\theta K$, where R denotes the market interest factor. Thus generally

$$c_2^i = X + Rs - K - b^i + \theta \qquad (4)$$

with b^i as bequests to the child. The parent maximizes equation (1) subject to equations (2)–(4). Assuming $K < RW^P + X$ ensures that $EU^P > -\infty$. Given the two-period certain lifetime, it is clearly economically meaningless to restrict savings s to be non-negative. Thus, equations (2)–(4) only require all consumption and bequests to be financed out of individual net lifetime wealth. However, given the notion 'retirement' attached to the second period, it also appears plausible to assume that youth income plus interest payments on net youth income, subjectively discounted, should always be strictly greater than old-age income – hence, introducing a desire to shift income from youth towards retirement:

$\rho R[W^P - \theta\frac{P}{R}K] > X$. This can be satisfied for all $\theta \in [0, 1]$, if

$$X < [RW^P - pK] \tag{5}$$

As for the child, it observes the health status of the parent before deciding upon the care level a. The child's preferences can be expressed by the utility function

$$U^C = \ln(I) - v^C \ln(a) \tag{6}$$

with I denoting income and $v^C > 0$. This utility function for the child is again clearly motivated by the intention to keep the analysis as simple as possible. It should be noted, however, that the structural form in equation (6) could be derived as an indirect utility function from equation (2) in a full-grown overlapping generations model introducing care for the parent an income-generating activity during the youth period.[13] It is convenient to define $a \in [\underline{a}, \infty)$, with $\underline{a} = 1$ referring to a minimum level of attention necessitated by the simple fact of being a child. Like the parent, the child will be assumed to be perfectly self-interested. Thus, normalizing $\underline{a} = 1$, it will only exert the care level, a^j if

$$\ln(W^C + b^j_l) - v^C\ln(a^j) \geq \ln(W^C) \qquad j = h, i \tag{7}$$

where $W^C > 0$ denotes wealth excluding the bequest. The (implicit) contract between parent and child concerning the supply of care levels a^j in exchange for bequests b^j is assumed to be perfectly enforceable. The parent can consume the intended bequest during her old age, if the child does not exert the agreed attention level. At the same time, the child can monitor the parent's consumption level and potentially withdraw from supplying care upon observing a contract breach.[14] Hence, equation (7) constitutes additional constraints on the expected utility maximization of the parent. Furthermore,

$$b^j \geq 0 \quad \text{for} \quad j = h, i \tag{8}$$

$$a^j \geq \quad \text{for} \quad j = h, i \tag{9}$$

must obviously be satisfied as well.

5.4   Individually optimal insurance coverage

The main effect of introducing a public LTC-insurance may be seen in abolishing the 'rational non-purchase' motive as analysed by Pauly (1989, 1990). This is due to the fact that a system in which LTC-cost subsidies are paid conditional upon becoming an LTC-patient *and* contingent on the individual's wealth is replaced by a social insurance guaranteeing benefit receipts conditional only on the realized health state. Consequently, the parent may actually be able to choose an individually optimal coverage in the LTC-state *i* as combination of public and private insurance.

Formally this implies:[15]

Proposition 1

Let the solution of maximizing equation (1) subject to equations (2)–(4) and (7)–(9) be denoted $\{\tau, S, B^i, B^h, A^i, A^h\}$. Then the optimal insurance coverage τ always equals unity. Moreover, optimal bequest and care levels satisfy: $B^i = B^h \equiv B, A^i = A^h \equiv A$. Thus, it is possible to distinguish two cases:

(I) *If*

$$W^C \leq \frac{\rho v^P \left[RW^P + X - pK \right]}{v^C [1 + \rho]} \equiv L^I \tag{10}$$

there exist interior solutions with respect to A and B. The optimum is characterized by

$$S = \frac{(v^C + v^P)\rho \left[RW^P - pK \right] - v^C \left[X + W^C \right]}{R \left[v^C (1 + \rho) + v^P \rho \right]} \tag{11}$$

$$B = \frac{v^P \rho}{\left[v^C (1 + \rho) + v^P \rho \right]} \left[RW^P + X - pK - \frac{v^C (1 + \rho)}{v_P \rho} W^C \right] \tag{12}$$

$$\ln(A) = \frac{1}{v^C} \ln \left(\frac{v^P \rho}{\left[v^C (1 + \rho) + v^P \rho \right]} \left[RW^P + X - pK + W^C \right] \right) - \frac{1}{v^C} \ln(W^C) \tag{13}$$

(II) *If*

$$W^C > \frac{\rho v^P \left[RW^P + X - pK \right]}{v^C [1 + \rho]} \equiv L^I \tag{14}$$

the attention by and bequest to the child attain the corner solutions $A = 1$ and $B = 0$, respectively. The optimum savings level is given by

$$S = \frac{\rho(RW^P - pK) - X}{R(1 + \rho)} \tag{15}$$

First, because the optimal insurance coverage in this case always implies perfect income insurance with respect to the LTC risk, the parent's health status does not influence her choice to engage in a bequest/care exchange with the child. Rather, the distinction between cases (I) and (II) only hinges on whether or not the parent can improve her well-being by '*purchasing*' attention by way of satisfying the participation constraint equation (7). The benchmark income L^I for the child generally depends on the parent's discounted net lifetime wealth, however – thus, constitutes a measure of the child's relative wealth compared with its parent. Therefore, when children (parents) are relatively wealthy (poor) $W^C > L^I$ – the high price of care associated with inducing voluntary participation of the children, prevents the bequest/care contract. More-over, irrespective of whether the bequest is positive or not, optimal savings S will always yield the well known condition for the efficient inter-temporal allocation of resources by the parent: $C_1 = \rho R C_2$ with C_t, $t = 1, 2$, referring to optimal consumption levels under the perfect LTC-insurance regime.

5.5 Non-Existence of an LTC-Insurance

If for any one of the arguments noted in the introduction, there does not exist LTC-insurance, the parent maximizes equation (1) subject to equations (2)–(4) and (7)–(9), with $\theta = 0$ introduced as an additional institutional constraint. The characteristics of respective solution can then be summarized as:

Proposition 2

Let $\{\sigma, \beta^h, \beta^i, \alpha^h, \alpha^i\}$ denote the solution to the parent's optimization problem given no LTC-insurance. Then there exist limits L_i^{NI} and L_h^{NI}, with $L_i^{NI} < L_h^{NI}$, for the child's income W^C such that:

(1) If $W^C \geq L_I^{NI}$,

$$\beta^h = \frac{v^P[R\sigma + X] - v^C W^C}{(v^P + v^C)}; \quad \beta^i = \frac{v^P[R\sigma + X - K] - v^C W^C}{(v^P + v^C)} \tag{16}$$

(2) If $L_i^{NI} < W^C \geq L_h^{NI}$,

$$\beta^h = \frac{v^P[R\sigma + X] - v^C W^C}{(v^P + v^C)}; \quad \beta^i = 0 \tag{17}$$

(3) If $L_h^{NI} < W^C$,

$$\beta^h = 0; \beta^i = 0 \tag{18}$$

Further, inserting from equations (16)–(18) according to the distinction of cases (1)–(3), the unique optimal savings level is implicitly given by

$$-\frac{1}{W^P - \sigma} + \frac{\rho R(1-p)}{R\sigma + X - \beta^h} + \frac{\rho Rp}{R\sigma + X - K - \beta^i} = 0 \qquad (19)$$

Finally, the optimal attention levels must satisfy:

$$\ln(\alpha^h) = \frac{1}{v^C}\ln\left(\frac{v^P}{v^C + v^P}[R\sigma + X + W^C]\right) - \frac{1}{v^C}\ln(W^C), \text{ if } \beta^h > 0 \qquad (20)$$

$$\ln(\alpha^i) = \frac{1}{v^C}\ln\left(\frac{v^P}{v^C + v^P}[R\sigma + X + W^C - K]\right) - \frac{1}{v^C}\ln(W^C), \text{ if } \beta^i > 0 \qquad (21)$$

and

$$\alpha^i = 1 \text{ if } \beta^i = 0, j = h, i.$$

According to Proposition 2, a child which is relatively poor compared with its parent's net lifetime wealth will supply care in both health states in exchange for bequests. As the child's income increases, it will ultimately withdraw from the care contract if the parent becomes an LTC patient. The care-bequest exchange now only applies to healthy parents. Increasing the child's wealth even further will in the end then lead to a complete withdrawal from providing care for the parent. In short, as under optimal perfect insurance, poor children will 'care' more about their parents, since they marginally benefit more from receiving bequests. With no LTC-insurance available, children will also prefer to 'care' for healthy parents, since this is less costly to them. Note also that, whenever the parent intends to bequeath some wealth in exchange for care in state $j = h,i$, the optimal bequest will be a fraction $v^P/(v^P+v^C)$ and the optimal parent consumption – hereafter denoted $\{Z_1, Z_2^i, Z_2^h\}$ – a fraction $v^C/(v^P + v^C)$ of the respective parent net income in this state.

5.6   Comparing regimes with and without LTC-insurance

As set out above, the main purpose of the analysis consists of allowing a comparison of the individual accumulation, consumption, and bequest behaviours as the institutional setting changes from providing no LTC-insurance at all – due to market failure – to allowing for optimal (perfect) insurance of the medical LTC costs. In the following, let $E\{Z_2\} \equiv pZ_2^i + (1-p)Z_2^h$; $E\{Z\} \equiv RZ_1 + E\{Z_2\}$ and $E\{\beta\} \equiv p\beta^i + (1-p)\beta^h$. Although not exhaustive, owing to the inability to derive an explicit solution with respect to σ, conclusions concerning the optimal levels of savings (expected) bequests, consumption, and care can then be summarized as follows.

Proposition 3

The limits on the child's income introduced in Propositions 1 and 2 satisfy

$$L_i^{NI} < L^I < L_h^{NI} \tag{22}$$

Thus, there exist four possible combinations of cases (I)–(II) of Proposition 1 and (1)–(3) of Proposition 2 which are relevant for investigating the effect of a regime change

(A) $W^C \leq L_i^{NI}$:

$$S + \frac{P}{R}K < \sigma < S + \frac{1}{R}K \tag{23}$$

$$E\{Z_2\} > C_2; \ E\{Z\} < RC_1 + C_2 \tag{24}$$

$$\beta^i < B; \ \beta^h > B; \ E\{\beta\} > B \tag{25}$$

$$\alpha^i < A; \ \alpha^h > A \tag{26}$$

(B) $L_i^{NI} < W^C \leq L^I$:

$$S < \sigma < S + \frac{1}{R}K \tag{27}$$

$$E\{Z\} < RC_1 + C_2 \tag{28}$$

$$0 = \beta^i < B < \beta^h; \ 1 = \alpha^i < A < \alpha^h \tag{29}$$

(C) $L^I < W^C \leq L_h^{NI}$:

$$S < \sigma < S + \frac{1}{R}K \tag{30}$$

$$E\{Z_2\} < C_2; \ E\{Z\} < RC_1 + C_2 \tag{31}$$

$$\beta^h > \beta^i = B = 0; \ \alpha^h > \alpha^i = A = 1 \tag{32}$$

(D) $L_h^{NI} < W^C$:

$$S + \frac{P}{R}K < \sigma < S + \frac{1}{R} \tag{33}$$

$$E\{Z_2\} > C_2; \ E\{Z\} = RC_1 + C_2 \tag{34}$$

$$\beta^i = \beta^h = B = 0; \ \alpha^i = \alpha^h = A = 1 \tag{35}$$

Thus, it is guaranteed that savings will decrease upon introduction of the LTC-insurance. This is clearly due to the risk reduction implied by the insurance: in order to ensure an adequate consumption level in state i the individual would have to provide savings in excess of those needed in state h. Hence, with probability $(1 - p)$ the savings level will turn out to be inadequately high. This risk of over-savings is eliminated by the LTC-insurance. Given case (A) with purely interior solutions and case (D) entailing corner solutions under both regimes, the risk-reduction effect can be seen to be strong enough such as to over-compensate the premium costs associated with the insurance: $\Delta = \sigma - S > \frac{p}{R}K$. This contrasts with cases (B) and (C) in which the parent desires positive bequests only in the healthy retirement state, given the regime without an LTC-insurance. Because old-age income in state h always equals old-age income given perfect insurance, inter-temporally efficient accumulation necessarily only yields $\sigma > S$ in these cases.

It should be noted that the availability of LTC-insurance generally decreases the probability of observing positive bequests as $L_h^{NI} > L^I$. Further, the level of (expected) bequests tends to be depressed as well. At the same time, $L_i^{NI} < L^I$ implies that care for LTC-inflicted parents will become more common, however. As for the welfare effect, if should finally be recalled that introducing the LTC-insurance always increases the parent's expected lifetime utility. This simply follows from $\tau \neq 0$ according to Proposition 1.

5.7 Summary and conclusions

In order to discuss the savings effects of introducing an LTC-insurance, first consider the group of consumers who will bequeath positive wealth as 'healthy' retirees and as LTC-patients under both institutional regimes. The parent's wealth constitutes a very significant initial endowment for the child. This should be true rather for rich families than for poor. The prime example clearly is of the self-employed parent bequeathing a business. Thus, it is likely that the parent will not be required to participate in the pay-as-you-go financed social LTC-insurance. Instead they will turn to private insurers. However, the sum of savings and premium payments – hence, total wealth accumulated during youth – will decrease under the mandatory insurance regime for this consumer group.

As the relative wealth position of the child improves, a similar clear-cut conclusion with respect to the sum of savings and premium payments cannot be obtained. Nevertheless, this may not be necessary in order to show an induced decrease in total wealth accumulation. Note that these cases should be associated with moderate to low income brackets for the parent and child. These individuals will likely be covered under the new social LTC-insurance. But, pay-as-you-go financing implies no accumulation of funds anyway. Assume, for example, that additional private LTC-insurance is in principle available, but the social LTC-insurance provides an optimal perfect insurance. Consequently, actually accumulated wealth during youth equals private savings and will, thus, decrease as well. If the social insurance coverage falls short of providing perfect income insurance, the conclusion will hinge on the exact amount of additional private insurance necessary to achieve optimum coverage. Higher social insurance coverage always increases the probability that accumulated wealth decreases.

Finally, consider families in which the parents do not contribute a positive bequest to the children's initial endowment because the child is already relatively wealthy. This case will likely apply to rather low-income groups in which individuals almost exclusively rely on labour income. The sum of private savings and insurance premium again falls short of the private savings level under the no-insurance regime. Thus, the accumulated wealth will decrease irrespective of the financing method employed to provide LTC-insurance coverage.

This final case only applies to families who do not possess strategic savings for the bequests motive under either scenario. The first three cases in the analysis above are clearly most important in discussing the possible effects of introducing an LTC-insurance on the bequest/care exchanges. It should be noted that such exchanges will generally be observed less frequently over all income groups. However, this only reflects the fact that, without such insurance, the children for which the possible bequests constitute significant endowments are subject to more effective incentives to care for 'healthy' parents. In particular, family care for elderly LTC-patients will become more common. The insured parent will be willing to devote more income in the LTC state to purchase the child's attention.

Furthermore, the bequest volume will certainly decrease in families with relatively and very wealthy parents. Given the classification above, the same holds true for moderate income groups for families in which the child is relatively wealthy compared with its parents. For families with moderate income parents in which the child is relatively less wealthy, this may not hold true. In this case, bequests will occur in both retirement health states when the insurance is introduced. However, it will be recalled that the probability of LTC infliction is rather small. Furthermore, without insurance the optimal bequests received from 'healthy' parents always exceed the optimal bequests under the insurance regime, and it is very likely that the bequest volume will decrease in this case as well.

APPENDIX

Proof of Proposition 1

First, it should be emphasized that the problem imposes no non-negativity constraints on s or requires θ to be less than or equal one. Although not explicitly shown below, it can be verified that both variables always actually attain an interior global maximum. Second, note that, due to the non-satiation of the parent's expected life-time utility, equations (7) always holds as equality. Thus, equations (8) and (9) constitute equivalent constraints. Hence, substituting from equation (7) for $\ln(a^j)$ into equation (1), the first-order conditions assuming interior solutions for all variables can be rearranged as

$$\frac{1}{W^P - S - \frac{P}{R}\tau K} = \frac{\rho R p}{RS + X - B^i - (1-\tau)K} + \frac{\rho R(1-p)}{RS + X - B^h} \tag{A.1}$$

$$\frac{v^P}{v^C}\left[RS + X - (1-\tau)K - B^i\right] = W^C + B^i \tag{A.2}$$

$$\frac{v^P}{v^C}\left[RS + X - B^h\right] = W^C + B^h \tag{A.3}$$

$$R\rho\left[W^P - S - \tau\frac{P}{R}K\right] = RS + X - B^i - (1-\tau)K \tag{A.4}$$

Now, equations (A.2) and (A.3) yield

$$B^h = B^i - \frac{v^P}{(v^P + v^C)}(1-\tau)K \tag{A.5}$$

while inserting equation (A.4) into equation (A.1) generates $B^h = B^i + (1-\tau)K$. Since $v^P, v^C > 0, \tau = 1$. Thus, optimal savings S can be calculated as exposed in equation (11) and it is possible to evaluate a limit income L^i_i compatible with an interior solution with respect to b^i. Explicitly it is given by the expression L^i in the proposition.

Next, suppose $B^j = 0$ and, hence, $A^j = 1$, for both states $j = i,h$. Inserting from equation (A.4) into equation (A.1) then yields $0 = -(1-\tau)K \Rightarrow \tau = 1$. Optimal savings S as spelled out in equation (15) then follow upon insertion. Further investigation confirms that the limit L^i_h compatible with the corner solution $b^h = 0$ must also be identically equal to L^1 defined in Proposition 1. Thus, it must only be distinguished whether $W^C \leq L^i$ or $W^C \geq L^i$ when characterizing the optimum. In both cases the optimal insurance coverage is $\tau = 1$. The remaining characteristics of the optimum can now easily be verified by inserting to obtain explicit solutions. Q.E.D.

Proof of Proposition 2

First, note again that equation (7) must hold with equality and, hence, equations (8) and (9) constitute equivalent constraints for states $j = h,i$. Assuming an interior solution with respect to s and $\{b^j, a^j\}$, equation (19) can easily be identified as the respective first-order condition with respect to s, while equation (16) follows from simple rearrangements of the respective first-order conditions for bequests b^j. Hence, in this case optimal bequests in both retirement health states can be expressed as a function of savings: $\beta^j = \beta^j(s)$. Thus, the parent's expected lifetime utility only depends on s. Inserting and differentiating with respect to s yields

$$
\frac{\partial EU^P(s)}{\partial s}\Big|_{s=\sigma} = -\frac{1}{W^P - \sigma} + \frac{\rho(1-p)\left[R - \dfrac{\partial \beta^h(\sigma)}{\partial s}\right]}{R\sigma + X - \beta^h(\sigma)} + \frac{v^P \rho(1-p)\dfrac{\partial \beta^h(\sigma)}{\partial s}}{v^C[W^C + \beta^h(\sigma)]}
$$

$$
+ \frac{\rho p\left[R - \dfrac{\partial \beta^i(\sigma)}{\partial s}\right]}{R\sigma + X - K - \beta^i(\sigma)} + \frac{v^P \rho p\dfrac{\partial \beta^i(\sigma)}{\partial s}}{v^C[W^C + \beta^i(\sigma)]} = 0,
$$

(A.6)

if σ is in the interior. The respective second-order derivative can be rearranged as

$$
\frac{\partial^2 EU^P(s)}{[\partial s]^2} = -\frac{1}{(W-s)^2} - \frac{\rho(1-p)\left[R - \dfrac{\partial \beta^h(s)}{\partial s}\right]^2}{[Rs + R - \beta^h(s)]^2} - \frac{v^P \rho(1-p)\left[\dfrac{\partial \beta^h(s)}{\partial s}\right]^2}{v^C[W^C + \beta^h(s)]^2}
$$

$$
- \frac{\rho p\left[R - \dfrac{\partial \beta^i(s)}{\partial s}\right]^2}{[Rs + X - K - \beta^i(s)]^2} - \frac{v^P \rho p\left[\dfrac{\partial \beta^i(s)}{\partial s}\right]^2}{v^C[W^C + \beta^i(s)]^2} < 0
$$

(A.7)

and, thus, confirms that the parent's expected lifetime utility is strictly concave in s for $\beta^j \geq 0, j = h, i$. Hence, σ defined by equation (A.6) characterizes an interior maximum. Moreover, it can be obtained that

$$
\lim_{s \to \frac{1}{R}[K-R]} EU^P(s) = -\infty; \quad \lim_{s \to W^P} EU^P(s) = -\infty
$$

(A.8)

This suffices to show the existence of exactly one limit for W^C denoted L_i^{NI} such that, for $W^C > L_i^{NI}$, the optimum entails a corner solution. Investigating the functions equation (16) at the optimal savings level σ reveals that necessarily $\beta^i = 0$. Setting $b^i = 0$ in EU^P and deriving first-order conditions with respect to $\{s, b^h, a^h\}$ yields equation (17) and restates equation (19). Hence, again in the optimum $\beta^h = \beta^h(s)$. Repeating the procedure from above, confirms the characteristics noted as case (2) and yields the additional limit L_h^{NI}. Case (3) then follows upon verifying that there exists a unique optimal savings level σ, given $n^j = 0$, for $j = h, i$. Q.E.D.

Proof of Proposition 3

Given Propositions 1 and 2, assume $W^C \leq \min\{L_i^{NI}, L^I\}$. Hence, case (1) of Proposition 1 and case (1) of Proposition 2 apply. From equations (12) and (16) obtain:

$$
\beta^i = B + \frac{v^P}{(v^P + v^C)}[R\Delta - K]
$$

(A.9)

$$
\beta^h = B + \frac{Rv^P}{(v^C + v^P)}\Delta
$$

(A.10)

with $\Delta = \sigma - S$. Inserting into equation (19) then yields

$$
\frac{1}{W^P - \sigma} = \frac{\rho R(1-p)}{RS + X - B + \left(1 - \dfrac{Rv^P}{(v^c + v^P)}\right)[\sigma - S]}
$$

$$+ \frac{\rho R p}{RS + X - B + \left(1 - \frac{Rv^P}{(v^C + v^P)}\left[\sigma - S - \frac{1}{R}K\right]\right)}$$

$$> \frac{\rho R}{RS + X - B + \left(1 - \frac{Rv^P}{(v^C + v^P)}\right)\left[\sigma - S - \frac{p}{R}K\right]}$$ (A.11)

accounting for Jensen's inequality. The equality confirms the upper limit for σ, while the lower limit follows from the inequality.

Quite clearly, this also implies $\beta^i < B < \beta^h$ and therefore, yields $L_I^{NI} < L^i < L_h^{NI}$. The distinction of cases in the proposition above then follows. Thus, turning to case (B) it can similarly be established that

$$\frac{1}{W^P - \sigma} = \rho R \left[\frac{p}{R\sigma + X - K} + \frac{(1-p)}{RS + X - \left\{\frac{(v^c + v^p)}{V^p} - 1\right\}\{b^h - B\}} \right]$$

$$> \rho R \left[\frac{1}{pR\sigma + (1-p)RS + X - pk + (1-p)\left\{\frac{(v^c + v^p)}{V^p}\right\}\{\beta^h - B\}} \right]$$ (A.12)

Yet, given equation (A.4), equation (A.1) implies

$$\frac{1}{W^P - S - \frac{p}{R}K} = \frac{\rho R}{RS + X}$$ (A.13)

As before $S \geq (<)\sigma \Rightarrow B \geq (<)\beta^h$. Thus, comparing equation (A.12) with equation (A.13) proves $S < \sigma < S + \frac{1}{R}K$ for case (B).

Following the same routine the remaining conclusions with respect to the savings levels for cases (C) and (D) can be verified easily as well. All other results reported follow from simple insertion. Q.E.D.

References

Beck M., 'Sozialhilfeempfänger 1992', *Wirtschaft und Statistik* (1994) 466—71, and 557–68.

Bernheim D. B., A. Shleifer and L. H. Summers, 'The Strategic Bequest Motive', *Journal of Political Economy*, XCIII (1985) 1045–76.

BMF, *Stellungnahme des Wissenschaftlichen Beirats beim Bundesministerium der Finanzen zur Finanzierung der Pflegekosten*, BMF Dokumentation n. 6 (Bonn: German Federal Ministry of Finance, BMF, 1990).

Breyer F., 'Verteilungswirkungen unterschiedlicher Formen der Pflegeversicherung', *Finanzarchiv*, IL (1992) 84–103.

Buchholz W. and W. Wiegard, 'Allokative Überlegungen zur Reform der Pflegeversicherung', *Jahrbücher für Nationalökonomie und Statistik*, CCIX (1992), 441–57.

Bundesbank, 'Zur Vermögenssituation der privaten Haushalte in Deutschland', *Monatsbericht – Okt. 1993* (Frankfurt a.M: Deutsche Bundesbank, 1993) pp. 19–32.

Cohen M. A., N. Kumar and S. S. Wallack, 'Who Buys Long term Care Insurance?', *Health Affairs*, XI (1992) 208–23.

Cremer H., D. Kessler and P. Pestieau, 'Intergenerational Transfers within the Family', *European Economic Review*, XXXVI (1992) 1–16.

Cutler D., *Why doesn't the Market Fully Insure Long-Term Care?*, NBER Working Paper n. 4301 (Cambridge, MA: National Bureau of Economic Research, 1993).

Deininger D., 'Sozialhilfe und Kriegsopferfürsorge', *Wirtschaft und Statistik 1993*, (1993) 786, 916–23.

Eisen R., 'Alternative Sicherungsmöglichkeiten bei Pflegebedürftigkeit', *Sozialer Fortschritt*, XLI (1992) 236–41.

Fabel O., *The Economics of Pensions and Variable Retirement Schemes* (Chichester: Wiley, 1994) ch. 5.

Friedman B. M. and L. M. Manheim, 'Should Medicare Provide Expanded Coverage for Long-Term Care?', in M. V. Pauly and W. L. Kissick (eds), *Lessons from the First Twenty Years of Medicare: Research Implications for Public and Private Sector Policies* (Philadelphia, PA: University of Philadelphia Press, 1988) pp. 151–79.

Gabanyi M., 'Absicherung des Pflegefallrisikos in Westeuropäischen Ländern: Ein Vergleich von Struktur- und Finanzierungsmerkmalen', *Arbeit und Sozialpolitik*, 47.11 (1993) 57–64.

Gaulke J., *Kursbuch Versicherung: Risikovorsorge auf dem Prüfstand* (Frankfurt a.M: Fischer, 1992).

Heise G., 'Im Jahrzehnt der Erben', *Deutsches Allgemeines Sonntagsblatt*, 1993/41 (1993).

Infratest, 'Hilfe- und Pflegebedürftige in privaten Haushalten', *Sozialforschung, Infratest Epidemiologie und Gesundheitsforschung*, 20.2 (Stuttgart: Kohlhammer, German Federal Ministry for Families and Senior Citizens, 1993).

IWG, *Archiv* (Institut für Wirtschaft und Gesellschaft, Feb. 1990).

IWG, *Archiv* (Institut für Wirtschaft und Gesellschaft, Jan. 1994).

Jacobs B. and W. G. Weissert, 'Helping Protect the Elderly and the Public Against the Catastrophic Costs of Long-Term Care', *Journal of Policy Analysis and Management*, V (1985) 378–83.

Körber K. O., 'Pflegeversicherung – staatlich oder privat?', *Versicherungswirtschaft*, XLVI (1991) 721–27.

Krug W. and G. Reh, *Pflegebedürftige in Heimen: Statistische Erhebungen und Ergebnisse* (Stuttgart: Kohlhammer, German Federal Ministry for Families and Senior Citizens, 1992).

Noelle-Neumann E., 'Wenn die Kasse bezahlt, Kommen die Kranken ins Heim', *Frankfurter Allgemeine Zeitung*, 1993/215 (1993) 6.

Pauly M. V., 'Optimal Public Subsidies of Nursing Home Insurance in the United States', *Geneva Papers on Risk and Insurance*, XIV (1989) 3–10.

Pauly M. V., 'The Rational Non-Purchase of Long-Term Care Insurance', *Journal of Political Economy*, LXXXII (1990) 153–68.

PKV, *Die Private Krankenversicherung: Zahlenbericht 1992/93* (Cologne: Verband der Privaten Krankenversicherungen, 1993).

Richter W. and K. Ritzberger, 'Optimal Provision against the Risk of Old Age' *Finanzarchiv*, N. F., LII (1995) 339–56.

Rüdiger D. and D. Seiler, 'Veränderung der Einkommenssituation von Pflegebedürftigen nach Einführung einer Pflegeversicherung', *Zeitschrift für Gerontologie*, XXV (1992) 178–85.

Scanlon W. J., 'Possible Reforms for Financing Long-Term Care', *Journal of Economic Perspectives*, VI (1992) 43–58.

Schmähl W., 'Zur Finanzierung einer Pflegeversicherung', *Deutsche Rentenversicherung* (1993) 358–74.

Schubert R., 'Das Fehlen von Versicherungsnachfrage – Eine entscheidungstheoretische Anomalie?', *Jahrbücher für Nationalökonomie und Statistik*, CCVII (1990) 496–509.

Segerer G., 'Pflegefallversicherung: Ein Blick über die Grenzen', *Versicherungswirtschaft*, XLVII (1992) 1449–54.

Sinha M., 'Umsetzung des Pflegegesetzes: Zur Nutzung empirischer Analysen', *Arbeit und Sozialpolitik*, XLVII (1993) 60–67.

Statistisches Bundesamt, *Statistisches Jahrbuch (1992) für die Bundesrepublik Deutschland* (Stuttgart: Metzler-Poeschel, German Federal Office for Statistics, 1992).

Strüwe W. and P. Zweifel, 'Pflegeleistung und Pflegeversicherung in einem Zwei-Generationen Modell', *Finanzarchiv*, LI (1994) 28–48.

Uhrig N., 'Ambulante Pflegeversorgung: Pflegebedürftige präferieren häusliche Pflege', *Arbeit und Sozialpolitik*, XLVII (1993) 57–9.

Wahl S., 'Der Materielle Wohlstand vieler älterer Menschen in Deutschland', in G. Verheugen (ed.), *60 plus – Die wachsende Macht der Älteren* (Cologne: Bund, 1994) p. 91–106.

Wasem J., 'Der Mögliche Beitrag der Versicherungswirtschaft zur Lösung der Pflegefallproblematik – Perspektiven, Probleme, Lösungsansätze', *Zeitschrift für Versicherungswesen*, XLII (1991) 378–91.

Notes

1. Körber (1991).
2. Eisen (1992).
3. Uhrig (1993).
4. At the same time, there appears to exist only a single empirical study investigating the individual motives (not) to purchase private LTC-insurance. Cohen, Kumar and Wallack (1992) focus exclusively on consumers who have ordered information packages from insurers, however.
5. Sinha (1993).
6. Wasem (1991).
7. Beck (1994).
8. At the same time, LTC-cost subsidies accounted for an additional 69 per cent of the DM 1.5 billion budget of the Kriegsopferfürsorge which constitutes yet another tax-financed annex to the German social security system available for 'victims of war'.
9. Schmähl (1993) provides a comprehensive discussion of the effects of PAYG-financing.
10. Infratest (1993).
11. BMF (1990).
12. Fabel (1994).
13. Hence, Cremer, Kessler and Pestieau (1992) analyse a model in which parents invest in their children's human capital in exchange for care, for instance.
14. Bernheim, Schleifer and Summers (1985).
15. In order to save space all proofs for propositions have been relegated to the Appendix.

6
Innovation, Growth, and Co-ordination Through Institutions: A Discussion on 'Innovation Systems'

*Michel Quéré**

The aim of this paper is to discuss the recent emphasis on national and local systems of innovation. First, it argues that both concepts contribute to the understanding of the various ways in which institutions support innovation and growth. One can consider the literature on national systems of innovation as a kind of 'top-down' approach wherein national institutions have a predominant role in supporting innovation processes. Conversely, local systems of innovation can be considered as a kind of 'bottom-up' approach emphasizing the role of decentralized institutional initiatives aimed at supporting innovation processes. Second, such 'alternative' approaches highlight the relevance of institutional arrangements in favouring suitable growth regimes, suitable in such cases being related to the establishment of incentives able to maintain co-ordination failures in an acceptable viability corridor in order to ensure long-term growth. As a consequence, it will be argued that the interest in this concept of innovation system essentially lies (1) in the specific interplay between firms and institutions, which defines the frontiers of a specific innovation system (whatever its geographical dimension), and (2) in the role that those institutions play in favouring relationships between a given system and its external environment.

6.1 Introduction

Within the so-called new growth theory, a second generation of models developed an emphasis on innovation as the engine for growth. In contrast to the first generation, where growth was endogenous due to the existence of a general stock of knowledge that indirectly benefited to the whole economy, this second generation tries to cope with a more plausible explanation for the endogenous character of growth mechanisms (see Gaffard and Quéré, 1998, for an overview). As such, innovation has been the central candidate, following the attempts of Romer (1990) and Aghion and Howitt (1992). The purpose of this contribution is not to add to the proliferating elaboration of either such models that include an emphasis on learning (Young, 1991), product variety and/or quality (Grossman and Helpman, 1991), or of any deeper considerations on external complementarities allowed by international trade (see especially the illuminating contribution of Lucas, 1993).

The purpose of this paper is to deal with a complementary line of thinking referring more explicitly to an evolutionary perspective regarding the innovation process. Evolutionary theory has traditionally placed emphasis on innovation as a micro- and firm-specific phenomenon. However, this evolutionary perspective has become increasingly critical for a deeper account of the role played by institutions. Recently, the appreciative theory by Nelson clearly stressed the importance of understanding better the co-evolution of technological innovation and institutions. Among the significant contributions to this approach, the analysis of national systems of innovation is possibly one of the most interesting and important. Since Freeman's (1987) book on the analysis of Japan's competitiveness, the concept of national system of innovation has been of a growing interest especially through the contributions of Lundvall (1992) and Nelson (1993). In fact, Freeman offers an interesting discussion on the role of institutions in the process of economic growth, emphasizing this central role in co-ordinating economic activity, especially in the case of companies facing innovation processes. But interestingly, too, the literature on innovation systems is not homogeneous. It groups different kinds of approaches, depending on the geographical scale of the analysis (either national or local).

This paper therefore considers the analysis of national systems of innovation as a kind of 'top-down approach', where national institutions are centrally considered in the analysis. But there are also some complementary attempts focusing on the role of local institutions supporting innovation processes; these can be associated with a kind of 'bottom-up' approach analysing 'local' systems of innovation (Gaffard, 1990; Longhi and Quéré, 1993; Antonelli, 1995). In other words, innovation systems can refer equally to national or 'local' systems of innovation. Focus on local systems of innovation is based mainly on the microeconomics issue claiming that the economic representation of technical change is not considered in a sufficiently satisfactory way. As far as innovation is associated with the change of techniques that agents choose from a given basket, the essential features of technological innovation cannot be captured. Thus, the search for a better understanding of the nature of the innovation process becomes the central aim of these bottom-up approaches.

The concept of innovation system appears somewhat ambiguous due to its ambition to consider the role of different kinds of institutions supporting innovation, both at the local and at the macro-institutional levels. In fact, these two main ways of thinking about innovation systems (top-down versus bottom-up) are far from being complementary. First, the interests and the limits of each dimension of innovation systems are successively addressed. In a second part of the paper, the focus is on the ability of both approaches to provide a better understanding of the role of institutions within the process of economic growth. The conditions required by such approaches in order to cope more fruitfully with growth mechanisms are finally particularly addressed.

6.2 Economic analysis and the concept of national systems of innovation: a top-down approach

The development of the literature devoted to the analysis of national systems of innovation is largely related to the increase in the process of globalization, because it redefines the role of nations in supporting economic growth. The relationships between national economies and multinational companies have continued to change in recent years; hence, the emphasis on the concept of the national system of innovation can be considered as a response to this new interplay, and to the need for more effective means by national public institutions to support innovation and growth.

Since 1987, the economic literature has had a clear interest in the concept of national systems of innovation. This started with the analysis of Freeman (1987), aimed at explaining Japan's competitiveness and has been extended mainly by the attempts of Dosi *et al.* (1988), Nelson (1992, 1993), and Lundvall (1992). It is beyond the scope of this paper to characterize each of these attempts and their specific contributions for coping with the concept of national system of innovation; incidentally, this can be found partially in MacKelvey (1992), Niosi *et al.* (1992) or Edquist (1997), among others. However, one can try to emphasize some of the analytical difficulties related to the use of this concept by discussing the basic hypotheses of the three essential scholars initially involved (Freeman, Nelson, and Lundvall).

Freeman aims to understand the success of the Japanese economy in the previous 40 years. The most impressive feature of Japanese growth lies in the interventionist role of public actors and its effectiveness to complement the action of private companies. Freeman indicates three main reasons for that: first, the development of public goods and services for which the Japanese state has to control and co-ordinate private companies; second, international trade which requires negotiation between national economies: the Japanese state seems very effective in bargaining and controlling this 'global' co-ordination for the benefit of its own companies; third, public intervention is used to ensure long-term growth by compensating for firms' myopic behaviour. 'Firms which are not in more perfect competitive markets situations would not be able to amass or to allocate resources for long-term objectives. Indeed, there would be strong pressures from the capital markets for them to improve short-term profitability by sacrificing long-term investments' (1987, p. 51).

Indeed, the success of the Japanese economy lies for Freeman in (1) this pragmatic intervention of public actors to ensure long-term objectives for the Japanese companies' growth by co-ordinating the main national companies by way of the role of MITI, (2) the capability of companies to import new techniques and to do 'reverse engineering' in order to design new products and processes, and (3) a continuous interaction between the educational system and companies, which enables the professional retraining of a large number of employees within the production system.

This organizational mode of production is centred on what Freeman calls 'Group Mode of Transactions', which is to some extent the capability of organizing market imperfections. If this capability appears as the main source for long-term growth, it clearly needs to be co-ordinated by public institutions. This mix-development of the Japanese economy is the main explanation for its recent international success. Shinohara (1982; quoted by Freeman, 1987, p. 52) notes that the Japanese economy is 'a long way from the textbook model of atomistic small firm perfect competition. But within a framework of oligopolistic competition, characteristic of all major industrial countries, it offers a potent combination of decentralized flexibility and initiative with many scale economy advantages'. In fact, what seems essential to the Japanese economy is that the selection process of productive options is not defined at the firm's level as it appears in most European countries. On the contrary, productive options are defined at the national system's level. Therefore, it is this crucial mix-dimension of Japanese economic growth, the capability of companies and public institutions to co-ordinate initiatives within international competition that allows Freeman to describe the Japanese national system of innovation as 'the network of institutions in the public and private sectors whose activities and interactions initiate, import, modify, and diffuse new technologies' (1987, p. 1). Thus, he uses it as a central concept to explain this economy's successful competitiveness. As such, Freeman provides us with an institutional explanation for Japanese economic performance. The Japanese economy has exhibited such a catching-up effect owing, to some extent, to the fact that Japanese institutions are better suited to cope with major changes in available resources – that is a new techno-economic paradigm based on the development of information technologies. Specifically, Japanese institutions are effective in furnishing guidelines for adapting national companies that, otherwise, would appear myopic in their necessary focus on short-term profitability. In this way, institutional arrangements between private and public interests contribute to avoid firms' myopic behaviours and to ensure long-term effectiveness, accounting for Japanese competitiveness in the long run. Thus, in order to explain economic growth, Freeman substitutes an institutional explanation for the technological dimension traditionally involved in evolutionary approaches.

This shift of focus from technology towards institution will appear even clearer when looking at complementary attempts to qualify national systems of innovation through the contributions of Dosi, Freeman, Nelson, Silverberg and Soete (1988). But there the debate also changes its nature. National systems of innovation, to which one part of their book is devoted (Dosi *et al.*, 1988), are used for comparing economic systems in order to discuss whether institutional decentralization versus centralization is suitable for economic growth. Indeed, national features are not characterized *per se* (that is, specifically for a country) but understood in a comparative perspective, especially emphasizing the differences between a J-form and an A-form of national innovation systems. But, then, it is not the internal cohesion of one national system of innovation that is considered. On the contrary, the central focus is on a comparative institutional analysis for discussing the advantages of nations in a line of thinking which is not really far from that of Porter's further work (1990).

The specific contributions of Nelson (1992, 1993) on national systems of innovation make this point even more explicit. His comparative study of institutional infrastructures supporting innovation in 15 different countries puts the emphasis on the similarities versus differences encountered by these countries. According to the author this has only produced very general results. As such, the common characteristics of national systems of innovation arise essentially due to the constraints induced by the functioning of a market economy:

• firms are the dominant producers of goods and services that are motivated by a search for profitability;
• direct planning and control from institutions are weak;
• the educational system is organized by public actors;
• basic research institutions are financed by public actors; and
• there is a long inertia of national public institutions such that, even when institutional change exists, it appears limited and smooth over time, involving a kind of historical determinism in the evolution of national systems of innovation.

However, differences between national systems of innovation are essentially:

• the demographical pressure that generates differences in consumers' behaviours;
• the distribution of earnings in so far as it influences the rate and direction of technological innovation (differentiation in the relative price of production factors);
• the relative access to natural resources which also influences the rate of change of technological innovation; and
• the importance of defence policy, which largely directs the evolution of industry (thus, security concerns appear important in shaping innovation systems).

These are the very general similarities and differences between national systems of innovation stemming from Nelson's analysis. Considering national systems of innovation in such a comparative perspective induces an important concern for the traditional approach of comparative advantage which seems able to capture these differences between national systems. This is not sufficient, however, because it is meaningless to compare elements of national systems such as educational training, basic research institutions, and so on, in quantitative terms. The essential characteristics that regulate the internal dynamics of national systems are not really taken into account, contrary to Freeman's attempt, since the internal mechanisms of one national innovation system are specified mainly in comparison to another. However, the crucial issue at stake is to understand the intrinsic characteristics of each national system of innovation.

To some extent, Lundvall's view of national systems of innovation seems, on the surface, to go a step further to relax this limitation of the comparative methodology. Lundvall's approach of national systems of innovation is dominated by his definition of innovation as a 'socially embedded process' which cannot be understood without considering its institutional and cultural contexts. Starting from a reflection on users-producers relationships, Lundvall emphasizes the mechanisms that produce new knowledge within the firm. Then, innovation becomes a process that depends jointly on the productive and institutional environment. 'We will argue that most important forms of learning may fundamentally be regarded as interactive processes, and that together the economic structure and the institutional set-up form the framework for, and strongly affect, processes of interactive learning, sometimes resulting in innovations' (Lundvall, 1992, p. 12). While this objective does seem very attractive, upon more careful scrutiny, it remains just an analysis of understanding 'why technology develops in a certain direction, and at a certain rate' (ibid.).

Companies engage in innovation also because the institutional (national) infrastructure offers them some guidelines for their innovative choices. However, in Lundvall's analysis it is not so easy to understand the nature and the frontiers of this institutional infrastructure and the mechanisms by which it influences firms' innovative behaviours. This environment is a mix of micro-external factors, including other companies, and their associated relational contracting (one has clearly in mind Lundvall's emphasis on users-producers relationships) as well as of macro-external factors because innovative strategies also must take into account other kinds of institutions and their influence on firms' behaviours. The latter justifies the interest in national systems of innovation; however, it is unclear why the national level is the essential one to be taken into account when the starting point is the viewpoint of the firm. In other words, which kind of institutional infrastructure appears important to support firms' innovative behaviours and what kinds of mechanisms have to be favoured in order to increase a firm's economic performance? This issue arises essentially because the practical objective developed by Lundvall (understanding the direction and rate of technology evolution) seems hardly compatible with innovation under-stood as a process. In addition, the Lundvall attempt does not bypass the difficulty of capturing the economic essence of the innovation process, despite its emphasis on interactive learning; in particular, it neglects the institutional devices that appear central to ensure long-term economic growth.

This brief and critical review of the three different approaches of national systems of innovation aims only at developing the basis for a more general discussion. Each of these approaches gives an essential role to national institutional infrastructures in favouring innovation, structural change, and thereby national economic performance. However, these approaches do consider in the same way the role played by those institutional infrastructures. Thus, one can stress two different issues and perspectives.

On the one hand, if the comparative perspective in the analysis of national systems of innovation is considered as central, this must be a more or less similar approach to traditional growth analysis. In other words, national systems of innovation can provide a deeper explanation of differences in initial conditions and also a different explanation of why a process of growth convergence is difficult to reach among countries or why differences in the economic performance of countries tend to persist. In that respect, the discussion of national systems of innovation goes hand in hand with the encouragement of a process of institutional convergence through learning and borrowing from other contexts (where each national system could benefit from the most interesting features of the others). But, then, an innovation system approach cannot be but a descriptive complement to the new growth theory approach in the sense that it provides a more subtle explanation for the diversity of national economic performances.

On the other hand, if the focus is not put on a comparative perspective but, as in the lines initiated by Freeman, on the internal mechanisms that drive the diversity of economic growth and performance, this points to a different central question. By assuming that historical inertia resulting from national economic institutions matter, such an approach can provide an explanation for the persistence of structural disparities between countries as well as their growth performances. The significance of structural diversity across nations is not that they should necessarily reach different levels of performance. On the contrary, the diversity of countries' structural characteristics may justify the diversity of local and national institutions, while also explaining why the coherence between firms and institutions (characterizing an innovation system) can provide a diversity of economic contexts even when they reach a similar level of economic performance. The essential issue lies in understanding the way by which firms interact with institutions because the latter are very different from one country to the other. What is crucially at stake when discussing national systems of innovation is the internal coherence that can be established between firms' innovative behaviours and the incentives schemes provided by national institutions in order to favour the former.

Introducing the concept of national systems of innovation can justify the absence of convergence among economic systems. However, such an explanation can be understood in two different ways: first, it can become a descriptive justification for the impossibility to converge because institutions matter, constituting the main source of distortion in the expected convergence process; in that respect, disparities between economic systems will persist, because of the disparities of institutions; second, it can offer a richer perspective by justifying the diversity of national economic infrastructures that can reach a comparable level of economic performance without standardizing their institutional infra-structures.

The way in which the debate about national systems of innovation has developed, especially in its comparative dimension, has largely favoured the first line of thinking, although maybe the second is the most interesting. The latter largely still needs to be encouraged and this is partially the aim of this contribution. To go further on this second line of thinking about national systems of innovation, one can learn from complementary attempts based on an interplay between firms and institutions (broadly defined) to provide a satisfying explanation for innovation at a micro (but systemic) level.

The latter emphasis implies that institutions matter not only *per se* (through their own characteristics and actions) but essentially because they encourage innovative strategies of firms by providing and adjusting incentives over time. Understanding this interplay between firms and institutions is central to explain the diversity of national infrastructures supporting innovation processes. It also induces a focus for the analysis on the co-ordination modes governing both companies' relationships as well as those between national institutions and companies. Both are really country-specific as each national system of innovation establishes different types of interrelationships between its organizations and institutions. For instance, each country has more or less the same objectives in terms of performance of the educational, research, or banking systems, and so on. But each country has its own traditions, habits, and constraints in order to reach this common objective; consequently, despite similar kinds of comparative advantages, each country exhibits very different characteristics and results.

Therefore case studies are essential, and one needs to learn about the internal mechanisms which complement firms' and institutions' strate-gies in a specific country. However, if we accept such a view, it must immediately be complemented by another argument related to the scale of the analysis: nations are not homogeneous entities, especially as regards their structural characteristics. Obvious infranational differences justify the need to cope with infranational disparities. Further, national institutions matter in order to support innovative behaviours of companies, but one must also cope with other complementary institutional devices that importantly influence companies' strategies. One can learn about this interplay by considering a complementary body of the economic literature devoted to local systems of innovation rather than national systems.

6.3   Bottom-up approaches: the economic analysis of local systems of innovation

It is possible to distinguish between two different types of 'bottom-up' approaches. The first emerges from evolutionary approaches to firms' innovative behaviours. Dosi (1988) emphasizes the 'local' character of technological innovation, the term 'local' referring to the tacit character of knowledge involved in the innovation process rather than to a geographical meaning. Following that perspective, evolutionary approaches are a means of qualifying a firm as a local system of innovation, by considering that technology embodies not only a codified but also a partially tacit, specific, and cumulative knowledge. As such, organization matters because it allows to manage strategic choices between routines and innovative behaviours. Then, a firm facing innovative strategies, that is facing structural change, can be associated in a local system of innovation, where the organizational design it chooses in order to implement new learning is a key determinant of this innovation process. In this way, the interacting relationships between the different stages of a production process become central to defining an innovation process (Kline and Rosenberg, 1986). A lot of works in that perspective aim to make explicit the role of knowledge in firms' innovative strategies. One may note that the understanding of the localized character of knowledge creation has progressively become a structured research area (see Antonelli, 1996, 1998) emphasizing the articulation between knowledge and technological innovation rather than the geographical aspect of firms' innovative strategies.

   We wish to stress the idea that such evolutionary approaches can be complemented by institutional approaches of innovation. We argue that a firm's innovative strategy is not centrally determined by technological characteristics (that is those of the technological paradigm that it is confronted with). This is not to deny the importance of technology itself (and especially its cumulative character), but it seems preferable to conceive a firm's innovative strategy as one that widens the possible productive options through the learning process in which the firm is engaged. An innovation process is much more dependent on the organizational design that a firm chooses in order to implement new learning. It depends much more on the complementarity between the firm's organization and its related markets than to some intrinsic technological characteristics. And therefore, a firm's innovative strategy also involves some geographical or spatial implications that largely influence the choice and the feasibility of the organizational design needed to implement its strategy.

Following this second perspective, some attempts have already been made to qualify a firm as a local system of innovation, and we do not add too much to this discussion (cf. Amendola and Gaffard, 1988; Gaffard *et al.*, 1993). However, two important points need to be stressed. First, a firm's innovative strategy is defined by its ability to cope with structural change, that is the firm's ability to make the modification of its productive activities in a profitable way when the associated decision-making processes are taken in a situation of structural uncertainty. This crucially involves the time dimension of the production process, conceived as a sequential balance between learning processes (construction phases) and production (utilization phases) of the firm's activity. Indeed, the essential issue is the viability problem faced by the firm in the sense that past productive decisions constrain the current learning capabilities, which, in turn, will constrain future productive options and so on. Second, an innovative firm has to be considered as an open system of innovation, where the interacting relationships with its environment are a necessary part of the process of moving its productive activities. The nature of the process of change is structured through these relationships, and in turn, the environment itself is also structured by the new options found by the firm (Amendola and Bruno, 1990). Therefore, the determinants of innovative behaviours of firms are not only to be found in the market environment, but they are also more largely dependent on different kinds of institutional arrangements. This is the reason why a firm *per se* can be thought of as a local system of innovation.

More precisely, as a firm progressively structures its environment through the implementation of its innovative strategy, the way its relationships evolve over time goes hand in hand with geographical implications in terms of 'mapping' the territorial area involved in this implementation. This can also have important consequences in terms of locational effects. One can offer the hypothesis that the greater the number of productive relationships, the greater are the incentives to locate them in proximity of each other. This is intrinsically part of the argument for a co-structuring of the firm and its environment when dealing with the understanding of the organizational design implementing a firm's innovative strategy.

Finally, there are good arguments for considering a spatial area as a local system of innovation, local referring here to a geographical meaning. But then, a sort of methodological shift is required because it is not a firm, even including its active environment, that has to be considered as a system. It becomes a spatial area *per se* and the sole way to define it from an economic viewpoint is to consider the spatial area to be defined by specific institutions as they are providing incentives to companies and, as such, are geographically defined. However, in this perspective, the essential issue is to understand the open character of such local systems, namely the relationships they are organizing with other active external components (mainly other companies located outside those areas or other external institutions that regulate the internal working of the systems). Indeed, the innovative working of a local system is highly dependent (1) on the relationships between the internal components of the system itself, which focus on how to benefit from local relationships, and (2) on the interdependency between different spatial areas, that means taking into account the interacting dimension between an area and the active components of its environment. One can provide an alternative discussion about the understanding of the role of public policy in facing the diversity of innovation systems. For instance, this analysis allows provision of an original explanation to the obvious diversity of European regions in facing structural change (cf. Gaffard *et al.*, 1993). Moreover, such a view is very close to that of Freeman when dealing with the mixed strategy between private companies and public institutions to define the Japanese national system of innovation.

6.4   The relevance of analysing innovation system

Clearly, Freeman's influence is still of a relevant importance for the debate on innovation systems. What is at stake is mainly the understanding of the interplay between private organizations (companies) and private or public institutions in order to adapt an economic system to structural change. Of course, the major changes to which economies need to adapt are not simply technological shocks (in Freeman terms, a new techno-economic paradigm due to the development of information technologies). Without referring to the dominance of a technological regime, one prefers to consider that firms continually adapt their productive capacity to the evolution of their markets. Therefore, the problem an innovation system is facing (be it a firm or a spatial area) is first of all a problem of growth regime, including some technological considerations but not exclusively. This is the essential motive for engaging in innovative strategies, in a continuous search for adaptation. This also appears as the essential source of difficulty for institutions supporting these innovative strategies in order to design effective incentives, effective meaning coherent according to the firms' continuous search for adaptation to their markets' constraints. Therefore, microeconomic considerations about innovation processes are necessary and one needs to learn from bottom-up approaches in order to move away from the structuralist trap implicitly dominant in the top-down approaches that consider nations as given entities. Indeed, one central issue lies in discussing the possibility of linking both types of reflections on innovation systems.

Certainly, when considering the institutional environment of local systems of innovation, the national dimension of institutions involved in innovation support (such as the banking, the educational, and the academic research systems and/or the regulatory framework, industrial relations, and other types of business associations) is essential. The national system necessarily structures the relationships that exist between local systems inside a specific country. However, things are more complicated, and it is obviously possible to find some interesting examples of local initiatives in innovation processes that are the result of interactions with extra-national institutions or with multinational companies located outside a local system. In fact, the local dimension of a system of innovation is that of the productive environment necessary to the learning which characterizes firms' innovative behaviours. As such, it is not a geographical meaning which can fit in the economic analysis of innovation processes; on the contrary, the open character of learning is a key issue to understand local innovative dynamics.

This is why it is not possible to consider both kinds of systems of innovation (top-down and bottom-up approaches) as being intertwined, simply in the way national systems of innovation could be thought of as external constraints for the structuring of local systems. Situations exist where the national dimension is the relevant one, even when the objective is to consider infranational (local or regional) initiatives; but there are also cases where the national dimension is not the relevant one because the skills necessary to implement innovative strategies need to be organized worldwide; lastly, there are also cases where local initiatives are relevant, despite the structuring effect of the national dimension in the implementation of the firms' innovative behaviours.

Therefore, two crucial points appear in order to reconcile both types of analyses of innovation systems (top-down versus bottom-up approaches). The first is the dynamic dimension of an innovation process, which implies a continuous redefinition of the relevant components interacting with the firm in order to organize learning processes, that is new productive capacities. Consequently, from an analytical viewpoint, the geographical dimension of a specific system of innovation would always have to be redefined over time. The second point is that, whatever the definition of the system (be it national or local), it must cope centrally with the open character of the set of components that are defined as an innovation system.

An essential methodological problem can now be stressed. From the firm's viewpoint, the institutional environment activated to organize an innovation process is always moving within its frontiers. Therefore, the concept of innovation system must be thought of as an open system in order to cope with all these modifications in the firm's environment over time. Despite such an open character, it is still necessary to recognize that some institutions supporting innovation are hardly moving and, on the contrary, are a means of stabilizing the firm's environment. Obviously, this is the case with national institutions. Despite the continuous moving of the frontiers of an innovation system from the firm's viewpoint, one needs to characterize innovative firms from the viewpoint of the relevant set of institutions influencing their innovative strategies. The methodological issue arises since it is necessary to determine the geographical dimension by associating the analysis with the set of relevant institutions influencing these innovative behaviours. Then, it is impossible to capture the actual geographical dimension of innovative strategies implemented by firms. It is, however, possible to focus on the scope of the related influencial institutions in order to understand the characteristics of the relationships existing between these institutional infrastructures and firms' innovative behaviours.

As a consequence, when considering local or national systems of innovation, it is important to learn from empirical studies in order to go beyond some of these analytical limits. Particularly, the crucial aspect to be understood is the interacting character between organizations (firms) and institutions (here local, regional, national, or even international, but depending on a determined methodological choice) that characterizes the scope of an innovation system as well as the viability problem it is facing over time. What is centrally at stake is the problem of co-ordinating market imperfections through the role of an institutional infrastructure. Innovative firms' behaviours require, or are associated with, market imperfections 'by definition'. The latter are the only means of ensuring a sufficient level of profitability for a firm's new productive capacity resulting from the innovation process to be expected and reached. This is a necessary condition for a suitable co-ordination of economic activity in the sense that these market imperfections are the only means of allowing companies to engage in innovative behaviours as they will be certain that the expected profitability can be maintained during the time necessary to set up their new productive capacity. In this respect, institutional infrastructures take part more or less actively in ensuring a suitable co-ordination such as to favour the implementation of firms' innovative behaviours. Further, one has only a weak understanding of the influence of institutional infrastructures (local or national as well). A lot of work is still required to clarify how institutions interact with firms in order to establish a suitable co-ordination of economic activity when the latter is facing a continuous evolution in a context of structural change. This appears as the basic component to be tackled in order to identify the characteristics of the growth regimes faced by innovation systems.

6.5 Conclusion

The concept of innovation system has recently been of increasing interest in the economic literature, but its analysis remains unsatisfactory because of the various definitions and methodologies applied for qualifying this concept. In order to define a local or a national system of innovation, the essential issue is the kind of relationships existing between innovative organizations (firms) and institutions (private and public) that provide the latter with innovation incentives and support. This is essential because an innovation process cannot be but a disequilibrium process that disrupts the pre-existing coherence within the economic system. What is central for consideration are the mechanisms by which the coherence (that is a suitable co-ordination) between companies and institutions supporting innovation is restored, that is how growth viability can be ensured in the long-term. In that respect, one needs to learn about such adaptive and systemic mechanisms from case studies. Thus, there is an important need for empirical work to be done in order to contribute to the required clarification of the concept of innovation system. In this paper an attempt has been made to establish the conditions by which such empirical work can be profitable for the analysis of this concept.

References

Aghion P. and P. Howitt, 'A Model of Growth through Creative Destruction', *Econometrica*, LXIII, 2 (1992) 323–51.

Amendola M. and Bruno S., 'The Behaviour of the Innovative Firm: Relations to the Environment', *Research Policy*, IX, 5 (1990) 419–33.

Amendola M. and J. L. Gaffard, *The Innovative Choice: an Economic Analysis of the Dynamics of Technology* (Oxford: Blackwell, 1988).

Antonelli C., 'Localized Knowledge Percolation Processes and Information Networks', *Evolutionary Economics*, VI (1996) 281–95.

Antonelli C., *The Economics of Localized Technologies Change and Industrial Dynamics* (Batton: Kluwer, 1995).

Dosi G., C. Freeman, R. Nelson, G. Silverberg and L. Soete (eds), *Technical Change and Economic Theory* (London: Pinter Publishers, 1988).

Edquist C., *Systems of Innovation: Technologies, Institutions and Organizations* (London: Pinter, 1997).

Freeman C. *Technology Policy and Economic Performance* (London: Pinter Publishers, 1987).

Gaffard J. L., ' Toward a Theory of the Creation of Technology as an Out-of-Equilibrium Process', Discussion Paper (CNRS-LATAPSES, 1990).

Gaffard J. L., S. Bruno, C. Longhi and M. Quéré, 'Cohérence et Diversité des Systèmes d'Innovation en Europe – Synthesis Report', E.C. Working Paper, FAST Dossier, XIX (1993) FOP 349.

Gaffard J. L. and M. Quéré, 'Coordination, Croissance, et Géographie Économique', *Revue Economique*, IL, 3 (1998) 857–65.

Grossman G. M. and E. Helpman, *Innovation and Growth in the Global Economy* (Cambridge, MA: MIT Press, 1991).

Kline S. and N. Rosenberg, 'An Overview of Innovation' in R. Landau and N. Rosenberg (eds), *The Positive Sum Strategy* (Washington, DC: National Academy Press, 1986) pp.275–305.

Longhi C. and M. Quéré, 'Systèmes de Production et d'Innovation, et Dynamique des Territoires', *Revue Economique*, XLIV, 4 (1993) 713–24.

Lundvall B. A., *National Systems of Innovation* (London: Pinter, 1992).

Lucas R., 'Making a Miracle ', *Econometrica*, LXI (1993) 251–72.

Mac Kelvey M., 'How do National Systems of Innovation Differ?: A Critical Analysis of Porter, Freeman, Lundvall, and Nelson' in G. Hodgson and E. Screpanti (eds), *Rethinking Economics* (Aldershot: Edward Egar, 1992) pp. 117–37.

Nelson R., 'National Innovation Systems: A Retrospective on a Study', *Industrial and Corporate Change*, I, 2 (1992) 347–74.

Nelson R., *National Systems of Innovation: A Comparative Study* (Oxford: Oxford University Press, 1993).

Niosi J., B. Bellon, P. Saviotti and M. Crow, 'Les Systèmes Nationaux d'Innovation: à la Recherche d'un Concept Utilisable ', *Revue Française d'Economie* (1992) 215–50.

Porter M., *The Competitive Advantage of Nations* (London: Macmillan, 1990).

Romer P., 'Endogenous Technological Change', *Journal of Political Economy*, XCVIII, 5 (1990) 71–102.

Young A., 'Learning by Doing and the Dynamic Effects of International Trade ', *Quarterly Journal of Economics*, CVI (1991) 369–406.

Notes

* CNRS, Valbonne/France.

7
Intersectoral Innovation Flows Within and Between Nations and Regions: Network Analysis and Systems of Innovation

*Mario A. Maggioni**

This paper analyses the innovative systems of different territorial entities: two European countries (Italy and Germany) and two Italian regions (Lombardy and Piedmont). The analysis of the intersectoral innovation flows within the systems is based on an input-output database rearranged in vertically integrated sectors and studied through network analysis methodology and indicators.

The paper shows that Germany is characterized by a higher level of systemic connection and a more evenly distributed structure of intersectoral innovation flows both in absolute and (generally) in relative terms. The Italian technological system is segmented in a dualistic structure where few high-tech sectors coexist along with a pool of traditional ones, rather peripheral in the innovation flow network.

Another type of analysis is conducted with respect to the interactions between different regional systems of innovations within Italy, the scope being to highlight the role played by the two most industrially advanced regions. The results suggest that Lombardy acts truly as the 'engine' of the Italian technological system – being strongly pervasive – while Piedmont is a rather isolated entity with limited innovative contacts with the rest of the country.

7.1 Introduction

The recent literature on the economics of innovation and technical change increasingly stresses the role of national systems of innovation in shaping the technological trajectories and paradigms of entire industries and in determining the overall performance of countries (Lundvall, 1992; Nelson, 1993).

However, nations seem to become less and less the reference level for economic and technological policies being pegged in the middle by subnational components (such as regions, counties, provinces), which call for a process of decentralization and territorial flexibility, and supranational organizations (such as UE, OCSE, NAFTA) which stress the importance of harmonization and co-ordination in a world of increasing international interdependence.

It is beyond the scope of this paper to enter the debate of the optimal level for designing and implementing economic policies supporting firms' innovative activity (whether national, subnational or supranational); however, it seems important to acknowledge the existence and the role of international, national and regional dynamics in determining 'the rate and direction (not to forget the economic outcome) of technological change'.[1]

The aim of this paper is therefore to show the power and versatility of an innovative methodology when analysing different national systems of innovation at different territorial levels. To achieve this aim, on the one hand, the Italian and the German technological systems have been compared; while, on the other hand, the technological structure of the two most industrialized Italian regions (Piedmont and Lombardy), have been analysed.

The systemic nature of the topic at study – within technological intersectoral relationships often matter more than single industry's attributes – required a structural and holistic approach, so that network analysis indexes and methodology have been applied to the appropriate matrices of intersectoral innovation flow.

The paper is organized as follows. Section 7.2 briefly reviews the notion of 'systems of innovation', sections 7.3 and 7.4 deal with the application of input-output techniques and network analysis to the study of innovation flows, sections 7.5 and 7.6 present the main results at the national and regional level, while section 7.7 concludes the paper.

7.2   The notion of system of innovation

In a systemic perspective (von Bertalanffy, 1968), the economic system of a country (or region) is conceived as a set of components whose relationships define a global behaviour with characteristics of its own, that cannot be inferred by the single unit features. This simple statement implies two main consequences: (i) the system has its own structural peculiarity (a sort of 'identity') and it must be studied accordingly; (ii) the relevance of a single unit lies in its interactions with other units and it cannot be isolated from the system or be separately analysed.

As a consequence, in the economics of technological change, it has been assumed that innovation is not the product of the atomistic behaviour of maximizing agents, but is the result of complex dynamics determined either at the sectoral or at the global (regional, national or international) level (Antonelli and De Liso, 1997, Bramanti and Maggioni, 1997). The sectoral characteristics, in terms of positive externalities, cumulativity and synergy determine the peculiar performance of the single firms (Pavitt, 1984).

The innovative performance of any economic system derives from the confluence of particular institutional, economic, social and cultural characteristics. However, the possibility of identifying a stricter definition of the system of innovation refers solely to the interactions of the innovative and the productive subsystems.

7.3   Input-output and innovation flows

Each innovation system is thus assumed to be largely dependent on the input-output flows of the relative productive system. Therefore it is convenient to conduct the quantitative examination of the technological linkages within an economic system at a sectoral level of disaggregation. The matching of the different databases (the input-output tables and the statistics on the R&D activity at the various territorial levels involved in the analysis) resulted in the consideration of two different sets of data. Thirteen manufacturing macro-sectors: 1. Energy; 2. Non-energy minerals; 3. Chemicals; 4. Metal products; 5. Machinery; 6. Office automation and precision instruments; 7. Electrical and electronics; 8. Motor vehicles; 9. Aerospace and other transport; 10. Food, beverage and tobacco; 11. Textiles and clothes; 12. Wood and furniture; 13. Rubber and plastics were used for the comparison between Italy and Germany; while other 13 productive macro-sectors: 1. Agriculture; 2. Energy; 3. Metallic minerals; 4. Non-metallic minerals; 5. Chemicals; 6. Metal products, Machinery, Office automation and precision instruments, Electrical and electronics; 7. Motor vehicles and other transport equipment; 8. Food, beverage and tobacco; 9. Textiles, clothing and footwear; 10. Wood and furniture, Paper and printing, Rubber and plastics; 11. Building; 12. Trade, transport, credit and insurance; 13. Other market services, have been chosen for the Italian regional case.

The intersectoral innovation diffusion process has been in turn analytically examined through intersectoral innovation flow matrices.

These are the result of the standard diffusion of input-output approach with input indicators: innovations are embodied in the exchanged intermediate goods and services, while one sector's innovative activity is measured by its innovative efforts (measured by the sectoral R&D employment and expenditure) (Montresor, 1994).

Intersectoral innovation flow matrices $R(13*13)$ have been obtained through the following algorithm (Momigliano and Siniscalco, 1982; Marengo and Sterlacchini, 1990; Leoncini, Maggioni and Montresor, 1996):

$$R = r^\wedge B \tag{1}$$

where $r^\wedge(13*13)$ is the diagonal matrix of sectoral R&D employment, while the $B(13*13)$ matrix transforms each sectoral variable in vertically integrated terms,[2] and is defined as follows:

$$B = (x^\wedge)^{-1}(I - A)^{-1}d^\wedge \tag{2}$$

In equation (2), $x^\wedge(13*13)$ is the diagonal matrix of sectoral output, $(I - A)^{-1}(13*13)$ is the Leontief inverse and $d^\wedge(13*13)$ the diagonal matrix of final demand.

Row i of R matrices indicates the amount of R&D performed by sector i to innovate the re-employed output (elements on the principal diagonal) and the remaining output required by the other sectors (elements out of the principal diagonal). Its column j is symmetrically described in terms of requirements.

In the national analysis, countries have been treated as 'closed' systems.[3] This limitation has been overcome in the regional analysis where the attention has been explicitly focused on the pattern of innovative relationships between different regions (and between different sectors of different regions). For this reason, the regional level of analysis has involved a more complex treatment of the original dataset constituted by a series of input-output bi-regional tables (Formez, 1992) built at a seventeen sectors disaggregation, one for each of the 20 regions, and by the vector of the Italian R&D employment subdivided by region and sectors (Istat, 1991).

Following a painstaking procedure[4] – involving a tridimensional RAS – a macro table (see Table 7.1) has been obtained for a system composed of three 'regions', Lombardy, Piedmont and Rest of Italy (ROI),[5] where the matrices on the main diagonal correspond to the national analogues described above (and depict the innovation flows existing within each technological system of Lombardy, Piedmont and Rest of Italy), while the

Table 7.1   Interregional matrix of innovation flows

	Lom	*Pied*	*ROI*
Lombardy	R^{LL}	R^{LP}	R^{LI}
Piedmont	R^{PL}	R^{PP}	R^{PI}
Rest of Italy	R^{IL}	R^{IP}	R^{II}

off-diagonal matrices reflect the innovation flows between a couple of regions (to describe, for example, the innovation flows contained in the exports from Lombardy to Piedmont).

Several strong assumptions – concerning the proportionality between imports and total inputs of a given good, the inexistence of re-exporting activities, the proportionality of the innovative content of imports to a region with the sectoral R&D intensity of the other regions' exports[6] – had to be made in order to obtain such a complete and disaggregated matrix from the original aggregated dataset.

7.4   Network analysis: micro and macro indexes

Network Analysis[7] (NA) uses quantitative techniques, derived from graph theory, to study and describe the structure of interactions (edges) between given entities (nodes) (Maggioni, 1994). Therefore, in this paper, the 13 sectors of the Italian and German technological system are treated as nodes, while their innovation flows are treated as edges.

Orthodox approaches describe the innovation process through an atomistic principle that assumes the existence of individual utility maximization procedures and does not take into account the wider social, economic and institutional framework. By contrast, NA highlights some relevant structural features (Bramanti and Maggioni, 1997).

The 'behaviour' of a node (in terms of strategy and performance) has to be interpreted in terms of both structural limits and internal features; internodal relationships must be examined from two complementary perspectives: the single node's and the whole system's perspective; neither a single node nor a pair of nodes can be meaningfully analysed, when isolated from the system framework; systems display a surprisingly intrinsic fractal nature: both the macro level (whole system) and the micro level (nodes) are composed by a plurality of structurally interrelated elements; the interdependence of observations does not hinder NA techniques, allowing a wider use of this methodology when more traditional statistic and econometric tools are unusable.

Two are the most common representation techniques utilized within NA: the graphic and the matricial. In the paper both representations have been used: the graphic directly allowed a visual comparison of the different structures of intersectoral innovation flows in the two countries; the second has been used indirectly, through a specific computer package (UCINET 1.4/X), to calculate all the reported indices in both regional and national analysis.

In the following analysis, as the index of systemic connection, the density of a network is used, and this is defined as the ratio between the actual number of edges e and the maximum number of directed edges in a network composed by n nodes or, in formula:

$$\frac{D = e}{n(n-1)} \tag{3}$$

The networks analysed in the paper describe the intersectoral innovation flows; thus the fact that one sector transfers innovations to another one does not imply that also the reverse is necessarily true. In this case, for each node an outdegree (number of outward connections) and an indegree (number of inward connections) must be calculated.

Furthermore, NA indexes have been calculated from a dichotomized version[8] of the original intersectoral innovation flow matrices. The customary procedure implies the choice of an 'appropriate' (often *ad hoc*) threshold; however it must be considered that the choice of a given threshold is strategic because different values produce different dicotho-mized networks. For this reason the dichotomization has been conducted, for the national case, through a whole range of cut-off values in order to identify and study the most representative outcomes; while, for the regional case, three different thresholds (referring to three different perspectives of analysis) have been identified.

In order to detect the most central sector within the system and the definition of a scale of hierarchy (inequality), centrality and centralization indexes have been designed.[9] Formally, the degree centralization of a network (system) of n nodes (sectors) $(\overline{\overline{C}}_g^i)$ can be defined as follows:

$$\overline{\overline{C}}_g^i = \frac{\sum_i (C_g^* - C_g^i)}{(n-1)(n-2)} \tag{4}$$

where C_g^* is the centrality value of the most central sector in the system and the denominator reflects the maximum level of centrality obtainable in a system of n sectors. The centralization indices measure the difference in centrality levels between the most central sector and the other ones. A high centralization index therefore identifies a very hierarchic system where differences in positions are large. A low centralization index identifies a structure where most of the positions are similar and interchangeable.

In the paper, innovation flows are measured on the basis of vertically integrated sectors. therefore, despite the existence of a plurality of dimensions of centrality,[10] the only indexes used are those built according to the degree.[11] The value of the edge spilling from one sector to the other accounts for every innovation flow – both direct and indirect (that is through any other sector).

7.5   Empirical results at the national level

The comparison between the productive-innovative sub-systems of the two countries, based on the examination of the innovative flows, has been carried out both in absolute and relative terms.[12] The two approaches present both advantages and disadvantages. The absolute perspective allows to directly employ the original database and underlines the existence and relevance of critical mass phenomena. This perspective is, however, strongly affected by the dimension of the innovative sub-system, so that the German system, being larger in size, appears to be generally more connected than the Italian one.

The utilization of relative flows takes into account the structural characteristics of each system by overcoming the dimension effect. This methodology, however, needs a criterion to re-proportionate the original flows and therefore it entails some arbitrary elements.[13]

Because both methodologies are mutually relevant, stressing different aspects of the topic at study, a twofold analysis has been carried out by applying a set of indicators to the whole range of thresholds or cut-off values.

In the analysis, three different indicators have been used to measure and compare the degree of systemic connection displayed by Italy and Germany: variance, density, and centralization.

The first indicator, variance, measures the dispersion of the elements of a matrix around an average value (that is the arithmetic mean for the absolute value matrix and the harmonic mean for the relative term matrix). It has been assumed that the polarization of intersectoral innovation flows – measured by a dispersion index as the variance – is a good proxy for the inverse of the connection of a system (high dispersion means low systemic connection).

The second index, density, is defined as in equation (3); the greater its value, the more connected is the system.

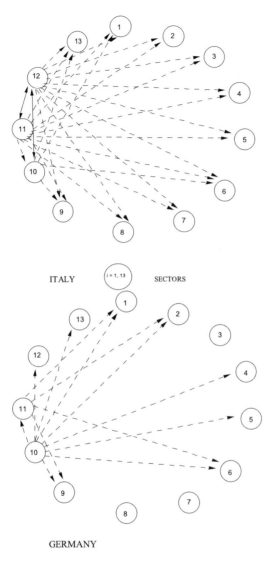

Figure 7.1 Absolute values, cut-off equals to 0.86573, (lines represent missing intersectoral links)

Centralization – as defined in equation (4) – is the third systemic indicator used in the paper. The higher its value, the more connected the system, as it has been assumed that symmetry among the sectors is proportional to the connection of a technological system.

The analysis of these indicators is complemented with a sectoral examination that evidences, for selected cut-off values, both qualitative and quantitative aspects of the pervasiveness/dependency of each macro-sector.

7.5.1   Absolute value matrix (dimension effect)

A preliminary evaluation of the systemic connection can be carried out on the basis of the variation coefficients ($V_I = 4.02$; $V_G = 4.76$); by considering nearly all the flows in both systems, Italy is slightly better connected than Germany.

For relatively low cut-off values, the two systems begin to diversify and show different intersectoral relationships (Figure 7.1). Germany appears to be better connected than Italy, according to the density index ($D_I = 0.8284$; $D_G = 0.9231$).

The centrality indexes analysis shows the low pervasiveness of traditional sectors in both countries. However, in Italy this is mainly due to the poor innovative performances of sector 10 (Food, beverage and tobacco) and especially of sectors 11 (Textiles and clothes) and 12 (Wood and furniture), while in Germany, the low pervasiveness of traditional sectors regards marginally sectors 10 and 11. Sector 12, despite its traditional character, is rather pervasive in Germany whilst completely dependent in Italy. A similar dynamic involves also sector 11, even if it is not so pervasive in Germany. On the contrary, the food and beverage sector is more pervasive in Italy than in Germany.

The indegree analysis – measuring sectoral dependence – stresses that, despite their substantial similarity, the two systems hold some distinctive features. Sectors 1 (Energy), 6 (Office automation and precision instruments) and 9 (Aerospace and other transport) are the least dependent sectors for both systems. Nevertheless, the minimum dependency value is higher for Germany. Moreover, sector 13 (Rubber and plastics) for Italy and sector 2 (Non-energy minerals) for Germany belong to the same low dependent class. Centralization index analysis ($\overline{\overline{C}}_{g,G} = 0.098$ per cent; $\overline{\overline{C}}_{g,I} = 0.220$ per cent) confirms Germany's higher systemic connection.

By increasing the dimension of the retained flows (Figure 7.2), Germany shows again higher density values ($D_I = 0.1361$; $D_G = 0.3314$). The skeletal framework of each system becomes apparent.

The outdegree centrality analysis highlights the pervasive nature of the Italian Chemical sector (sector 3) with respect to other seven sectors. Flows from sector 4 to sectors 5, 7 and 8 are still relevant and this stresses the basic role of the Metal products for high-intensive capital and

157

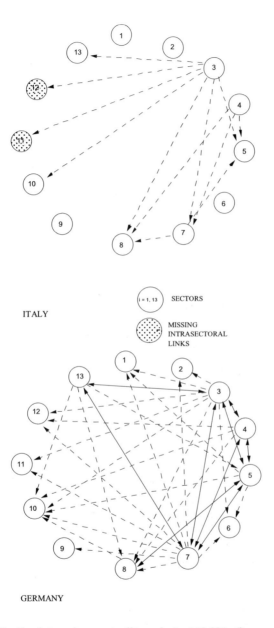

ITALY

i = 1, 13 SECTORS

MISSING
INTRASECTORAL
LINKS

GERMANY

Figure 7.2 Absolute values, cut-off equals to 165.081, (lines represent existing intersectoral links)

technologically-intermediate sectors. Chemicals is a highly pervasive sector for Germany too: nearly all its outflow values are retained (11 out of 12). The most pervasive German sector is, however, sector 7, whose crucial role for the country is in this way confirmed. Its pervasiveness is instead limited for Italy to Motor vehicles and Metal products. Looking at inflows, Italy is characterized by a dichotomy between specialized suppliers and scale intensive sectors (5, 7 and 8) and supplier-dominated sectors (10, 11 and 12 sectors): the former are in fact typically more dependent than the latter. Germany is not so polarized with respect to dependency. All the inflows are in fact around the average; those for sectors 4 (Metal products), 5 (Machinery) and 13 (Rubber and plastics), in particular, confirm once again the importance of such technologically-intermediate sectors, based on process innovation.

The 'standard' centralization index shows a more 'symmetric' and systemic situation for Italy ($\overline{\overline{C}}_{g,I} = 0.598\%$; $\overline{\overline{C}}_{g,G} = 0.856\%$). However, for the above-mentioned reasons, the Bonacich index was used and on its basis Italy shows a greater centralization ($\hat{C}_{B,I} = 19.00$; $\hat{C}_{B,G} = 16.40$). In brief while the Italian system at first sight seems less hierarchical, by using network analysis indices its results are polarized and less systemic.

For very high cut-off values, density and centrality indexes tend to zero, leaving only intrasectoral flows. This type of flow does not 'survive' the dichotomization in Italy (by construction), while it does in Germany for sectors 3, 5, 7 and 8. This confirms the important role of technologically-intermediate and high capital-intensive sectors within the German productive and innovative systems.

7.5.2   Relative value matrix (proportional effect)

The dispersion degree around the harmonic mean shown by the relative flow distributions is a first rough inverse indicator of the relative systemic connection ($Disp_{Ma,1} = 7.693$; $Disp_{Ma,G} = 6.963$): as for the absolute values, it appears to be greater for Germany than for Italy.

Because of these reasons, the analysis has been performed by considering the structure of the preceding section, and various cut-off values have been considered. At modest cut-off values, both density ($D_I = 0.888$; $D_G = 0.929$) and centralization indices ($\overline{\overline{C}}_{g,I} = 0.144\%$; $\overline{\overline{C}}_{g,G} = 0.091\%$) show a higher systemic connection for Germany.

For greater cut-off values, entering the switching area, density and centralization are as follows: $D_I = 0.609$; $D_G = 0.467$; $\overline{\overline{C}}_{g,I} = 0.5\%$; $\overline{\overline{C}}_{g,G} = 0.682\%$; $\hat{C}_{B,I} = 7.52$; $\hat{C}_{B,G} = 19.51$.

The analysis of the centrality indexes shows that two particular sectors are responsible for the switch: sectors 2 and 6 are in fact more pervasive in Italy than in Germany where their outflows value is less than the mean value; although sector 13 is more pervasive in Germany, it is not, however, enough to compensate the weaker systemic connection determined by the other two sectors. The German Office automation sector is confirmed by this analysis as isolated, given its introductory commercial phase, while the traditional strength of Rubber and plastics, directly linked to the Chemical sector, also emerges. Considering the indegrees, the high dependency of the Italian traditional sectors and the role of technology for Aerospace are noteworthy. Aerospace in Germany is not so involved in the technological process and this is plausible in the light of the sanctions imposed to the defence-related sectors in Germany after the Second World War.

By considering cut-off values higher than the second turning point

$$(D_I = 0.183; \ D_G = 0.207; \ \overline{\overline{C}}_{g,I} = 0.652\%; \ \overline{\overline{C}}_{g,G} = 0.72\%;$$
$$\hat{C}_{B,I} = 0.828; \ \hat{C}_{B,G} = 2.692)$$

very relevant structural differences emerge.

Chemicals is the most pervasive source of innovations in both systems. However, while in Italy its pervasiveness is limited to traditional sectors, in Germany other middle-tech sectors are net receivers (e.g. 6 and 8). The role of the second diffuser is held differently in the two systems: in Italy it is performed by sector 4 (Metal products), while in Germany by sector 7 (Electrical and electronics). The latter diffuses both to low-tech and high-tech sectors.

Further differences emerge if the centrality index analysis is performed for the remaining sectors.

Sector 5. Machinery. In Italy it depends only on sectors 4 and 7, while in Germany it is also pervasive with regards to sectors 1 and 2, showing an innovative dynamic of the producer-user type.

Sector 6. Office automation and precision instruments. In Italy, this sector is totally isolated: on the output side, this shows how the traditional sectors in Italy are scarcely influenced by information technology; on the input side, this suggests that a low degree of integration is displayed by the Italian system. In both cases, it must still be verified if this anomaly is strictly linked to the foreign production system. As will be shown, this isolation is not shown by the German system.

Sector 7. Electrical and electronics. A qualitative analysis of this sector-which is pervasive by its very nature – shows for Germany how its 'output' is employed by almost all the other sectors (only sectors 3, 9 and 13 are

160

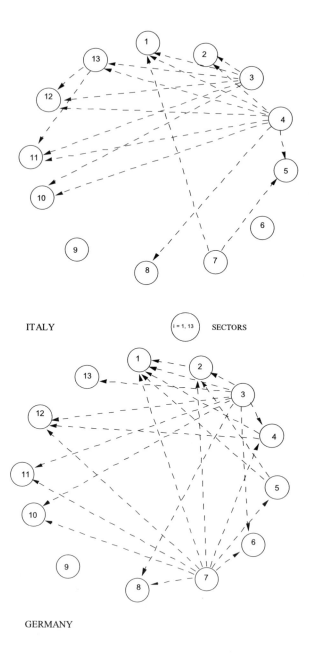

ITALY

SECTORS

i = 1, 13

GERMANY

Figure 7.3 Relative values, cut-off equals to 0.05, (lines represent existing intersectoral links)

excluded by this diffusion process). In Italy the same sector pervades only two sectors (1 and 5).

Sector 8. Motor vehicles. Although technologically dependent in both systems, this sector represents two different innovative and productive processes. In Italy, innovations flow from the Metal sector (a typical intermediate inputs sector for traditional production processes); in Germany, these flows come from Electronics and chemicals, confirming these sectors as high-tech ones.

Sector 9. Aerospace and other transport. This sector is totally isolated in both systems. As already mentioned, a very important 'shaping' factor refers to the historical and institutional context.

Sector 13. Rubber and plastics. In both systems, this sector shows a natural dependency on Chemicals. On the pervasiveness side, however, while in Italy it pervades two traditional sectors, in Germany it is limited to the intrasectoral flows. This situation may be due to the more basic nature of the German research system in the Plastics sector in comparison to the Italian one, where this material is used as an intermediate or a final good within traditional sectors (such as 11 and 12).

The Italian and the German technological systems have often been paired, in relation to a similar context of technological opportunities, though exploited in different ways. In this paper too, striking differences pointing in the direction of two antithetical systems have not emerged. Nevertheless, some significant differences have been highlighted by the analysis.

First, all the indicators used have generally shown a higher degree of systemic connection for Germany. In particular, the polarization of the Italian technological system seems to be its main characteristic which influences both its technological and economic performance.

Second, the technological specialization of the two systems obtains further evidence by the present study: towards traditional sectors for Italy and towards specialized supplier sectors for Germany (and especially the chemical sector). This seems to confirm the trends observed in the last years regarding an improvement in the international position of traditional sectors for Italy, that increased their market share in a totally declining market; for what regards Germany, the low-to-high tech specialization is confirmed, connected to a progressive weakening of the traditional sectors.

Third, as far as the main technological flows are concerned, the most significant channel of diffusion follows the path of utilization of material inputs in Italy, while in Germany, it mainly follows the characteristics of the manufacturing processes.

7.6   Empirical results at the regional level

Recent contributions on the inner structure of the Italian technological system (see Antonelli, 1984; Antonelli, 1988; Archibugi and Pianta, 1992; Malerba and Orsenigo, 1990; Malerba, 1993, Leoncini, Maggioni and Montresor, 1996) underline its dualistic structure both from a dimensional and a sectoral perspective.

The Italian industrial and innovative structure is heavily polarized: few large firms and few advanced sectors record the highest indicators of innovative activity, while the great majority of firms (which in Italy are SMEs) and of sectors (Italy is specialized in mature and traditional sectors) are involved in traditional technologies and are locked in mature technological trajectories doomed to extinction. These conclusions are supported through the analysis of R&D indicators both at a sectoral and firm level. However, in all these works, the territorial dimension is not analysed, the only reference being some general remarks of the effect of an underdeveloped southern Italy, which heavily influences the overall performance of the Italian technological system.

A greater emphasis on the geographical aspects can be found in Ciciotti (1992), where the productive and innovative structure of all Italian regions is examined. In this work three different indicators of regional innovative activity are used (namely: R&D expenditure, number of innovative firms and number of patents) to show that Lombardy and Piedmont are always recording values largely higher than any other region.

The official Istat statistics, devoted to the survey of the innovative effort (such as the *Statistiche della Ricerca Scientifica e Tecnologica*) do not focus explicitly on the territorial perspective. The most relevant data concern the R&D expenditure: more than 60 per cent of the total is performed by the two industrial regions (Lombardy, 31.7 per cent, and Piedmont, 31.6 per cent). The Rest of Italy, with the sole exception of Lazio (recording a figure of 10 per cent) shows one-digit figures or often values of less than 1 per cent. If one considers the R&D expenditure of the public sector, only Lazio (where the Italian capital, Rome, is situated) increases its rank.[14]

The established literature tends to explain these three dualisms (dimensional, sectoral and geographical) as three aspects of the same structure. The largest and the most innovative firms in Italy are located in Piedmont and Lombardy; as a consequence, these two regions account for the majority of the innovative efforts and are ranked in the first two positions.

What has not been analysed is the interregional structure of innovative flows, and this section of the paper is therefore devoted to the examination of this issue; for one thing is to say that the firms of Lombardy and Piedmont account for more than 60 per cent of Italy's national total; another is to investigate the intersectoral and interregional effects of these expenditures. If 'these two regions show a location quotient larger than one for all three indicators [patents, R&D expenditure, number of innovative firms] confirming their national leadership for what concerns the innovative activity' (Ciciotti, 1992), what is left to be explained is how this technological leadership is transformed into effective innovative influence. This part of the paper is therefore devoted to the identification of the regional engine of technological progress in Italy; consequently, the level of the analysis must be intersectoral as well as interregional.

7.6.1 Three different perspectives

The regional analysis has been conducted from the innovation flows matrix (where flows are measured in number of R&D employees embedded in goods exchanged within sectors and regions, through three different adjacency matrices obtained by using three different criteria for dichotomization). Leontief (1965) indirectly suggests that the average should be used as a threshold. However, this suggestion does not entirely solve the problem, the second question being, what sort of average must be used?

The answer cannot be unique; it depends on the specific aspect to be addressed within the analysis of the matrix of the innovation flows.

If one wants to assess – from a macro-territorial or systemic perspective – the most relevant innovative flows in Italy, then one should consider the scale or absolute effect and use the appropriate matrix MATSCAL (Table 7.2), which is dichotomized according to the national average (the arithmetic mean of the 1521 cells of the 39×39 matrix). This matrix emphasizes the most relevant innovation flows and gives a very synthetic representation of the total innovative and productive structure of a country. Such a matrix overvalues the role of sectors such as Chemical and Mechanical, which enjoy larger technological opportunities.

If, alternatively – from a micro-territorial or subsystemic perspective – one wants to analyse the relative performance of sectors within a single region or a subsystem made by two regions, then one should refer to another matrix, MATPRO (Table 7.3), which is built by using as a threshold value the average of each single 'geographical sub-matrix' 13×13. Such a matrix allows the analysis of the relative role played by

Table 7.2   MATSCAL (black cells represent relevant flows)

each sector within the subsystem and can highlight the performance of peculiar sectors which would be neglected by the absolute perspective.

If – from a sectoral-territorial perspective – one wants to analyse the relative specialization or diversification of both origins and destination of the innovation flows of a specific spatially defined sector (that is the Chemical and Pharmaceutical sector of Lombardy), then, following the suggestion provided by Campbell (1975), one would refer to a third matrix[15] MATRICO (Table 7.4) which summarizes the outcome of three complementary dichotomizations operated via the sectoral average of both rows and columns.[16] Such a matrix allows the analysis of forward and backward linkages within the Italian technological system at a regional level.

All three matrices show a common sectoral structure: sectors 5 (Chemicals) and 6 (Metal products) are the most pervasive sectors both in absolute and in relative terms in every geographical area. The sectoral perspective confirms their centrality: these sectors show the most

Table 7.3 MATPRO (black cells represent relevant flows)

| | | Lombardy | | | | | | | | | | | | | Piedmont | | | | | | | | | | | | | Rest of ITALY | | | | | | | | | | | | |
|---|---|1|2|3|4|5|6|7|8|9|10|11|12|13|1|2|3|4|5|6|7|8|9|10|11|12|13|1|2|3|4|5|6|7|8|9|10|11|12|13|

differentiated pervasiveness. Sectors 11 (Building) and 12 (Trade, transport, credit and insurance) are the largest destination for the flows of innovative goods in the whole economy.

All three matrices give also a clear description of the geographical areas under study:

• Lombardy has a technological system that is very compact, but in the meantime highly intertwined with the Rest of Italy. This relationship shows a function of Lombardy as the main source of innovation flows for the whole Italian technological system.
• Piedmont has an 'unbalanced' inner structure heavily concentrated around a hard core of heavy manufacturing sectors (5, 6 and, to a lesser extent, 7 and 8) and tends to privilege Lombardy, with respect to the Rest of Italy as a destination of its own innovation flows.
• The Rest of Italy (ROI) is a very non-homogeneous system, dualistic and polarized with a series of manufacturing sectors which, being open to exchange with the northern regions, act as a sort of bridge between

Table 7.4 MATRICO (black cells represent relevant flows)

the northern high-tech sectors and the underdeveloped southern traditional sectors.

Here follows a short description of the matrices: each section is opened by a table which shows the relative density of nine sub-matrices; the section is completed by the analysis of the general matrix and is concluded by the exam of the role of each region, as shown by the dichotomized matrix.

7.6.2 MATSCAL: The systemic perspective

This matrix shows the leadership of Lombardy as the 'engine of technological innovation' in Italy. The absolute level of innovation flows to the ROI more than triples the relative figure of Piedmont and confirms the cohesiveness of its internal structure. Two northern regions as a whole have an internal structure comparable to the ROI which, in turn, has a highly connected internal structure; this, however, is also heavily dependent on two northern regions.

Table 7.5 Relative density of all sub-matrices

Relative density	Lombardy	Piedmont	Rest of Italy
Lombardy	0.154	0.006	0.101
Piedmont	0.006	0.059	0.030
Rest of Italy	0.018	0	0.231

From a sectoral perspective, chemical and metal products are the most pervasive sectors while the building and the service sectors are the most dependent. The northern regions seem to replicate their inner structure in the exports. Therefore, the intraregional technological feature of a sector (dependence or pervasiveness) is confirmed by the export sub-matrices.

Examination of the centralization indexes confirms the extreme polarization of the ROI (0.689 per cent), an intermediate situation for Lombardy (0.591 per cent), owing to the strong pervasiveness of three sectors, and a relatively more parithetic situation for Piedmont (0.318 per cent), where all sectors are rather similar.

The most pervasive sectors in Lombardy are (in decreasing order): 5 (Chemicals), 6 (Metal products) and 13 (Other market services). This shows the double technological nature of Lombardy, which still holds a national leadership in the more established technologies in the manufacturing sectors, but which is already well advanced in the process of tertiarization of the economy. With the exception of sectors 1 (Agriculture), 4 (Minerals), 9 (Textiles, clothing and footwear), 11 (Building) and 12 (Trade, transport, credit and insurance) – which are structurally dependent sectors – all other sectors show an inner strong overall pervasiveness and an external diagonal pervasiveness. Innovation flows directed towards Piedmont are excluded by this threshold, while flows towards ROI replicate the inner structure. This could confirm Porter's theory (Porter, 1990) which states that internal characteristics of a country (here a region) determine the international (here the interregional) competitiveness.

This matrix also highlights the technological isolation of Piedmont, a quasi-autarkic system, with no inflows and no relevant outflows. From a sectoral perspective towards the ROI, only sectors 5, 6 and 7 seem to play a diffusive role.

The Rest of Italy is heavily dependent on both northern regions (and especially on Lombardy). The innovative imports are 56.4 per cent of the inner ones. The inner structure is compact, triangular and polarized. In other words, within ROI there is a clear distinction between pervasive sectors (2, 3, 5, 6) and dependent sectors, which are influenced only by inner technological dynamics. In particular, sectors 11, 12 and 13 are part of an autarkic technological circuit without any contact with the northern regions.

7.6.3   MATPRO: The sub-systemic perspective

The analysis of proportion (or relative) effects reduces the geographical differences while stressing the sectoral characteristics within mono and/or bi-regional subsystems. For this reason, the pervasiveness of sectors 5 and 6 is emphasized in any subsystems (both intra- and interregional).

Table 7.6   Relative density of all sub-matrices

Relative density	Lombardy	Piedmont	Rest of Italy
Lombardy	0.112	0.130	0.053
Piedmont	0.124	0.077	0.018
Rest of Italy	0.130	0.136	0.136

Lombardy shows an inner diagonal structure with horizontal tendencies limited to sectors 5 and 6. This behaviour is confirmed with respect to Piedmont, where these traditional export sectors are accompanied by sector 2 (Energy). Similar results hold for ROI where the diagonal structure of the innovative exports is prevalent.

The inner structure of Piedmont is very similar to that of Lombardy (diagonal plus horizontal pervasiveness for sector 5). Towards Lombardy, its best technological partner, Piedmont shows the relevance of the manufacturing hard-core (sectors 6 and 7) which is very active both in imports and in exports and which accounts for more than 80 per cent of all selected flows. Towards ROI few flows are concentrated in the usual sectors 6 and 7.

This peculiar threshold allows to underline the existence of some inflows from ROI to the northern regions. These flows are concentrated in sectors 5 and 6, while sectors 11, 12 and 13 of Piedmont and Lombardy seem to show a relative dependency on ROI imports. It must be stressed, however, that these flows have a negligible size in absolute terms.

7.6.4   MATRICO: The sectoral perspective

This is the less synthetic and richer matrix. The relative density indexes show that Lombardy and Piedmont have some elements of similarity (their density is equal to 0.337). The innovative interaction between the northern regions shows a clear integration of Lombardy and Piedmont. The sectoral perspective confirms the leading role of Lombardy with respect to ROI (exports from Lombardy are more than one and a half times

Table 7.7   Relative density of all sub-matrices

Relative density	Lombardy	Piedmont	Rest of Italy
Lombardy	0.337	0.118	0.183
Piedmont	0.112	0.337	0.118
Rest of Italy	0.036	0	0.396

larger than those from Piedmont). Complementarity between Lombardy and Piedmont is also shown by the exports towards ROI. The vertical dependence of ROI on Lombardy is concentrated in sectors 5 and 6, whereas its dependence on Piedmont is focused on sectors 3 and 7.

Lombardy performs a horizontally diffuse pervasiveness towards Piedmont (in sectors 5 and 6), while the export structure tends to be diagonal with respect to ROI. This difference can be attributed to the fact that, while Piedmont is a technological partner and the relationship with Lombardy is modelled on a complementarity level, the innovation exports to ROI are based on a technological superiority of sectors in Lombardy with respect to the same sectors in ROI.

Piedmont seems to be a closed system; its technological diffusion is limited and more selected. Piedmont does not import any innovation from ROI and, from a quantitative point of view, it seems to consider Lombardy and ROI as equivalent partners. However, the analysis of the exports structure reveals that the pattern towards Lombardy is horizontal and polarized in sectors 5 and 11, while it is diagonal and vertical (sector 3, Metallic minerals, and 7, Motor vehicles and other transport equipment) towards ROI. The inner structure shows a relative dependence of mature sectors such as 9 (Textiles, clothing and footwear) and 11 (Building).

ROI appears as a compact but dependent structure which relies on external inflows from the northern regions. The triangular shape of the matrix confirms the polarization of the technological structure of ROI, where a sector is either producer (2, 3, 5, 6, 10) or user (1, 8, 11, 12, 13) of innovations and no intermediate role is allowed.

7.7 Conclusion

This paper has shown the power of network analysis as a valid and innovative methodology to enquire about the structure and the dynamics of systems of innovation at different territorial levels. The main results of the paper can be summarized as follows: the use of network analysis techniques has allowed to identify and measure some structural differences between systems of innovation that are traditionally considered as similar.

The national analysis has shown that the systems of innovation of Germany and Italy, despite some similarities in terms of technological opportunities, are structurally different. In particular, Germany has a higher degree of systemic connection, while Italy is characterized by a dualistic structure where the technological gap between the so-called advanced and traditional sectors is wide. Secondly, the analysis of the productive and innovative subsystems has confirmed the traditional German leadership both in the specialized suppliers and in the chemical sectors, while the comparative advantage of Italy is based on the traditional ones. Finally, the transfer of innovation in the German system occurs mainly through the manufacturing process, while in Italy the foremost channel of innovation diffusion is the use of raw materials and intermediate inputs.

The regional exercise represents a radical innovation in the analysis of innovative systems, being focused on the simultaneous analysis of the innovation flows (measured at a sectoral level) that exist both within and between different (but connected) economic systems. In this way it is possible to give an exact quantitative content to the notion of 'technological leading region' with specific empirical reference to the role played by such a region – in the network of intersectoral innovation flows – with respect to other regions and to the whole country. The use of relational data, which explicitly refers to the contents of technological relations, allows an objective measure of the technological dependence and pervasiveness of different territorial subsystems in a way that cannot be reached through the use of traditional indicators of territorial concentration and localization of innovative inputs (R&D outlays and employment, percentage of higher degree in the labour force) or outputs (patents and innovations).

References

Antonelli C., 'I Determinanti della Distribuzione Territoriale dell'Attività Innovativa in Italia', in C. Antonelli, R. Cappellin and R. Jannaccone Pazzi (eds), *Le Politiche di Sviluppo Locale* (Milano: Franco Angeli, 1988).

Antonelli G. (ed.), *Innovazioni Tecnologiche e Struttura Produttiva: la Posizione dell'Italia* (Bologna: Il Mulino, 1984).

Antonelli G. and N. De Liso, *Economics of Structural and Technological Change* (London: Routledge, 1997).

Archibugi D. and M. Pianta, *The Technological Specialization of Advanced Countries* (Dordrecht: Kluwer, 1992).

Bonacich P., 'Power and Centrality: a Family of Measures', *American Journal of Sociology*, V, 5 (1987) 1170–82.

Bramanti A. and M. A. Maggioni, 'The Dynamics of Mileux: from Governance Structures to Network Analysis', in R. Ratti, A. Bramanti and R. Gordon (eds), *Structural Dynamics of Milieus* (London: Harwood, 1997).

Campbell J., 'Application of Graph Theoretic Analysis to Interindustry Relationships. The Case of Washington State', *Regional Science and Urban Economics*, V, 1 (1975) 91–106.

Ciciotti E., 'Le Prestazioni Innovative delle Regioni Italiane', in A. Boitani and E. Ciciotti (eds), *Innovazione e Competitività nell'Industria Italiana* (Bologna: Il Mulino, 1992).

Coleman J. S., *Introduction to Mathematical Sociology* (New York: Free Press, 1964).

FORMEZ, *Tavole delle Interdipendenze Settoriali delle Regioni Italiane. Anno 1987* (Naples: Progetto Formez-ISTAT, 1992).

Freeman L. C., 'Centrality in Social Networks: Conceptual Clarification', *Social Network*, I (1979) 215–39.

ISTAT, 'Statistiche della Ricerca Scientifica: Consuntivo 1988. Preventivo 1989–1990', *Collana d'Informazione*, XXIX (1991).

Leoncini R., M. A. Maggioni and S. Montresor, 'Flussi Innovativi Intersettoriali e Sistemi Tecnologici: Metodologie Reticolari per un Confronto Italia-Germania', *Rivista di Politica Economica*, LXXXVII, 3 (1997) 3–54.

Leoncini R., M. A. Maggioni and S. Montresor, 'Intersectoral Innovation Flows and National Technological Systems: a Network Analysis for Comparing Italy and Germany', *Research Policy*, XXIII, 7/94 (1996) 2–15.

Leontief W. W., 'The Structure of US Economy', *Scientific American*, CCIX (1965) 148–66.

Lundvall B. A., *National Systems of Innovation. Towards a Theory of Innovation and Interactive Learning* (London: Pinter, 1992).

Maggioni M. A., 'Metodologie Reticolari per l'Analisi della Dinamica Industriale Regionale', in G. Garofoli and R. Mazzoni (eds), *I Sistemi Produttivi Locali: Struttura e Trasformazione* (Milan: Franco Angeli, 1994) pp. 154–86.

Maggioni M. A. and C. Miglierina, 'Dov'è il Motore del Sistema Tecnologico Nazionale? Un'Analisi Spaziale dei Flussi Innovativi Intersettoriali', in G. Gorla and O. Vito Colonna (eds), *Regioni e Sviluppo: Modelli, Politiche e Riforme* (Milan: Franco Angeli, 1996) pp.79–114.

Malerba F. and L. Orsenigo, 'Technological Regimes and Patterns of Innovation: A Theoretical and Empirical Investigation of the Italian Case', in A. Heertje and M. Perlman (eds), *Evolving Technology and Market Structure. Studies in Schumpeterian Economics* (Ann Arbor, MI: University of Michigan Press, 1990) pp. 283–305.

Malerba F., 'The National System of Innovation in Italy', in R. Nelson (ed.), *National Innovation Systems. A Comparative Analysis* (Oxford: Oxford University Press, 1993) pp. 230–59.

Marengo L. and A. Sterlacchini, 'Intersectoral Technology Flows. Methodological Aspects and Empirical Applications', *Metroeconomica*, XXXXI, 1 (1990) 19–39.

Momigliano F. and D. Siniscalco, 'Note in Tema di Terziarizzazione e Deindustrializzazione', *Moneta e Credito*, XXXV, 138 (1982) 143–81.

Montresor S., 'Un'Analisi Input-Output dei Sistemi Nazionali di Innovazione Italiano e Tedesco', *L'Industria*, 3 (1994) 475–502

Nadel S. F., *The Theory of Social Structure* (London: Cohen & West, 1957).

NBER, *The Rate and Direction of Inventive Activity* (Princeton, NJ: Princeton University Press, 1962).

Nelson R. (ed.), *National Innovation Systems. A Comparative Analysis* (New York: Oxford University Press, 1993).

Pavitt K., 'Sectoral Patterns of Technical Change: Towards a Taxonomy and a Theory', *Research Policy*, XIII (1984) 343–72.

Porter M., *The Competitive Advantage of Nations* (London: Macmillan, 1990).

von Bertalanffy L., *General System Theory. Foundations Development Applications* (London: Allen, 1968).

Wasserman S. and C. Faust, *Social Network Analysis* (Cambridge: Cambridge University Press, 1995).

Notes

* ISEIS, Università Cattolica, Milano and IDSE – CNR, Milano. This paper draws from previous research where network analysis has been applied in great detail to the analysis of national (Leoncini, Maggioni and Montresor, 1996) and interregional (Maggioni and Miglierina, 1996) intersectoral innovation flows. Readers interested in the analyses of the specific cases can therefore refer to the quoted papers. The present contribution offers an original methodological viewpoint by showing how network analysis can improve the understanding of the inner dynamics and structure of technological systems both at a national and at a regional level. The author is grateful to the co-authors of the above mentioned papers and to the participants to the EUCompEcs International Conference held in Warsaw for useful comments and discussions. Nevertheless, the usual caveats apply.

1. To quote the title of a seminal contribution in the economic literature on technological change (NBER, 1962).

2. The total unitary output of each sector is thus decomposed separately in shares representing its direct and indirect contribution to the satisfaction of each component of the final demand.

3. Although in Leoncini, Maggioni and Montresor (1996) a brief section is devoted to the analysis of the technological contents of imports and exports.

4. Described in detail in Maggioni and Miglierina (1996).

5. Calculated as a residual.

6. In particular, the vector of the labour coefficient imported by region i from regions j and y has been calculated as follows: $r_m^i = (r^j + r^y)(x^j + x^y)^{-1}$

7. A methodology originally developed in the 1950s within two independent fields of research: the British ethnology (Nadel, 1957) and the American sociometry (Coleman, 1964).

8. '1' is substituted to the actual value of the edge when it is greater than or equal to the cut-off; '0' when the actual value is smaller than the cut-off. The use of valued versus unvalued networks is widely discussed in the literature (Wasserman and Faust, 1995).

9. If both degree centrality (for the single node) and centralization (for the whole system) indexes are used on a directed network, then it must be stressed that inward and outward measures (relative to the inward and outward links of a node) are, in general, not equal. In the paper, therefore, centrality and centralization indexes – without any further specification – identify the outward measure of the indexes.

10. Degree refers to the number of other nodes directly connected with a given node; closeness measures the distances (that is the number of edges) between two nodes; betweenness relates to the frequency with which a node falls between pairs of other nodes in the network (Freeman, 1979).

11. In particular, together with the above mentioned degree centrality index, an alternative measure proposed by Bonacich ($\hat{C}_B$) has also been used; it is calculated by substituting C_g^i in equation (4) with an expression ($\sum_i l_{ij} C_j^i$) that 'weights' each edge with a centrality measure of the associated nodes. Such an index, therefore, values differently two nodes, with the same degree centrality, if one node is linked to very central nodes, while the other has connections limited to the peripheral area of the network (see Bonacich, 1987).

12. A detailed analysis of the outcomes obtained for a wider spectrum of cut-off values can be found in Leoncini, Maggioni and Montresor (1996).

13. For the relative perspective, a matrix R' has been obtained, whose general element *ij* indicates, for sector *j*, the incidence of its acquisitions from sector $i(R_{ij})$ on its total acquisitions ($\sum R_{ij}$).

14. 'Lazio is a region in which the R&D activity has a peculiar institutional nature given that public-owned enterprises and national research centres, both private and public, are often localised in Rome' (Ciciotti, 1992).

15. 'A demand link exists if a given industry sells $1/n$ or more of its inputs to another industry, whereas a supply link exists if a given industry purchases $1/n$ or more of its inputs from another industry, where n equals the number of industries represented in the interindustry matrix. ... In each row of an input-output matrix, the cells which meet the definitions for a demand link can be identified. ... Similarly, in each column of an input-output matrix, the cells which meet the definition for a supply link can be identified. Two industries may be considered linked if either the demand or the supply link condition is satisfied .... [Finally] a matrix was developed in which each of those cells representing either a supply or a demand link were set equal to "1", whereas all other cells ... were set equal to "0"' (Campbell, 1975).

16. In order to obtain MATRICO, we have firstly built two matrices, MATRIG and MATCOL by using, respectively, the average of the row and of the column. These two matrices have then been 'condensed' in the third matrix (MATRICO) by proceeding in the way described above.

PART III

Transition, Two Sample Paths

8
Structure and Productivity During a Simulated Transition: The Polish Case

*Jan Gadomski and Irena Woroniecka**

This paper aims at an analysis of structural changes in the Polish economy. The economic transformation in Poland entailed changes at both the macro and the micro levels. These changes have involved the privatization of the national economy, liberalization of foreign trade and technical progress. In the model used for this analysis the privatization and technical progress take the form of autonomous technical progress affecting all of the installed capital or new capital from investment. An evaluation of the impact of particular factors is often impossible; yet an effort aimed at their separation is necessary. In the model, the privatization of the economy as well as technical progress are treated in a similar way as processes which induce changes in the parameters of the production function. Simulation results are presented and the envisaged progress of the transformation process is assessed using the criterion of convergence of sectors to their optimum paths.

8.1 Introduction

This paper is aimed at an analysis of structural changes during the transformation process of the Polish economy. The transformation consists in redefining goals of enterprises as well as the economic role of the government; privatization and demonopolization; price liberalization; opening of the economy and intensive development of the financial sector. The purpose of this research was to produce forecasts enabling identification of the bottlenecks as well as the insufficient or excessive development of certain sectors of the Polish economy. In working out the analysis the authors have also wished to answer questions concerning the duration of the economic transformation process given the scale of benefits and time profile of the liberalization and privatization of the economy.

It is necessary to mention models of Polish economy developed recently in other scientific centres, such as: the Institute for Econometrics and Statistics of the Lódz University (Welfe *et al.*, 1996; Tomaszewicz *et al.*, 1996; Juszczak *et al.*, 1993), the Poznan Economic Academy (Czerwiński, 1996), the Institute for Development and Strategic Studies (Barteczko, 1996), and the Gdansk Institute for Market Economics (Gronicki, 1997; Charemza, 1998). The models developed in these centres are diversified as they were built for different purposes.

This model is distinguished from the others by a link between the macro and microeconomic levels. This link has enabled an analysis of the interrelationships between the sectoral and macroeconomic structures and equilibria. The model is of the Systems Dynamics type.

In this research two aspects of the structural changes are analysed. The first aspect is related to the proportions between economic sectors. The second aspect is connected with the intrasectoral proportions of inputs of the capital and labour.

The initial conditions of the economic transformation were characterized by a disproportional part of the sectoral development and a deep disequilibrium of the production factors employed within the production sectors. The disproportional part of the sectoral development concerned an excessive size of certain sectors, for example, that of mining and heavy industry, or underdevelopment of other sectors. This was the case, for example, of sectors producing consumer goods. The consequences of this disproportion are the bottlenecks that slow down or halt economic growth. In the proportions of the inputs of capital and labour, the situation of particular sectors varied. There was a strong over-investment in certain sectors, as in the case of mining and metallurgy. There was significant under-investment in other sectors, for example in agriculture and sectors producing consumer goods. An inappropriate structure of the inputs of the production factors was one of the main reasons for low productivity.

Redefinition of the goals of enterprises consists in the maximization of financial surplus while diminishing the uneconomic roles (social and political ones). However, adjustments to actual production and the demand for inputs to the optimum values are not instantaneous. In the case of employment, delays at a time when production is expanding usually result from the time necessarily taken to recruit and train new workers. With regard to decreasing production, the delays occurring in the reduction of employment are the consequence of group cost reductions, resistance of trade unions and so on. The delayed adjustment of capital results mostly from the length of time taken in the investment process.

It can be assumed that both the scales of effects and duration of the systemic reforms are constrained. Positive effects can be treated as a rent on the systemic transformation. However, it is worth indicating that the higher rates of implementation of reforms, although politically desirable, are not necessarily technically feasible. Higher weight attributed to the efficiency of production contributes to higher productivity of both capital and labour. The autonomous technical progress as well as that embodied in the new capital generation are involved.

Both systemic factors and technical progress influence the improvement of the efficiency of production. This impact can be expressed through the changes of the parameters of the sectors' production functions.

The criterion used in this research for the assessment of advancement of the structural changes is based on an analysis of the divergence of the actual and long-term optimum values of the capital-to-labour ratio. The capability of a sector to adjust the capital-to-labour ratio to its short-term optimum is an indicator of the short-term performance of the sector in the changing economic conditions. Convergence of the actual value of the capital-to-labour ratio to the long-term optimum value is interpreted as an achievement of the long-term equilibrium. A moment when the actual values of the capital-to-labour ratios enter the production factors' substitution range in all analysed sectors is treated as the completion of the process of economic transformation. In terms of the production theory this convergence is achieved whenever the value of the capital-to-labour ratio belongs to the production factors' substitution range.

This paper consists of two parts. The first includes the description of the model, with an emphasis given to the new solutions. In the second part, simulation results are presented and discussed.

8.2 Outline of the Model

The model is designed for the simulation of the economic development given the initial condition and the simulation scenario. Such a scenario includes assumed changes in the economic environment of the Polish economy (world prices and demand), technical progress, effects of 'marketization' and privatization of the national economy, demographic processes and economic policy represented by the regulation rules and their parameters.

The model consists of sectors grouping aggregated economic agents playing similar roles and having similar functions in the economic system. Sectors interact with one another, however not all relations form closed loops. The following sectors are distinguished: five sectors producing goods and services; public sector; households; banking sector and the foreign trade sector. The household sector is the supplier of labour, savings, revenues from direct and indirect taxation, and the consumer of goods and loans. The market relations determine supplies and purchases of goods and services provided by the producing sectors, money and foreign trade.

Demand for foreign goods and services in the producing sectors and households is determined by appropriate preference functions and relations of world and domestic market prices. It is assumed that Polish exports and imports do not affect supply and prices in world markets. Relations of the world and domestic market prices as well as other factors, such as the progress of economic co-operation and integration, determine the export demand for goods and services.

Macroeconomic policy is represented by the rules of balancing the budget and the admissible level of the budget deficit in relation to the revenues and GDP, the exchange rate mechanism in relation to foreign reserves and the rules of interest rate determination.

A full description of the model was published in Gadomski and Woroniecka (1995), while preliminary results were presented in Fleissner *et al.* (1996).

8.2.1   Structure of the model

It is assumed that there are five products being produced by five separate sectors.

Sector A produces agricultural intermediates. Sector M produces non-agricultural intermediates. Sector I produces investment goods while sectors F and C produce respectively food being the result of processing intermediate A and industrial consumer goods F produced by M. The model includes also the banking sector B, the household sector H, the public sector G (government plus public services) as well as the labour market. Flows of goods, money and labour between sectors and the world economy are presented in Figures 8.1 and 8.2.

The above figures indicate only the structure of links between the sectors. The rates of flows between the sectors are determined by an interaction between these sectors.

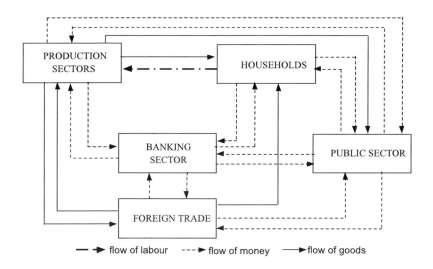

Figure 8.1   Flows of goods, money and labour in the model

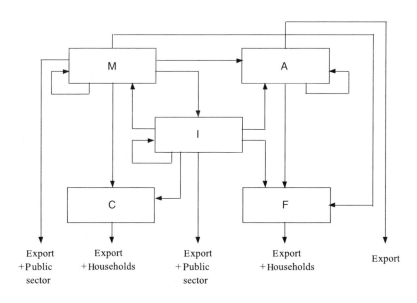

Figure 8.2   Flows of goods between production sectors

8.2.2   Production

The production sector determines an optimum production rate by maximizing the expected short-term profit:

$$max \prod_{L}^{*} = max_{L} \; P^* \cdot Q(L) - C[Q(L)] \} \tag{1}$$

where P^* is the index of the expected sales price based on the freely determined price and $C[Q(L)]$ is the cost of producing $Q(L)$ at the full production capacity:

$$C[Q(L)] = P_K \, a \, K(t) + wL + (p_A \, q_A + p_M q_M)(1 + r)Q(L) + D \tag{2}$$

where a is the depreciation rate; w is the gross wage rate; L is the number of employees; p_K is the price index of fixed assets; p_A is the price index of supplies of product A to a given sector; p_M is the price index of supplies of product M to a given sector; q_A is the intensity of input A in a given sector; q_M is the intensity of input M in a given sector; r is the bank interest rate; D is the repayment of interest on long-term loans.

The production capacity of a given production sector is described by the following production capacity function (Gadomski, 1992):

$$Q = F(K, L) + L \cdot P_L(U) = L \cdot P_L^* \cdot \left[\frac{U}{U^*} \cdot exp\left(1 - \frac{U}{U^*}\right) \right]^\beta \tag{3}$$

where:

P_L^* is the parameter defining the maximum value of the average labour productivity; U is capital-to-labour ratio: $U = K/L$; U^* is the value of the capital-to-labour ratio for which $P_L(U^*) = P_L^*$; beta is the substitution coefficient $(\beta > 0)$; and U^{**} is the value of U determining maximum production capacity (if $\beta > 1$).

The above production capacity function is derived from the concept that wrong proportions of the production factors are a potential source of production inefficiency (see Gadomski, 1990 and 1992). It may be noticed that production is efficient whenever the value of the capital-to-labour ratio U, $U = K/L$, satisfies condition $U^{**} < U < U^*$, that belongs to the substitution range. An attempt to produce using a value of U from outside of the substitution range results in inefficiency because lesser input of at least one production factor can produce the same output.

In the intermediate-term analysis, that is when inputs of both production factors change while the production technique remains constant, average production costs under full utilization of the production capacities are a function of the capital-to-labour ratio and are independent of the scale of production (see Figure 8.3).

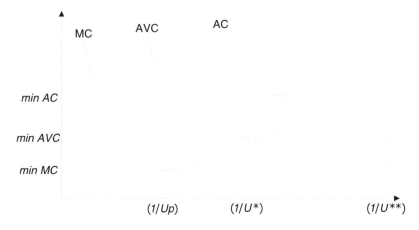

Figure 8.3 Intermediate-term average costs and the capital-to-labour ratio

In the long term, relations of the production factors as well as the production technique undergo changes. Technical progress is expressed by the changes of U^* and P_L^* parameters. The U^* and P_L^* parameters change as a result of autonomous technical progress affecting the existing stock of capital and of technical progress embodied in the new generation of capital. An increase of the parameter P_L^* reflects the general improvement of production efficiency, while an increase of U^* represents the long-term growth tendency of the capital-to-labour ratio.

It is assumed that autonomous technical progress increases the value of U^* by 0.75 per cent per annum and the value of P_L^* by 1.5 per cent per annum in all production sectors. It is also assumed that the effects of privatization on the total increase of the value of U^* and P_L^* parameters amount to 5 per cent over five years in A, C and F sectors, over eight years in the I sector and over ten years in the M sector. The difference between these time periods is related to the uneven rates of privatization in particular sectors.

Investments in given production sectors are the function of the expected interest rate and the bank interest rate. Investments are financed by the sector's own means, by bank loans and by direct foreign investment.

The demand for investment loans is assumed to be a constant proportion of the profit. Subsequent decisions concern the structure of demand for investment goods (imported – domestic). These purchases are influenced by the relation of the prices of imported to domestic products and by preferences as to the supply source.

Under such assumptions, the analysis of the long term efficiency of production is based on the value of the capital-to-labour ratio relative to the trajectories of U^{**}, U^* (respective limits of the substitution range) and U_P.

The actual production rate is defined as the minimum of the optimum production rate and production capacity. If the optimum production rate is smaller than the production capacity, employment is being reduced. Neither labour reduction nor increase can exceed an assumed level. Excessive employment causes higher average production cost.

8.2.3   Product market

Enterprises maintain inventories of products in order to provide a continuity of sales. Producers observe the production costs, changes of inventory, and the desired level of inventory, and react to them by adjusting the price. The desired level of inventory is a linear function of demand and is interpreted as a filling up of the distribution system that enables a continuity of sales.

Three categories of prices are used in the model: the freely determined price, the minimum price and the sales price. Each sector sets a sales price by observing the values of the freely determined price and the minimum price. The freely determined price p_t^s is the price set by supply and demand. The freely determined price p^s changes under the influence of inventory changes and the divergence of inventory from the desired level. The Δp_t^s price increase is caused by a decrease of inventory and/or a decrease of the actual inventory below the desired level of inventory:

$$\frac{\Delta p_t^s}{p_t^s} = \varsigma_1 \frac{\Delta Z_t}{Z_t} + \varsigma_2 \frac{Z_t - Z_T^*}{Z_t} \tag{4}$$

where Z_t is the inventory level; Z_t^* is the desired inventory level; and ς_1, ς_2 are parameters, $\varsigma_1, \varsigma_2 < 0$.

The p_t^{min} minimum price is the level considered by the producer to be the lower limit on the sales price. This price reflects supply conditions, determined by average production costs and the degree of monopolization within a given sector:

$$p_t^{min} = \delta AC_{t-1} \tag{5}$$

where δ is the monopolization coefficient $\delta > 0$; and AC_{t-1} is the average production cost.

In the case of perfect competition, the minimum price is defined by the minimum average variable cost. In the monopolistic case, a minimum price would provide profit despite the production cost.

The p_t^d sales price is equal to

$$p_t^d = \max(p_t^{\min}, p_t^s) \tag{6}$$

8.2.4 Labour market

The persistence of long-term unemployment is a prerequisite for the assumption of an inherent disequilibrium of the labour market, and application of the concept of natural unemployment. Actual employment is assumed to be the minimum of the supply and demand of labour.

The supply of labour depends on the number of economically active persons determined demographically. Moreover, the number of economically active persons is assumed not to depend upon the wage level.

The demand for labour is formed in the public and production sectors. The demand of a given production sector is determined by the optimum employment level and the constraint of a maximum admissible employment change. The total demand for labour is a sum of effective demands from all sectors.

The following categories of wages are distinguished: a freely determined wage, a guaranteed wage, and a minimum wage. The freely determined wage is an average wage that would result if the labour market were not regulated. The freely determined wage increases with the relative decrease of unemployment and grows when the unemployment rate falls below the natural level:

$$\frac{\Delta w_t^s}{w_t^s} = \chi_1 \frac{\Delta U_t}{U_t} + \chi_2 \frac{U_t - U^*}{U_t} \tag{7}$$

where w_t^s is the freely determined wage; U_t is unemployment; U_t^* is the natural unemployment rate; and χ_1, χ_2, are the parameters, χ_1, $\chi_2 < 0$.

The guaranteed wage is determined in negotiations between the social partners: government, employers and employees. A change of the Δw_t^g guaranteed wage depends upon the rate of growth of the GDP and the rate of the consumption price increase:

$$\Delta w_t^g = v_1 \frac{\Delta p_t^c}{p_t^c} + v_2 \frac{\Delta Y_t}{Y_t} \tag{8}$$

where p_t^c is the consumption price index; Y_t is GDP; and v_1, v_2 are the parameters, $v_1, v_2 > 0$.

The dependence of the guaranteed wage upon the price increase reflects the mechanism of wage indexation, while its dependence upon the GDP growth defines the long-term relation of wages and the GDP.

The effective average wage in the economy w_t^a is defined as the maximum of the freely determined and guaranteed wage levels:

$$w_t^a = \max(w_t^g, w_t^s) \tag{9}$$

Whenever a sector has insufficient means to pay full wages, the actual average wage is lowered beneath the normative average sectors' wages. The minimum wage is the lower limit for the case of financial losses in the production sectors and is related to the guaranteed wage. The average level of wages in particular sectors is determined in definite proportions to the average wage in the whole economy.

8.3   Simulated structural changes

The simulation scenario in general assumes a continuation of the economic policies and tendencies in both the Polish and world economies.

During the whole simulation period a homogeneous budgetary policy is continued. Interest rates, tariffs and social security rates are not changed. This also applies to corporate income tax, personal income tax, indirect taxes, social insurance and tariffs. Wages in the public sector, pensions, unemployment benefits and social benefits remain in the same proportion to the average wage in production sectors as that which prevailed in 1995.

Employment policy in the public sector is kept unchanged too. The number of persons employed in public sector service per one inhabitant remains constant over the whole period of simulation. Thus, employment in the public sector is stable and its changes result uniquely from demographic factors.

The scenario assumes zero real growth of investments in the public sector under an additional financial constraint concerning the proportion of investment expenditures and the value of GDP. It was also assumed that in the case of positive budgetary balance the whole surplus is proportionally dispensed on all kinds of expenses. In the case of negative budgetary balance not exceeding 5.5 per cent of the GDP, the actual expenditures are equal to those planned, while when the deficit exceeds 5.5 per cent of the GDP the sums disbursed are lowered proportionally in all the groups thus preserving the structure of budget expenditures.

The A sector producing agricultural intermediates is being subsidised during the whole simulation period. These subsidies take the form of debt restructuring as well as preferential loans. Such a solution was necessary, without it the model was unstable.

The model was calibrated on the basis of the input-output table for Poland in 1990. The starting point of the simulation was September 1996. Initial conditions were determined by results of the model run during 1991–96 and on the basis of actual data. The simulation scenario was then elaborated for the period 1996–2010. In general, the scenario assumes a continuation of the economic policy and trends of exogenous variables.

8.3.1 Structure of production and employment

The changing structure of production is shown in Figure 8.4. The share of sector C increases uniformly over the whole period from 7.6 per cent at the starting point up to 16 per cent in 2010. The increased share of sector C in output is accompanied by a decrease of the sector F share: from 20 per cent down to 14 per cent in 2010. The share of sector I in output increases slowly in the whole period, from 10.4 per cent at the starting point up to approximately 11 per cent in 2010. The share of sector M decreases from 60 per cent to 57 per cent in 2010. The share of sector A in output decreases from 4 per cent to 2.5 per cent in 2010.

The employment structure is presented in Figure 8.5. In the initial period, only in the case of sector A does the employment share decrease quickly (from 29 per cent in 1996 to 20 per cent in 1999). From 2000 on that decrease continues, although at a slower rate, down to 17 per cent. The share of sector F in total employment increases in the years 1996–99 and then decreases slightly over the remaining period. The shares of the sectors M, C and I in total employment increase over the whole period.

Special attention should be paid to the shrinking share of agriculture in the national economy, despite subsidies from the state budget. The share of the agricultural sector in both production and employment diminished by around 30 per cent. This indicates the need, in the long term, of an

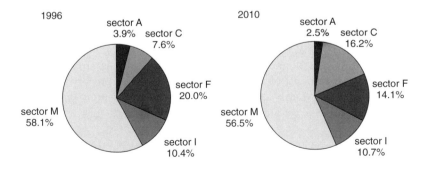

Figure 8.4 Production structure

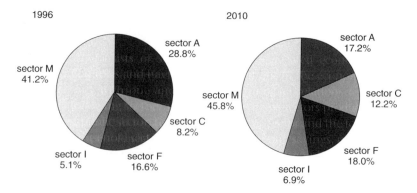

Figure 8.5   Employment structure

economic policy which duly considers the social aspects of the restructuring of Polish agriculture.

Opposite tendencies are observed in sector C, which grew exceptionally quickly over the whole period. In conclusion, the share of the raw material and food producing sectors in the total output shrinks, while the share and significance of the manufacturing sectors increase.

Labour productivity in sectors is presented in Figure 8.6. The lowest level of labour productivity is in sector A, while the highest is that of sector C. Labour productivity above the average in the economy is achieved in sectors C, I and M. Sectors C and I are the sectors with an increasing share of production and employment in the whole economy. However, sectors A and F having a relatively low productivity of labour, lose their position in the national economy and their shares in production and employment decrease.

The average productivity of labour in the whole economy increases by about 35 per cent in 1996–2010, the strongest growth occurring in 1996–99. This is because in that period, most benefits from an adjustment to the market economy (privatization, opening up of the economy, etc.) emerge. Sectors A and C are characterized by the greatest movements of labour productivity (increment of about 40–50 per cent). The biggest structural changes are observed only in these sectors. At the other end of the scale is sector F with the slowest growth of labour productivity (increase of about 18 per cent).

Similar results (sector A being an exception) were obtained for the case of capital productivity. Sectors C and I reveal a high growth rate of capital productivity (above the average rate in the whole economy), while sectors

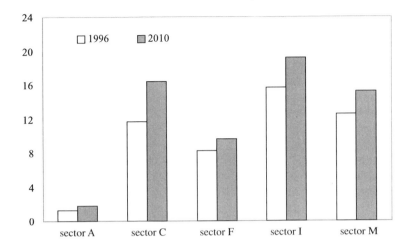

Figure 8.6 Productivity of labour, in thousand PLN per employee

A and F display a slow growth in the productivity of capital (below the average of the whole economy). The average productivity of capital in the whole economy increased by about 25 per cent – a little less than labour productivity. Special attention should be paid to agriculture. The increase of labour productivity in this sector is the strongest (about 50 per cent); however, after 15 years it will still lag behind other production sectors. Its capital productivity growth is the weakest one (about 10 per cent). Thus, in the whole simulation period the agriculture-food processing complex (agriculture proper and food industry) retains the lowest productivity of both production factors.

Comparisons of the actual with the optimum employment in sectors are presented in Figures 8.7–8.11.

Divergences between the actual and optimum employment levels are prominent at the starting point. The biggest discrepancy was in sector A. The excessive employment in this sector is the result of hidden unemployment. With the progress of restructuring agriculture, this form of unemployment transforms into explicit unemployment and causes on the one hand the decrease of employment in agriculture (about 25 per cent in the simulated period), and on the other hand, tensions on the labour market and temporary increase of unemployment. During the whole simulation period the actual employment pursues the optimum. The short-term equilibrium is approached about year 2001 and the divergence which occurs is relatively small.

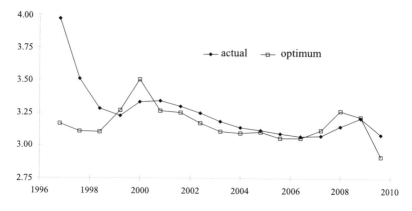

Figure 8.7 Actual and optimum employment in sector A

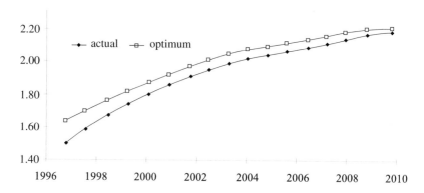

Figure 8.8 Actual and optimum employment in sector C

Other sectors reveal similar behaviour. The main difference consists in the initial stage. In other sectors optimum employment generally exceeds actual employment. This shows that the growth of these sectors is constrained by their inability to attract adequate workforce.

The increase of employment in all sectors beyond sector A is caused by growing demand for their products as well as improvement of productivity of the production factors. Increasing demand is the result of increasing export demand and growth in production. The marketization and privatization of the national economy as well as technical progress are the main causes of improvement of productivity in the production

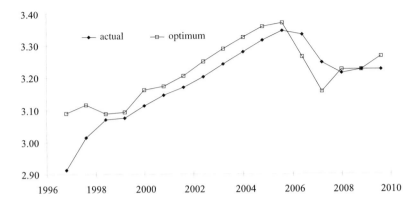

Figure 8.9 Actual and optimum employment in sector F

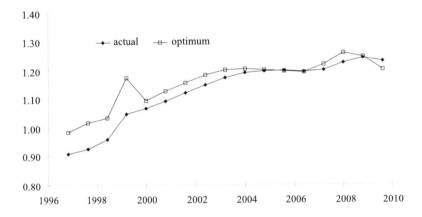

Figure 8.10 Actual and optimum employment in sector I

factors. At the end of the simulation period the former sources of the production efficiency are nearing exhaustion.

The fastest increase in employment, about 40 per cent during the whole period, is in sector C (producing industrial consumption goods). The employment in sector I (producing investment goods) grows over 30 per cent in that period. Slower growth occurs in sectors F (producing food) and sector M (producing non-agricultural intermediate goods) where employment increases by 10 per cent.

In assessing the efficiency of production, two elements are taken into consideration. The first is the distance between the actual and optimum

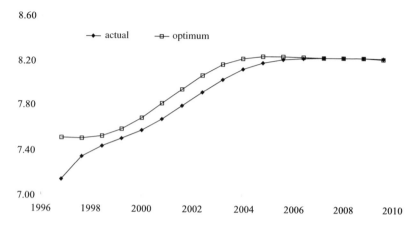

Figure 8.11   Actual and optimum employment in sector M

value of the capital/labour ratio, and the second is the location of the actual value of the capital/labour ratio in relation to the substitution range. The former indicates how successfully a sector adjusts to the changing market conditions, while the latter shows how effectively the production factors are being utilized.

The development of the capital/labour ratio in particular sectors is illustrated in Figures 8.12–8.16. The U^* and U^{**} lines represent, respectively, the upper and lower limit of the substitution range. U^* and U^{**} are parameters of the production function (see section 8.2).

In all figures, the greatest divergence between the actual and optimum values of the capital-to-labour ratio occurs in the initial period. In all sectors there were, at the starting point, inefficient proportions of production factors. The capital/labour ratio was out of the substitution range in each sector. There was strong under-investment (and relative over-employment) in agriculture – the actual level of capital-to-labour ratio in 1996 being 25 per cent below the lower limit of the substitution range. In other sectors, the situation is reverse: the value of the capital/labour ratio exceeds the upper limit of the substitution range, which indicates a relative overinvestment.

Subsequently, there is a tendency in all sectors of a gradual convergence of the actual and optimum values of the capital-to-labour ratio and the progress of these values into the substitution range. This efficiency improvement is induced primarily by the adjustment of employment and, to a lesser degree, by an increase in investment. This is particularly

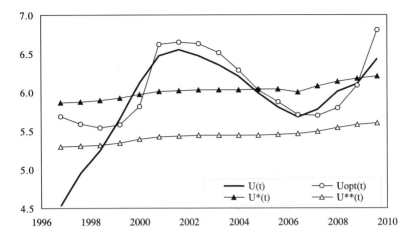

Figure 8.12   Development of the capital-to-labour ratio in sector A

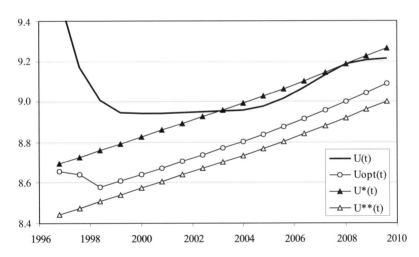

Figure 8.13   Development of the capital-to-labour ratio in sector C

evident in the case of agriculture. The results indicate that in 1996 agriculture was the last sector having a surplus of employment, and this was gradually reduced during the following years. As a consequence of these changes one can observe, on the one hand, an improvement of efficiency (especially significant being the increase of labour productivity,

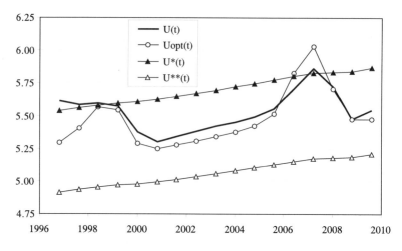

Figure 8.14 Development of the capital-to-labour ratio in sector F

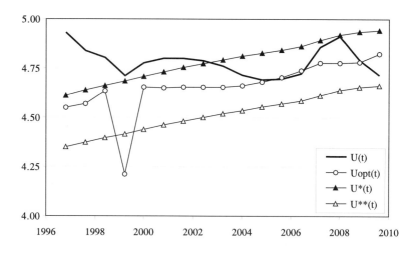

Figure 8.15 Development of the capital-to-labour ratio in sector I

see Figure 8.7), and, on the other hand, a decreasing share of agriculture in the whole economy.

Sector C displays an opposite tendency. Facing a strong consumption demand during the whole period, sector C undertakes investment outlays and also recruits new labour. In effect, the process of convergence of the

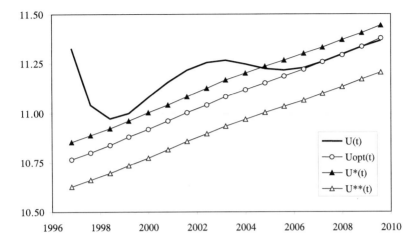

Figure 8.16 Development of the capital-to-labour ratio in sector M

actual value of the capital-to-labour ratio to the optimum lasts longer. The share of this sector in the whole economy increases significantly. The period of the fastest adjustments of production ends in about 2000 for sectors A, F and I, while in sectors M and C adjustment lasts until 2005. After that, the adjustment changes gradually disappear and the long-term stabilization in terms of technical efficiency of production is achieved. The values of the capital-to-labour ratio belong to the substitution range and a convergence to the optimum values continues.

8.4 Conclusions

The results presented show, subject to the assumptions of the simulation scenario, that the main part of adjustment of the Polish economy to the market environment will be completed in about ten years. In this period the most important quantitative as well as qualitative changes will take place. Later developments will resemble those of a stable market economy.

During the transition period, the largest development occurs in the domain of production efficiency and structural changes. The total productivity of labour in the Polish economy increases as a result of structural changes as well as a result of vast improvements occurring within production sectors. Production efficiency in sectors increases, on the one hand as an effect of the convergence of production to an optimum, and on the other hand as an effect of the improved proportions of production factors. In all sectors in the second part of the simulation period, the capital/labour ratio remains within the substitution range. In the adjustment period, the productivity of labour is the fastest increasing variable. The distribution of labour productivity does not change much during that period – the main change being the greatest expansion of the sector producing manufactured consumer goods. The biggest increase of the productivity of labour is observed in agriculture; however, this will still remain deficient in comparison to other sectors.

The most important structural changes consist in the increased relevance of manufacturing industries as well as the diminishing role performed by sectors producing intermediate goods and food. Agriculture loses its position in the national economy because its share in production, and particularly its share in employment, shrinks. According to the model, about half of the unemployed in the year 2000 will come from agriculture and this share should gradually increase in the succeeding years while in the economy as a whole, unemployment should decrease and employment grow. It is however necessary to emphasize that the simulation performed was based also on the unrealistic assumption of the invariable economic policy during the entire period.

References

Barteczko K. and A. Bocian, 'Makroekonomiczny Model Dlugookresowego Rozwoju Gospodarczego (Macroeconomic Model of Long-term Economic Development; in Polish)', in *Budowa i Implementacja Modeli Makroekonomicznych* (Warsaw: Institute of Development and Strategic Studies, 1996)

Charemza W. and S. Makarova, 'The LAM-3 Model of East European Economies: Initial Foundations and First Results', *Research Memorandum* (University of Leicester: ACE Project n. 98/1,1998).

Czerwiński Z., W. Gedymin, R. Kiedrowski and E. Panek, 'Makroekonomiczny Średniookresowy Model Gospodarki Polski KEMPO 94. Ogólna Charakterystyka i Równania Modelu (Macroeconomic Medium-term Model of Polish Economy KEMPO 94. General Characteristics and Equations of the Model; in Polish)', in *Budowa i Implementacja Modeli Makroekonomicznych* (Warsaw: Institute of Development and Strategic Studies, 1996).

Fleissner P., J. Gadomski and I. Woroniecka, 'Dynamic Model of Polish Economy During the Transition Period', in J. Owsiński and Z. Nahorski (eds), *Modelling and Analysing Economies in Transition* (Warsaw: Polish Operations and Systems Research Society, 1996).

Frączek R., J. Szafrański and Z. Żółkiewski, 'Long-run Projections for the Polish Economy Based on Computable General Equilibrium Model – Preliminary Results' Paper presented at the *MACROMODELS'94* conference, Łódź, 7–9 Dec. 1994.

Frisch R., *Theory of Production* (Dordrecht: D. Reidel, 1965).

Gadomski J., 'Selected Factors Determining Import of the Iron Ore, the Efficiency of Production and the Volume of Steel Consumption in Poland (in Polish)', *Ekonomia*, 54 (Warsaw: Wydawnictwa UW, 1990).

Gadomski J., 'Production in a Non-market Economy', *Control and Cybernetics*, XXI, 2 (1992) Warsaw.

Gadomski J. and I. Woroniecka, 'Poland Under Transition: A Systems Dynamics Model', Final Report, 1 (part IV), 2 (part V,VI) and 3, J. W. Owsiński (ed.), 'DYMOPET' Working group on dynamic macro-economic modelling of Polish economy in transition (Warsaw: Polish Operations and Systems Research Society, 1995).

Gadomski J., I. Woroniecka *et al.*, *A Dynamic Model of Polish Economy in Transition*, J. Owsiński (ed.) (Warsaw: Polish Operations and Systems Research Society, 1998).

Gronicki M., 'Zarys Kwartalnego Modelu Gospodarki Polski (Outline of Quarterly Model of the Polish Economy; in Polish)', seminar paper, The Gdansk Institute for Market Economics (Gdansk, 1 Dec. 1997).

Juszczak G., M. Kaźmierska and W. Welfe, 'Quarterly Model of the Polish Economy in Transition (with Special Emphasis on Financial Flows)', *Economic Modelling*, (April 1993).

Tomaszewicz L., C. Lipiński, M. Plich, A. Balcerak and M. Przybyliński, 'Zintegrowany Model Analityczno-symulacyjny IMPEC-CUP (Integrated Models of National Economy; in Polish)', in *Budowa i Implementacja Modeli Makroekonomicznych* (Warsaw: Institute of Development and Strategic Studies, 1996).

Welfe W., A. Welfe and W. Florczak, 'Makroekonomiczny Minimodel Gospodarki Polskiej (Macroeconomic Minimodel of Polish Economy; in Polish)', in *Budowa i Implementacja Modeli Makroekonomicznych* (Warsaw: Institute of Development and Strategic Studies, 1996).

Woroniecka I. and I. Gadomski, 'An Analysis of the Efficiency Changes in Polish Industry', in J. W. Owsiński, J. Stefański and A. Straszak (eds), *Transition to Advanced Market Economies. Strategic Options, Modelling Approaches and Operational Research Perspectives* (Warsaw: Polish Operational and System Research Society, 1992).

Notes

*   Polish Academy of Sciences, Warsaw, Poland.

9
Transition and the 'Speciation' of the Japanese Model

Ugo Pagano[*]

The Japanese model came about in a country that was at that time an isolated periphery of the capitalist system. In many respects, it was an unintended consequence of the policies followed during the American occupation of the country when the *zaibatsu* companies were at first nationalized and then privatized. The emergence of the Japanese species of capitalism implies that the transformations occurring in the former socialist countries cannot be seen as a transition from a unique model of socialism to a unique model of capitalism. The paper claims that capitalism is characterized by multiple 'organizational equilibria' characterized by different interactions between technologies and property rights. It is argued that the 'allopatric' form of speciation, that characterized the emergence of the Japanese model, should not be regarded as an uninteresting exception. It can be very relevant to the understanding of the processes occurring in the former socialist economies where different initial conditions and different institutional shocks can also lead to the emergence of new 'organizational equilibria'.

9.1 Introduction

After the end of the Second world war, Japan was considered to be a 'transition economy'. The American forces of occupation regarded it as a country coming from a feudal-*zaibatsu* past on top of which a centralized command economy had been developed during the war. The *zaibatsu* economic system had to be buried for ever because, according to the Americans, it was the ultimate cause of the militaristic characteristics that had been shown by Japanese society.[1] With the expropriation of the *zaibatsu* families, for a while Japan became a 'quasi-nationalized economy'; for this reason, the privatization of the former-*zaibatsu* firms was bound to involve problems that are now very familiar in the ex-socialist transition economies. The aim of the transition was to make Japan a standard capitalist country. However, Japan was not going to make a transition to an 'American-style' economy. Instead, the Japanese economy saw the 'speciation' of a new economic model that, after a few years, many American firms tried to imitate.

The postwar experience of Japan can be helpful in understanding what is happening in Central and Eastern Europe. While the change has often been viewed as the transition to a (unique) model of a market economy, each country is, in fact, producing its own species of capitalism. Of course, the success of the Japanese 'speciation' says nothing about the success of the new species that are emerging. Indeed, an analogy with natural selection would suggest that the emergence of successful species comes together with many other unsuccessful mutations. However, the experience of Japan shows that one should not take as given the species of capitalism that can survive and prosper in the world economy. One should not '*a priori*' assume that the new species, emerging after socialism, should necessarily be inferior 'transitional' arrangements to some unspecified form of 'pure' capitalism.

A puzzling aspect of the emergence of the Japanese model is that the 'new organizational species' did not come about in a country such as the US where market competition was vigorous but rather in a relatively backward country at the periphery of the world economy. This seems to cast serious doubts on the idea that competition tends always to select the best organizational outcomes. While major institutional shocks may often produce very inefficient organizational arrangements, they sometimes seem even necessary to stimulate the emergence of efficient organizational arrangements that would not have been selected by a competitive market process.

This paper tries to explore these complex issues by applying the concept of 'organizational equilibria'[2] to a comparative historical analysis of the 'Japanese model'.

It starts by considering two 'idealized' models: a 'Tayloristic-Fordist' or 'American model' (A-model) and a 'Toyotist' or 'Japanese model' (J-model) of production. The two models should be taken as 'thought-experiments': their schematic simplicity is intended to help focus on the nature of the interaction between rights and technology.

Section 9.2 considers the A-model and the J-model in the framework of New Institutional and Radical theory views. It shows that in the two theories causation runs in opposite directions. According to standard New Institutional theory, some 'technological' features of the resources (such as their monitoring and specificity characteristics) determine the structure of rights that characterizes the firm. According to standard 'Radical theory', the opposite is true: the structure of rights determines these 'technological' characteristics.

Section 9.3 considers the concepts of organizational equilibria and institutional stability, and shows that these concepts can integrate the Radical and New Institutional directions of causation. Joining together the two streams of the literature implies that property rights can 'regenerate' themselves by way of technology, and technology can regenerate itself by way of property rights. When this happens, we can say that we are in a situation of organizational equilibrium. The section shows that multiple organizational equilibria can exist. The A-model and the J-model can be considered as self-sustaining 'organizational equilibria'. These equilibria are 'institutionally stable' in the sense that they are resilient to 'weak' shocks to the technology or the property rights system. Organizational equilibria imply that history matters: initial institutional and technological conditions can reproduce themselves, and 'strong' shocks, upsetting the 'institutional stability' of the system, can bring about new organizational equilibria.

Section 9.4, in the framework of a very simple model, considers the interaction between property rights and technology. The 'new-institutional assumption' is expressed by observing that 'high-agency-cost factors' tend to acquire the control of organizations. The 'radical assumption' involves that owning factors tend to become high-agency-cost factors creating the conditions for the positive feedback that characterizes organizational equilibria. Also, the radical assumption can be easily captured by the language of standard economic theory. Owning factors pay for the agency costs of employing other factors whereas they save on their own agency costs; thus, ownership changes the relative prices of using the factors and induces a process of substitution. The non-owning high-agency-cost factors tend to be replaced by the owning high-agency-cost factors, and the 'speciation' of new ownership relationships is inhibited by this preventive substitution of alternative (possibly more efficient) owners.

The 'anti-speciation' mechanism that is built into each organizational equilibrium cannot be easily overturned by the forces of competitive selection. In section 9.5 we argue that the forces of competition tend to select the best members of a given species of organization but tend to inhibit the formation of a new species even when this is more efficient. In organizations as well as in natural species each characteristic tends to become optimal given the other characteristics. For instance, the A-model can be described as an organizational equilibrium where the property rights are optimal given the technology, and vice versa. In a competitive environment a change in property rights results (at least in the short-term) in an inferior hybrid that is very likely to be wiped away by competition before it is able to develop the other complementary mutations. This may explain why the speciation of the new organizational model occurred in a protected periphery like postwar Japan or, to use a biological terminology, it had an 'allopatric' nature.

In section 9.6, an attempt is made to apply this framework to the study of real-life Japanese history. Attention is concentrated on the strong 'institutional' shocks that have made Japanese history so different from that of the other capitalist countries. The focus is on the fundamental steps that after the war allowed Japan to develop the financial and labour market institutions that made possible a different self-reinforcing interaction between property rights and technology.

Section 9.7 consider some implications of the analysis for the 'institutional diversity' that is emerging in former-socialist economies.

9.2 Two 'ideal types': the A-model and the J-model

Both models will be described on the basis of two sets of data; the first concerns the technological characteristics of the resources that are employed in the firm, whereas the second concerns the rights that individuals have in these resources and in the firm where they are employed.

In the case of the Tayloristic-Fordist or American model (*A-model*) the resources that are employed within the firm have the following technological characteristics.

A very detailed division of labour is employed without any form of job rotation; labour acquires little job-specific or firm-specific skills. Workers are given precise and relatively simple commands which do not require the co-operation of their fellow workers; therefore, the contribution of each worker can be easily assessed. Thus, in the A-model labour is a 'generic' and 'easy-to-monitor' factor.

In the traditional Fordist A-model, capital tends to have characteristics that are opposite to those of labour. Machines are often firm-specific; they are often built to satisfy the needs of a particular product that is produced by the firm and can find little use outside of it. At the same time, machines are 'difficult to monitor' in the sense that it is difficult to assess their user-induced depreciation by observing their conditions before and after their employment. Their user-induced depreciation can only be indirectly assessed by observing how the machines are used by the workers. In this sense, in the A-model, capital is a specific and 'difficult-to-monitor' factor.

The characteristics of the factors employed in the *J-model*[3] firm seem to have characteristics very different and sometimes opposite to those employed in the A-model firm.

With regard to labour, much firm-specific investment in human capital is carried out: workers are encouraged to understand the technological problems of the firm and to suggest solutions for these problems. Job rotation and team-work are also encouraged; this requires human capital investments specific to the human capital of other individuals. The complexity of jobs and the existence of team-work implies that the productivity of an individual worker is difficult to assess for outside observers. In this sense, in the J-model, the workers acquire firm-specific and 'difficult-to-monitor' skills.

It is not clear whether the machinery adopted in the J-firm is substantially different from that adopted in the A-firm. However, another characteristic of the J-model seems to be the massive adoption of multi-purpose programmable machinery. Machines are less specific to a particular purpose. They have also some 'self-monitoring' characteristics that may make user-induced depreciation easy to assess.

Thus, the two firms are characterized by a tendency to adopt different technologies: the J-firm employs more specific and difficult-to-monitor labour (relatively to specific and difficult-to-monitor capital) than the A-firm.

The two firms are also characterized by a *different set of rights* and, in particular by a different set of (legal or customary) job rights.

In the *A-firm* the workers do not feel and, in many respects, they are not members of the organization: the firm 'belongs' to the owners of capital who have hiring and firing rights. The workers have 'weak' job rights in the organization.

In the *J-firm* the workers feel part of the organization: job rights are much stronger and many workers can expect that they will spend all their working life in the same organization. Capitalists do not 'own' the organization in the sense that they have hiring and firing rights.[4]

Assume that our schematic description of the A-model and of the J-model is correct. The following questions then arise. 'Is there a relation between the technology and the rights that characterize these two 'ideal' firms?' 'Can the technology used by each firm explain the set of rights? Or, can the rights that characterize each firm explain the nature of the resources that are employed?'

9.3 Two opposite views for two opposite models

In order to answer these questions, two theories that in recent years have emerged as alternatives to traditional neoclassical doctrine should be considered; there are the New Institutional and Radical theories.

In traditional neo-classical theory, under the assumptions of well-defined property rights and perfect competition, it can be shown that it does not matter who hires whom (Samuelson, 1957); the allocation of rights cannot influence or be influenced by the characteristics of resources that are adopted. In neo-classical theory it is implicitly assumed that resources are 'general-purpose' (that is they can be moved at zero cost from one use to some other alternative use) and they are 'easy to monitor' (so that problems due to asymmetric information do not arise).

New Institutional theory[5] has shown how, when these restrictive assumptions are relaxed, the monitoring and specificity characteristics of resources can influence the relative efficiency of different systems of rights. The firm is conceived as a governance structure; it can improve on market-type organization when the enforcement of simple market contracts becomes costly or impossible, because of the existence of specific or 'difficult-to-monitor' resources.

At the same time, the rights in or the control of the firm should be acquired by the owners of firm-specific or difficult-to-monitor resources. The owners of general-purpose or 'easy-to-monitor' resources should have no rights in the organization. If the former instead of the latter own the organization, monitoring or insurance expenses can be decreased and the value of the organization can be increased.

According to the New Institutional view, firms are there to mitigate asset-specificity and monitoring problems. For this reason, they are going to be owned by relatively more firm-specific and difficult-to-monitor factors. These factors can solve more efficiently the problems which are the cause of the very existence of the firm.

Consider the case of the owners of firm-specific assets. The value of their resources will increase or decrease with the success or the failure of the firm, will change with the policies of the firm and will be lost if they are fired from the organization. These circumstances do not hold for the owners of general-purpose resources. Thus, the owners of specific resources will be willing to offer a higher price for the control of the firm. Their control will save on the high insurance costs which should otherwise be paid to induce firm-specific investments.

Consider now the case of the owners of the difficult-to-monitor resources. If they own the firm, they will have an incentive to perform efficiently, and the high cost of measuring their contribution can be saved. Such saving will obviously be much less if the owners of the easy-to-monitor resources own the organization. Thus, if the owners of the difficult-to-monitor resources own the organization, they can run it more efficiently.

According to New Institutional theory, rights and safeguards will be given to the owners of 'difficult-to-monitor' and specific resources. In particular, in the case of the A-model and of the J-model, the structure of the rights and safeguards can be explained by referring to the different types of resources employed by the two organizations.

In the A-firm (difficult-to-monitor and specific), capital controls the organization because it would be inefficient to give the rights of control to 'easy-to-monitor' workers who have made no investment in firm-specific skills.

By contrast, it is efficient that workers have job rights and safeguards in the J-firm. Here, the workers make specific investments in human capital which would be very risky and, therefore, expensive in the absence of safeguards and rights on the organization. Moreover, given that the workers are relatively difficult to monitor, monitoring costs can be substantially decreased when the workers feel part of the organization.

Thus, in New Institutional theory, the direction of causality runs from the technological characteristics of the resources employed in the organization to the structure of rights. This direction of causality can be inverted on the basis of the arguments provided by Radical economists.

Radical economists have emphasized that 'easy-to-monitor' and 'generic' labour are not the neutral consequences of the dictates of technological efficiency but are the outcome of capitalist property rights.

The arguments of the Radical economists will not be examined in detail here, but the possibility that the arguments suggested by New Institutional economists themselves can be inverted following the direction of causality suggested by the Radical economists will be considered.

In New Institutional literature, the firm exists because of the costs of the market mechanism. At the same time, the efficiency of firms relies on the fact that the property rights in these organizations can be exchanged and acquired by the individuals who can rule them more efficiently. However, if market transaction costs exist, these gains may be lower than the costs of exchanging property rights. Moreover, exchange may take time. Because of the costs and the time taken by the transactions, changes in technology may have a weak or slow effect on the reallocation of property rights. And, if property rights are not immediately exchanged according to the dictates of technological efficiency, the opposite effect may take place. Property rights may influence the technology used by the firm and, in particular, the degree of specificity and the monitoring characteristics of the resources used by these organizations.

The influence of property rights on technology also has to be examined for a more fundamental reason. Technology is not created and adopted in a property rights and institutional vacuum. The technology adopted by the firm may well determine that some property rights have to be changed following the efficiency drive examined by New Institutional economics. But, in turn, this technology is always 'produced' and shaped within the framework of a certain ownership structure which influences the nature of the technology.[6]

For all these reasons, the influence of property rights on the technological characteristics of the resources deserves as much attention as the opposite line of inquiry.

Let us now consider more in detail how the specificity and the monitoring characteristics of the resources can be influenced by any given initial assignment of property rights. For example, consider the case of the A-model that is characterized by 'strong' capitalist rights and such a technology that, unlike machines, the workers are 'easy-to-monitor' and 'generic' factors.

In New Institutional economics this situation may be explained on efficiency grounds. Workers have no rights in the firms where they work because they are 'easy-to-monitor' and/or 'general-purpose' factors. Resources can be saved by having specific and difficult-to-monitor capitalists owning the firm.

However, it is perfectly legitimate to explain the same situation by inverting the direction of causation and by pointing out that, unlike machines, the workers may have become easy-to-monitor and general-purpose factors because they have no rights in the firm where they work.[7]

Under capitalism the development of difficult-to-monitor human resources may be inhibited by the fact that the workers have no rights on the organizations where they work. The high costs of monitoring labour will imply that capitalist technology will be biased against 'difficult-to-monitor labour. By contrast, no similar bias exists against difficult-to-monitor capital'[8] because the owners of the organization, owning the capital employed, have no incentive to misuse it. Thus 'classical' capitalism may be characterized by under investment in difficult-to-monitor labour.

Similarly, the development of firm-specific workers' skills, as well as the development of assets specific to the preferences of the present workers, may be inhibited because under classical capitalism the rights to these assets are ill-defined. These assets belong neither to the employers (who can lose them if the workers quit) nor to the workers (who can lose them if they are fired from the firm). Under capitalism no similar problem exists regarding the case of firm-specific machines.

Thus, the property rights of 'classical capitalism' imply underinvestment in difficult-to-monitor *and* firm-specific labour. In principle, the argument that the easy-to-monitor and general-purpose workers (coupled with specific and difficult-to-monitor capital) are the cause for the existence of capitalist property rights is as good as the argument that the latter are the cause of the former.

The 'inverted' argument considered above is quite general. Whichever factor happens to own the organization will have fewer inhibitions than the other factors to become difficult to monitor and specific to the organization. For instance, if the workers own the organization, there will be a tendency to under-invest in firm-specific and difficult-to-control capital. Difficult-to-control and specific capital is more likely to be developed under capitalist rights,[9] and difficult-to-monitor and specific human capital is more likely to be developed when the workers have some rights in the firm.

Thus, following the radical argument, the New Institutional explanations of the A-firm and of the J-firm could be inverted: the system of rights that characterizes each one of these models shapes the technological characteristics employed in these organizations. The J-firm, providing safeguards and job rights for the workers, finds it cheaper to develop firm-specific human capital and to use difficult-to-monitor labour. The A-firm inhibits the use of human capital because it does not provide an adequate structure of rights and safeguards for the workers.

9.4 The A-model and the J-model as organizational equilibria

The New Institutional argument can be schematized by saying that the technological characteristics of the resources T determine the structure of rights P or

$$T \longmapsto P$$

In Radical theory the argument is put upside down or:

$$P \longmapsto T$$

So the radical and New Institutional theories have an opposite direction of causation. However, their arguments are not incompatible. By contrast, the relationship between rights and technology can be properly understood only if the radical and New Institutional arguments are somewhat integrated in a single framework.

The fact that (T) causes (P) and (P) causes (T) are not mutually incompatible; rather, they imply that (T) can reinforce itself via (P) and (P) can reinforce itself via (T). When this occurs, the New Institutional and Radical mechanisms taken together imply that institutions of production such as the A-firm or the J-firm are self-sustaining. In this case we are in a situation of 'organizational equilibrium'.[10]

A situation of organizational equilibrium can be schematized as

$$\longmapsto T \longmapsto P \longmapsto T \longmapsto P \longmapsto \tag{F1}$$

In other words, in an organizational equilibrium the property rights reproduce themselves via technology[11] and the technology reproduces itself via property rights. According to the way in which we assume that the initial conditions of the system were given, an organizational equilibrium can be interpreted as a 'property rights equilibrium' or as a 'technological equilibrium'.

If we assume that the initial conditions of the system were given in terms of a 'strong' property rights shock, then an organizational equilibrium can be interpreted as a property rights equilibrium where the initial property right shock has reproduced itself via technology.

By contrast, assume that a technological innovation or a change in the structure of demand has changed the technological characteristics of the resources to be employed. In this case, the initial conditions have occurred in terms of a strong technological shock and an organizational equilibrium can be interpreted as a technological equilibrium where the initial technological shock has reproduced itself via property rights.

In many cases, after some time, it may be hard 'to know' whether an organizational equilibrium is a property rights equilibrium or a technological equilibrium.[12] Indeed, after the initial shocks no distinction between them is possible.

In this respect, independently of their historical origins (which may be different in different countries), the A-firm and the J-firm define 'organizational equilibria'.

In the case of the A-model, the exclusive rights of management and capital on the organization induce a 'Tayloristic' technology (difficult-to-monitor or specific capital and easy-to-monitor general purpose labour) that can only be cheaply operated under 'strong' managerial rights and capital ownership; or, alternatively, the Tayloristic technological specification of resources induces capitalist and managerial exclusive control under which it is optimal to choose a Tayloristic technology.

By contrast, in the case of the J-model, the existence of rights of the workers in the organization induce a 'Toyotist' technology (more intensive use of difficult-to-monitor and specific labour) that can only be inexpensively operated when workers are given some rights in the organization; or, alternatively, the Toyotist technological specification of resources requires rights and safeguards for the workers under which it is optimal to choose a Toyotist technology.

If we consider the A-model and the J-model as organizational equilibria, the self-sustaining character of these institutions becomes very clear. These self-sustaining characteristics imply that, under certain conditions,[13] multiple organizational equilibria can exist. They also imply that each organizational equilibrium can be 'institutionally stable' in the sense that it is resistant to 'weak' shocks on the rights or the technology. Organizational equilibria imply that history matters in the sense that 'strong' institutional or technological shocks can bring about different self-sustaining equilibria between rights and technology and may cause a qualitatively different path of institutional and technological interactions.

9.5   Organizational equilibria: a simple model

The scheme diagram (F1) describes an organizational equilibrium[14] where technology and rights reinforce each other. In this section a (very simplified) formalization of this concept will be considered and an attempt made to clarify the role of the distribution of assets on the selection of a particular organizational equilibrium.

According to the Radical literature, owning factors have a greater tendency to become specific and/or difficult factors or, in other words, high-agency-cost factors. This is because an owning factor has no 'inhibitions' to become firm-specific nor to develop situations of asymmetric information under which it becomes a difficult-to-monitor factor. The incentives due to ownership allow a saving of these agency costs.

In some ways, changes in property rights have an effect similar to changes in relative prices. They increase the agency costs of using the non-owning factors relative to those of the owning factors. Thus, similarly to changes in relative prices, changes in property rights have a substitution effect: the high-agency-cost resources of the non-owning factors tend to be substituted away; for this reason, non-owning factors tend to become low-agency-cost factors. Or, in other words, they tend to become less firm-specific and more difficult-to-monitor than owning factors.

Thus the changes in the technological characteristics of the resources can be explained by a familiar mechanism of standard economic theory. A change in property rights induces a process of technological substitution that tends to make non-owning agents a low-agency-cost resource.

The core of the 'radical' approach can be determined by the assumption that different agents face different costs when they own and run the organization and will, therefore, choose different technologies. This assumption can be formalized in a very simple way that clarifies why changes in property rights induce a process of technological substitution.

In order to simplify the analysis, it is assumed that there are only two types of agents: capitalists and workers that can own the organization, and four types of factors: low-agency-cost and high-agency-cost capital and labour.

Also assumed is the existence of a standard production function $Q(k, K, l, L)$, such that the output Q can be produced with different combinations of low-agency-cost capital and labour (k, l) and high-agency-cost capital and labour (K, L). However, according to David (1975), we assume that, in the short run, the agents know only the combinations of factors that they are actually using and that exploring new technologies may require time and effort. Thus, $Q(.)$ can be interpreted as a 'long-run' production function. Thus, the substitution effects induced by property rights are not immediate and it is possible to have short-term mismatches between property rights and the associated technology.

It is assumed that, when workers own the organization, they pay an additional agency cost Z in order to employ a unit of difficult-to-monitor or specific capital K – a cost that is saved when K is employed under capitalist ownership.[15] By contrast, when the capitalists own the organization, they pay an additional agency cost H when they employ a unit of difficult-to-monitor or specific labour L – a cost that is saved when L is employed under labour ownership. No such additional costs are paid for easy-to-monitor and general-purpose labour and capital k and l when they are employed by either capitalists or workers.[16]

The prices of respectively easy-to-monitor and/or general capital and labour are denoted by r and w and the prices (net of agency costs) of respectively difficult-to-monitor and/or specific capital and labour by R and L. The price of output is set equal to 1. Thus, it is possible to formulate the 'radical' assumption as follows.

Radical assumption

Under capitalist ownership firms maximize profits equal to

$$R^c = Q(k, K, l, L) - [rk + RK + wl + (H + W)L] \qquad (1)$$

Under labour ownership firms maximize profits equal to

$$R^L = Q(k, K, l, L) - [rk + (Z + R)K + wl + WL] \tag{2}$$

This method of formalizing the 'radical assumption' makes it very clear why property rights influence technology in a way similar to changes in relative prices; for instance, the relative prices of the high-agency-cost factors are $(H + W)/R$ under capitalist ownership and $W/(Z + R)$ under workers' ownership. Thus, under standard assumptions, the intensity of high-agency-cost capital relative to the intensity of high-agency-cost labour is higher under capitalist ownership than under labour ownership. In this framework, the value of the elasticity of substitution among factors becomes a measure of the 'strength' of the effects of changes of property rights on the nature of technology.

The 'New Institutionalist assumption' runs in a direction opposite to that of the 'radical assumption'; taking as given a certain technology the firm is supposed to be owned by that factor which can earn the highest ownership rent. This rent is equal to the difference between the cost of employing the factor in a firm that is property of the owners of the factor and the cost of employing it in a firm that is property of other owners.

New institutional assumption:

For any given combination of factors employed in the firm, ownership of the firm will be acquired by the factor which can get the highest ownership rent. Therefore, capitalist property rights can prevail if, given the factors currently employed, $R^c \geq R^L$ or, alternatively

$$ZK - HL \geq 0 \tag{3}$$

workers' property rights can prevail if, given the factors currently employed, $R^L \geq R^c$ or alternatively

$$HL - ZK \geq 0 \tag{4}$$

Thus 'the radical assumption' concerns the behaviour of the firm for any *given (capitalist or workers') ownership*. By contrast, the 'New Institutionalist assumption' concerns the ownership conditions of the firm for any *given combination of factors employed in the firm*. An *organizational equilibrium exists* when both the radical and New Institutionalist assumptions are simultaneously satisfied: in an organizational equilibrium, the behaviour of the firm under particular ownership conditions must bring about technologies characterized by factor intensities that do not upset the initial ownership conditions. The following definition of an organizational equilibrium can be given.

Definition of organizational equilibrium

An institution of production is an *organizational equilibrium* when it is defined by a system of property rights P and a technology T, such that T is the technology that maximizes rent under the property rights system P, and P is the property rights system that maximizes ownership rent with the factor intensities associated with T.

In particular, a capitalist organizational equilibrium exists when the capitalist rights P^c and the technology T^c are such that

$$\longrightarrow P^c \longrightarrow T^c \longrightarrow P^c \longrightarrow$$

and a labour organizational equilibrium exists when the labour rights P^L and the labour technology T^L are such that

$$\longrightarrow P^L \longrightarrow T^L \longrightarrow P^L \longrightarrow$$

In other words, there will be a capitalist organizational equilibrium (COE) if there is a technology that maximizes equation (1) and satisfies equation (3) and there will be a labour organizational equilibrium (LOE) if there is a technology that maximizes equation (2) and satisfies equation (4).

Let

$$(k^c, K^c, l^c, L^c) = \text{argmax } R^c(k, K, l, L) \tag{5}$$

$$(k^L, K^L, l^L, L^L) = \text{argmax } R^L(k, K, l, L) \tag{6}$$

Then a firm will be in *a capitalist organizational equilibrium* (COE) if

$$ZK^c - HL^c \geq 0 \tag{7}$$

and in *a labour organizational equilibrium* (LOE) if

$$HL^L - ZK^L \geq 0 \tag{8}$$

Condition (7) has an immediate intuitive meaning. Suppose that a firm is under capitalist ownership and the technique of production is such as to maximize profits. Condition (7) implies that, *with this technique*, the ownership rent occurring to capitalists is at least as great as the rent which workers could obtain if they owned the firm. Hence, *with this technique of production*, the workers would have no incentive to buy out the capitalists. This is what is meant by a capitalist organizational equilibrium. Condition (8) has an analogous intuitive meaning.

It will also be useful to write the conditions for COE and LOE in the following equivalent ways:

$$K^c/L^c \geq H/Z \tag{7'}$$

$$K^L/L^L \geq H/Z \tag{8'}$$

Conditions (7') and (8') have also an intuitive meaning; K/L is the ratio of high-agency-cost (H-A-C) capital to H-A-C labour or *the H-A-C capital intensity*; observe also that H/Z is the *agency cost ratio* between the capitalist's extra cost in employing H-A-C labour and labour's extra cost in employing H-A-C capital. Thus condition (7') means that a COE is feasible when the intensity of H-A-C capital is greater than the agency cost ratio and condition (8') means that a LOE is feasible when the intensity of H-A-C capital is lower than the agency cost ratio. For instance, high agency costs per unit of labour could be compensated by the employment of a great amount of H-A-C capital and make feasible a COE.

The conditions for the existence of organizational equilibria can also be interpreted as a Nash equilibrium. Organizational equilibria may be defined by the fact that 'production managers' choose the technology that maximizes profits given the existing property rights system and by the fact that 'financiers' arrange property rights that maximize ownership rent given the existing technology. In this sense, condition (7) says that capitalist property rights are the best response of 'financiers' given the technology chosen by the 'production managers'. The same condition says also that a H-A-C capital intensive technology is the best response of the production managers given the capitalist property rights chosen by the financiers. Condition (8) has an analogous interpretation.[17]

The strength of the effects on property rights on technology depend, by way of the radical assumption, on the value of the elasticity of substitution.

Under standard assumptions, the high-agency-cost capital intensity will be higher under capitalist ownership or

$$K^c/L^c \geq K^L/L^L \tag{9}$$

The value of the agency cost ratio H/Z either falls in the interval defined by these two values or outside it.[18]

Let us first consider the case in which it falls in this interval. In this case H/Z is such that

$$K^c/L^c \geq H/Z \geq K^L/L^L \tag{10}$$

Thus, both condition (7') and condition (8') are satisfied and there is multiple (capitalist and labour) organizational equilibria.

Consider now the cases in which H/Z does not fall in this interval. H/Z may be smaller than the high-agency-cost capital intensities. Or,

$$K^c/L^c \geq K^L/L^L > H/Z \qquad (11)$$

Then condition (7') is satisfied but condition (8') is not satisfied. In this case only a COE exists.

By contrast, if H/Z is such that

$$H/Z > K^c/L^c \geq K^L/L^L \qquad (12)$$

condition (8') is satisfied, but condition (7') is not satisfied. In this case only an LOE exists.

Observe that, since the ratio H/Z must necessarily fall in one of the three intervals considered above, for any H/Z ratio at least one organizational equilibrium must always exist.

It is possible to visualize the effects of the changes of the agency cost ratio H/Z on the nature of the organizational equilibria in the following F2. For H/Z that goes from zero to infinity there is the first unique COE equilibria, then multiple equilibria and, finally, LOE unique equilibria.

$$0 - (\text{COE}) - K^L/L^L - (\text{LOE} + \text{COE}) - K^c/L^c - (\text{LOE}) \rightarrow \qquad (\text{F2})$$

The scheme (F2) 'assumes' a certain value of the elasticity of substitution[19] and it can give some indication of the effects of its changes. An increase in the elasticity of substitution widens the values of the agency cost ratio for which multiple equilibria exist. It moves K^L/L^L leftwards and K^c/L^c towards the right, widening the interval of multiple equilibria defined by them. Within this interval, any initial set of property rights will induce technologies such that their interaction will define organizational equilibria. Thus, an increase of the elasticity of substitution widens the interval where property rights can shape technologies in a self-sustaining manner. Because of the 'radical assumption', the higher the elasticity of substitution the more powerful the effects of ownership on technology.

9.6 The speciation of organizational equilibria

The value of the elasticity of substitution does not only determine the range of the agency cost ratios for which there are multiple organizational equilibria. It influences also their 'institutional stability' and their possible inefficiency. A high elasticity of substitution acts like a good 'anti-speciation factor' in the sense that it favours the institutional stability of the existing ownership relations: it helps the rejection of the non-owning factors, that, because of the increase in their agency costs, threaten to upset the fitness of the existing species of organizational equilibrium. Unfortunately, the anti-speciation factor works particularly well with the factors that are the most efficient potential alternative owners and could generate a 'superior species' of organizations. These factors are efficient potential alternative owners because of the high agency costs that must otherwise be paid when they are employed by other factors. A high elasticity of substitution causes an unfortunate 'preventive treatment' against this possible mutation: these factors are promptly replaced by factors that are cheaper for the present owners.

Indeed, speciation theory offers a useful framework to understand the dynamics of organizational equilibria and the effects of competition. Organizational equilibria cannot gradually evolve into superior organizational arrangements. Because of the institutional stability of these equilibria it should be expected that long periods of 'stasis' characterize these equilibria that may be 'punctuated' by periods of sudden changes to new 'species' of organizations.[20] Thus, the analysis of the emergence of different organizational equilibria seems to be closer to that of the 'punctuated equilibria' discussed by Eldredge and Gould (1972) with reference to the evolution of new species than to any 'gradualist' approach.[21]

The analogy between the emergence of new organizational equilibria and speciation can be fruitful because the emergence of new organizational equilibria satisfies one of the typical aspects of speciation: the inferiority, or even the impossibility, of the 'hybrids' between the two groups that is a necessary condition for differentiating them into different species.[22] For instance, in our simple model, any combination of capitalist rights and labour technology 'genotypes' produces an organizational 'phenotype' that is inferior to both capitalist and labour organizational equilibria.

The property rights and the technology characterizing a capitalist organizational equilibrium can be denoted by (P^c, T^c) and those defining a labour organizational equilibrium can be denoted by (P^L, T^L). Moreover, the two 'hybrids' obtained by mixing together the technology and the property rights of each one of the two organizational equilibria can be denoted by (P^c, T^L) and (P^L, T^c).

Efficiency will rank organizational equilibria and 'hybrids' in one of

$$(P^C, T^C) \geq (P^L, T^L) \geq (P^C, T^L) \geq (P^L, T^C)$$

$$(P^C, T^C) \geq (P^L, T^L) \geq (P^L, T^C) \geq (P^C, T^L)$$
$$(P^L, T^L) \geq (P^C, T^C) \geq (P^C, T^L) \geq (P^L, T^C)$$
$$(P^L, T^L) \geq (P^C, T^C) \geq (P^L, T^C) \geq (P^C, T^L)$$

or, in other words, organizational equilibria can be inefficient in the sense that they may be inferior to another organizational equilibrium but they are always superior to the situations of organizational disequilibrium defined by hybrids.

In natural species as well as in organizational equilibria, after a period of one-by-one changes, each part of the whole becomes optimal given the nature of the other parts: for this reason, after this point, a better arrangement cannot be approached by a gradual change of each one of the parts but it requires simultaneous complementary changes. In this context, no gradual tendency to move away from inefficient equilibria can arise. Because of the 'complementarities' that are necessary for successful macromutations, these macromutations may never occur; if they do, they will be characterized by abrupt changes leading to the formation of other species that have a substantial number of different features. Like the evolution of natural species, the speciation of organizational equilibria is likely to be 'punctuated' by long periods of stasis and by sudden changes. In both cases, their 'efficiency' will be limited by the sequence of the mutations that were actually made or, in other words, by their history.

The inferiority of 'hybrids' does not only imply that macromutations improving efficiency may never occur. It does also imply that the same competitive pressure, that favours the micromutations improving the fitness of a given species, may inhibit the macromutations that are necessary for the beginning of a new species. Strong competitive pressure may wipe out hybrids before they have a chance to mutate into superior organizational equilibria. Moreover, if there are few members of the new species, 'interbreeding' with the old species will produce numerous inferior hybrids and may lead to the extinction of both mutations. Finally, the efficiency of each species of animals as well as organizations depends on its frequency. For instance, network externalities in property rights and in technologies may imply that few different organizational equilibria are not viable.

Since competition can inhibit the formation of new species, speciation is likely to be characterized by 'allopatric' conditions; or, in other words, it occurs when a physical barrier protects, for an initial period, the mutants from the competition of the members of the original species. Although competition can be very useful in selecting the micromutations that improve the efficiency of a given species of organizations, it can inhibit 'speciation' of new models of organization: we should not be surprised if a potentially more efficient organizational model was not generated in America where market competition was very vigorous. Indeed it is consistent with the theory of speciation that successful organizational innovations were more likely to occur in postwar Japan where strong property rights shocks were induced by the occupying forces and new models of organization were protected by competing arrangements for political reasons. However, the effects of these property right shocks cannot be understood without referring to the 'initial conditions' given by Japanese history. To this history we must now turn.

9.7　Institutional shocks and the 'speciation' of the Japanese model

The Meiji restoration has often been regarded as a peculiar kind of revolutionary 'modernization'.[23] The samurai class and the samurai ethos,[24] which characterized the Togukawa period, had also an important role in shaping the organizational structure of the modern Japanese economy. According to this interpretation, some relations of loyalty typical of the preceding period characterized the relationship of managers to the *zaibatsu families*, who repaid this loyalty with job security and promotions.

In other words, compared with Anglo-American experiences, the Japanese model of industrial economy shows greater continuity with the type of work relations which existed under feudalism. The Meiji restoration discredited the *shogun* but not the samurai class and its values; by contrast, it was largely a revolution from above. Many samurai were active in the revolution because they perceived that radical reforms were necessary to safeguard national independence even if they endangered their privileges. The struggle for the traditional 'market' freedoms had only a secondary role in the case of Japan.

After the Second World War, SCAP (the occupying authorities commanded by General MacArthur) believed the 'feudal' relations of the *zaibatsu* firms to be the main cause of Japanese militarism. SCAP tried to dissolve these relations by eliminating the control of the *zaibatsu* families and by breaking up the *zaibatsu* firms into smaller units. For the same reason, the senior managers of the companies whose feeling of 'feudal' loyalty was considered to be irreversible were fired by the occupying authorities. Moreover, in what it is known as the first phase of the style occupation, SCAP encouraged union activities and union rights. Some form of workers' ownership was also encouraged.[25]

The U-turn in the SCAP policies was hinted by General MacArthur's decision to forbid the general strike of February 1947. Some of the reasons for what has become known as the occupation 'reverse course' are stated very clearly in an article published in *Newsweek* in December 1947.

According to the American magazine, SCAP proposed to create in Japan what it termed a 'democratic economy'. *Newsweek* observed that no definition for such a term had been given in writing 'but, whatever that term may mean, in this instance it is proposed to distribute the wealth of Japan to the workers, farmers, and small traders through the medium of taxes, sales of valuable properties at nominal values, financial assistance, regimentation, and regulation...' (Livingstone *et al.*, 1976b, p. 107).

According to *Newsweek*, 'the tough reforms introduced by SCAP may cause the collapse of the Japanese economy'. In particular, the magazine criticized the Labour Standard Law, approved in April 1947: impoverished Japan could not afford the same labour standards enjoyed by American workers. Moreover, according to the magazine, Japanese labour contracts often went well beyond American standards: 'Many labour contracts go far beyond such agreements in this country. The agreement between the Japanese company in which a well-known American company had a controlling interest and the company union, in addition to the usual provisions for a closed shop, hours rights of dismissal, cost of living, wages and so on. States that part of the profits (not stating which part) shall be paid to the union, and the election and removal of directors, inspectors, and advisers of the company may be accomplished only after consulting the union' (Livingstone *et al.*, 1976b, p. 108).[26]

In December 1947, in a speech to Congress, Senator William F. Knowland commented on the document drawn up by State Department economists. The document was known as FEC (Far Eastern Commission) 230: 'If some of the doctrine set forth in FEC 230 had been proposed by the government of the USSR or even by the Labour government of Great Britain, I could have understood it.' (Livingstone *et al.*, 1976b, p. 113). What Senator Knowland found hard to believe, and it is for many people even harder to believe now, was that the *Americans* had been carrying out those policies.

The last period of the American occupation was not only characterized by the restriction of union activities but also by the relaxation of the anti-monopoly laws, disinflation and the 'red purge'. The international situation had dramatically changed. The issue was not anymore how to 'democratize' a former 'militaristic' enemy. Instead, it was how, in a short period, Japan could become a reliable partner which could help in the confrontation with the communists. The Korean War accelerated this re-assessment of the American policies.[27]

Before the 'U-turn', American policies were inspired by the idea that only a 'democratic' economy could favour the conditions for the development of a peaceful society. The American project of a 'democratic' economy involved the dissolution of the *zaibatsu* and a dispersion of stock to individuals that would have prevented any undesirable concentration of economic power. This limitation of economic power did not only involve a widespread ownership of securities but also some inside ownership especially by employees that would have made possible a control of the top management authority.

The dissolution of the *zaibatsu* companies was achieved by transferring the 50 per cent of the stock of the *zaibatsu* companies to the Holding Company Liquidation Commission (HCLC), a quasi-government agency. Government in ways similar to those of state-owned firms restricted the financial and operational decisions of the companies. Thus, in postwar Japan, a huge sector of quasi-state-owned firms was created, and SCAP had to pioneer privatization problems similar to those faced by the former socialist countries. Moreover, during the war years and the years of quasi-state-owned companies, insiders' control prevailed in ways similar to that experienced by the socialist economies.

The war, the purge and quasi-state ownership had greatly reinforced the rights of the insiders and had created the conditions for a 'pure' internal promotion system that was substantially different from the mechanisms by which control rights were transferred either under family capitalism or in the case of Anglo-American corporations.

The smooth and fast liquidation of the stock that had been transferred to HCLC did not involve the creation of any mechanism by which the internal promotion system could be monitored and changed in case of opportunistic behaviour. Following the SCAP plan, ownership became very dispersed and each individual shareholder became too small to exercise any outside control on management. At the same time, it was impossible to rely on the inside control of the workers-shareholders. Even if the 27 per cent of the whole disposed stock was bought by employees, it was heavily sold by them after the market collapse in August 1949. 'On average, only the 50 per cent of employees who bought their companies' stocks from January 1948 to June 1949 continued to hold their stock from more than two years' (Miyajima, 1995 p. 381).

According to the Americans, the classic agency problem of controlling management in a situation of dispersed individual share ownership was to be solved not only by employee ownership but also by the 'classic' means of equity finance and markets for corporate control. By contrast, while job tenure and the internal promotion system were retained, a drastically different system of corporate governance emerged: cross shareholding, debt (*keiretsu*) financing, and a main-bank-delegated monitoring system were going to be the key ingredients of Japan's postwar financial institutions.

Cross shareholding was explicitly outlawed by the Anti-Trust Law enacted in 1947. Moreover, in the same year the separation between banking and industrial concerns, modelled after the Glass-Seagall Act in the United States, was introduced in Japan: the Securities Trade Act prohibited banks from underwriting holding and dealing in corporate securities.

The stock market collapse happened in 1949 after the 'U-turn' of the policies of the occupation forces. By that time, the quick rebuilding of a stable anti-communist Japan had become far more important for the Americans than the implementation of the ideal institutions of their model of a 'democratic economy'. Companies faced a liquidity crisis and the threat of a take-over mechanism that was especially effective for the ex-*zaibatsu* companies whose stock was heavily liquidated. The stock market crash, occurring within the legal framework introduced by the Americans in 1947, was the first substantial threat to the pure internal promotion system of rights characterizing the Japanese companies.

The internal promotion system had emerged from a long experience of insider control. Insider control had, *de facto*, existed during the war, and, despite the 'interferences' of family capitalism, had also been substantially present in the *zaibatsu* experience. Under this system, not only high and lower-rank managers but also many workers had had the incentive to accumulate much irreversible human capital that was now at risk because of the stock market crash. The policies of the Americans had democratized the *zaibatsu* company and extended the incentive to invest in high-agency-cost human capital to many members of the company. Perhaps for the first time in their lifetime, managers and workers were risking the uncertain consequences of a takeover from outsiders who were not bound by any form of 'implicit' contract concerning their firm-specific assets.

For the Americans, upsetting the stability of the microrelation at firm level was made even more dangerous by the fact that, in the same period, they were engaged in a 'macro confrontation' with the central unions that they believed to be a dangerous congregation of potential enemies sympathetic to the new Soviet enemy. Thus, if the legal framework introduced in 1947 implied a very considerable danger for insiders' control, the reaction of the insiders was to try to make ineffective and eventually change that legal framework. At the same time, the Americans were too concerned with the stability and the recovery of Japan to impose the full consequences of the governance system that they had set up. It is not surprising that insiders were going to be successful.

Faced with the stock exchange crises and the risk of take-overs, managers tried to maintain their stock price by operations similar to 'company buyout' even if that was not allowed under Japanese law. While the Americans were mildly upset by this 'illegal' action, the Japanese government suggested various ways to maintain equity prices. The sale of the remaining *zaibatsu* stock by public tender was postponed and, in the process for maintaining stock prices, shareholding by institutions such as the insurance companies was not only permitted but also encouraged. Under some conditions, banks were also allowed to hold shares and the 1947 prohibition against industrial companies' shareholding was lifted. Moreover, cross shareholding became possible and helped to stabilize the power of top management against the risk of takeover.

Cross shareholding[28] made possible the reconstruction of a managerial version of the *zaibatsu* companies (the *keiretsu*) within which the role of the former *zaibatsu* banks became very important. Banks provided a way of solving the agency problems arising from insider control that did not upset the internal promotion governance system and its great potential for accumulating high-agency-cost human capital. The banking system that emerged was going to be known as the 'main bank system'. It involved the syndication of loans and the delegation of monitoring to a single bank that, in many cases, was going to be the bank of the *keiretsu* that had emerged from the cross shareholding of the companies of the former *zaibatsu* company. In other words, the main bank system allowed risk diversification without 'diluting' the monitoring activity among many banks.[29]

The implicit contracts, characterizing the Japanese firm, imply a 'truncation' of the rights of shareholders. Job security involves that the owners of the physical assets do not have the right to employ the assets of the firm without the managers and workers of the firm – a right that is well likely to be exercised in the case of hostile takeovers. In other words, the Japanese blend of capitalism has involved the 'unbundling' and the redistribution of a right on physical assets that belongs to shareholders under both family- and securities-based governance systems. The interaction between the rights of Japanese employees and the accumulation of their high-agency-cost human capital has produced one of the multiple self-reinforcing organizational equilibria considered in the preceding sections. Thus, the transfer of rights from 'insiders' to 'outsiders', that is associated to a securities-based decentralized financial system, may well be incompatible with the technology developed under the Japanese postwar production institutions.

By contrast, the main bank system has been compatible with the employees' rights system that has characterized postwar Japan. The main bank integrated *ex ante*, 'interim' and *ex post* monitoring that in a securities-based markets are performed by different agents. This allowed a contingent governance structure under which the bank intervened, having accumulated 'inside information', only in cases of financial distress. Thus, the bank did not interfere with the internal promotion system when it was delivering good results. Moreover, it did not upset the principles of the internal promotion system when intervention was necessary. The bank could act selectively, rewarding and punishing employees on the basis of the 'inside' information accumulated thanks to its *ex ante* and 'interim' monitoring activity. In other words, the main bank contributed actively to the exercise of rights that underlined the implicit contracts characterizing Japanese firms.

SCAP started by expropriating capitalist families and enhancing working rights and finished by forbidding general strikes and purging the unions. The combined effects of the two institutional shocks was that the workers acquired new rights, and developed new loyalties, but only within their companies. Thus, the unintended result of SCAP was that the 'feudal' relations of the *zaibatsu* economy were not replaced by impersonal market relations. They were rather 'democratized' and extended to all the 'core' workers of each firm.

The workers ended up enjoying rights and safeguards within their companies exceeding those that they have in standard capitalist economies. The loyalty to the *zaibatsu* families was replaced by the loyalty to the company and ultimately to the fellow workers. These rights and safeguards created the conditions under which team-work and difficult-to-monitor and specific human skills could flourish. In turn, the development of these skills increased the value of the rights and safeguards which the workers had within their companies.

This section is concluded by showing how this short account of the story of postwar Japan can be explained within the framework of the theory of organizational equilibria. The rights and safeguards, introduced by the institutional shocks of the occupation period, had the time to reinforce themselves through the development of the 'associated' technology. They become self-sustaining and a new 'organizational equilibrium' came about.[30]

The main steps of the 'speciation' of the new organizational model may be summarized as follows.

- The prewar organizations were characterized by the fact that a class of managers loyal to the firm already existed under the *zaibatsu* system and the war had enhanced the autonomy of management from the *zaibatsu* families.

- During the 'quasi-nationalization' of the zaibatsu companies, the rights of junior managers and workers were enhanced and had the time to favour the associated technology; going back to the *zaibatsu* was politically not feasible. The inferior hybrids between the new rights and the old technology could not be wiped out. By contrast, they had the opportunity to move to the speciation of a new organizational equilibrium.

On the other hand, while the insiders were incentived to become high-agency-cost factors, the kind of privatization promoted by the Americans was based on legislation allowing shareholders to exercise hiring and firing rights and the separation between commercial banking and industry. This created a situation of potential 'organizational disequilibrium' between formal rights and technology. The threat of takeovers, following the 1949 stock crash, made this disequilibrium evident and dramatic.

- The property rights system that emerged from the crisis was based on cross shareholding and the main bank system. The combination of this property rights system with the technology based on specific and difficult-to-monitor labour allowed the definitive 'speciation' of the new organizational equilibrium. Speciation was not only favoured by an initial protection of the new system of 'informal rights' but also by the fact that all the companies were involved in this change. Thus, the network externalities among property rights standards and technology did not inhibit but rather favoured the change. The network externalities in property rights were particularly evident in the cases of cross shareholding and of the main bank system whose emergence required that more companies were involved in the institutional change.

In terms of this evolutionary analogy, the 'speciation' of the Japanese model fits rather well with the biological emphasis on 'allopatric' speciation. A new species of organization did not evolve in the US in 'sympatric' conditions where market competition was more vigorous but rather in allopatric conditions in the periphery. There, a particular political situation protected the new model from the old models existing inside and outside the country.

The Americans, who had intended to export their institutions to Japan, had rather helped the speciation of new production institutions. At the time of the occupation, it would have been very difficult to forecast that, a few years later, the Americans should have to consider whether they had better import the 'Japanese model' and try to break their own self-sustaining organizational equilibria. However, importing some of the characteristics of the new organizational species would not necessarily lead to successful organizational innovations and could only produce inferior hybrids. Taking into account the 'complementarities' among property rights, technologies and other characteristics of the Japanese model was going to be a crucial factor either for successful imitations or for new successful organizational innovations.

9.8 Postwar Japan and the post-socialist speciation of organizational models

The problems that were faced by the Japanese economy after the war share some surprising analogies with those arising in the post-socialist 'transition' economies. In both cases the issue has been how to privatize nationalized enterprises (or quasi-nationalized ex-*zaibatsu* companies), and in both cases the role of insiders has been a fundamental problem for privatization policies. Moreover, in both cases an extra-national agent (SCAP in the case of Japan and the World Bank in the case of the former socialist countries) has had an important role in the reform process.[31]

While the success of the Japanese experience is difficult to imitate, it shows that economic evolution cannot be seen as a transition to an *a priori* given set of optimal institutional arrangements. The history of economic systems can diverge in ways that cannot be easily understood without referring to the complementarities between the agency attributes of the resources and the rights on these resources and without considering the different initial conditions that are faced by each economy. The Japanese experience[32] suggests that the desirability of the 'end-point' of the transition is not independent of the initial conditions and that there may be some initial conditions that can even produce desirable end states that we do not know *a priori*.

Different initial conditions characterized also the ex-socialist countries, for example Hungary, the Czech Republic and Poland, at the time of the 1989 revolution.[33]

In Hungary, as part of the reform process that had started in that country, substantial powers had been decentralized from above to the managers of the firms. The 'revolution' was initiated from above and 'negotiated' within the framework of the reforms introduced by the communist regime.

By contrast, in the Czech Republic, decentralization to the managers of the firms had been weak and late. The political shocks were far more abrupt and sudden than in the Hungarian case and came at the very end of the communist experience.

Finally, Poland was characterized by the existence of strong workers' councils that had acquired power as a consequence of the Solidarity movement. The political shocks came very early and involved a conflictual situation of power-sharing between the union and the regime. Unlike the case of Hungary, the change did not come from above and involved workers' active participation in the management of firms.

In other words, a different set of property rights characterized the 'socialist economies' in the last years of socialism; thus the type of links outlined in this paper would suggest that the high-agency-cost factors that had been developed in each country were very likely to have different characteristics.

In Hungary managers had the incentive to make firm-specific investments and acquire private information that made them difficult-to-monitor agents; in other words, by 1989 they had become high-agency-cost factors. No similar right to take autonomous decisions characterized the Czech economy where a fair degree of power centralization characterized the economy until the revolution; as a result, firms' managers were not high-agency-cost factors to any degree comparable to the Hungarian economy. Finally, the experience of working councils in Poland implied that fairly large groups of 'core' workers had become high-agency-cost factors. In other words, transition was characterized by very different political and property rights shocks before and after the 1989 revolution.

Thus, privatization was not taking place in a uniform environment. Property rights could be changed relatively quickly by the legislation of the new pro-capitalist state and by the conditions imposed by the international organizations. However, it was impossible to change, at least in the short run, the technology of agency characteristics that had emerged under the different socialist experiences. Thus, privatization assumed different meanings that reflected the nature of the resources inherited from the socialist past; instead of implying the transition to a uniform model of a 'private economy', it meant the 'speciation' of new forms of organizational models in each one of these countries.

The Hungarians developed a form of managerial capitalism with relatively little control by outsiders and by other insiders. In many cases privatization meant the transfer of ownership and control rights to those managers to whom very substantial power had already been transferred under socialism.

In the case of the Czech Republic, firms' managers were not high-agency-cost factors; it was relatively easy to transfer property rights to an outsiders' institution that, centralizing the control of the privatization vouchers, could eventually, paradoxically, inherit those forms of 'outsiders' control' that had characterized their own brand of socialism.[34]

Finally, in many cases, in Poland, privatization favoured the acquisition of ownership rights by insiders. A very active role in the privatization process was played by the enterprise management and employees' council that had already acquired substantial power during the long revolutionary struggle against the communist bureaucracy.[35] By the time that massive privatization was launched they had already become high-agency-cost factors.

9.9 Conclusion

Only further studies and the unfolding of the structural changes taking place in the former socialist countries will be able to tell whether the new 'organizational equilibria' will acquire a sufficient degree of 'institutional stability'. However, there is no reason why, in principle, 'organizational diversity' may not increase with the emergence of new species in the former socialist countries. The successes and the failures of the new arrangements should not be judged comparing each experience to the hypothetically given standard of a 'classic' private economy. The Japanese experience suggests that new organizational species should sometimes be given the benefit of the doubt. If these doubts are overcome and one decides that an active policy of institutional change is necessary, one should still try to consider the interactions between the changes that are being proposed and the situation that is inherited from past history. More specifically, the Japanese experience suggests that, in principle, in some production sectors, a property system where insiders have strong job rights may allow a fairly efficient technology based on 'high-agency-cost' labour by insiders, and that, vice versa, this technology requires property rights limiting some of the powers that shareholders enjoy under the classic Anglo-American model.[36]

References

Alchian A., 'Specificity, Specialization and Coalitions', *Journal of Institutional and Theoretical Economics* (1984) 34–9.

Alchian A., 'Property Rights', in J. Eatwell, M. Millgate and P. Millgate (eds), *The New Palgrave* (London: Macmillan, 1987) pp. 1031–4.

Alchian A. and H. Demsetz, 'Production, Information Costs and Economic Organization', *American Economic Review*, 62 (1972a) 777–95.

Alchian A. and Demsetz H., 'The Property Rights Paradigm', *Journal of Economic History*, XXXIII, 1 (1972b) 16–22.

Amsdem A., J. Kochanowicz and L. Taylor, *The Market Meets its Match. Restructuring the Economies of Eastern Europe* (Cambridge, MA: Harvard University Press, 1994).

Aston T. H. and C. H. E. Philpin (eds), *The Brenner Debate. Agrarian Class Structure and Economic Development in Pre-Industrial Europe* (Cambridge: Cambridge University Press, 1985).

Aoki M., *The Economic Analysis of the Japanese Firm* (Amsterdam: North-Holland, 1984).

Aoki M., 'Horizontal vs Vertical Information Structure of the Firm', *American Economic Review*, Dec. (1987a) 971–8.

Aoki M., 'The Japanese Firm in Transition', in K. Yamanura and Y. Yasuba (eds), *The Political Economy of Japan. Vol. 1. The Domestic Transformation* (Stanford, CA: Stanford University Press, 1987b).

Aoki M., *Information, Incentives and Bargaining in the Japanese Economy* (Cambridge, New York: Cambridge University Press, 1989).

Aoki M., 'Decentralization-Centralization in Japanese Organization: A Duality Principle', in S. Kumon and H. Rosovsky (eds), *The Political Economy of Japan. Vol. 3: Cultural and Social Dynamics* (Stanford, CA: Stanford University Press, 1992).

Aoki M., 'The Motivational Role of an External Agent in the Informationally-Participatory Firm', in S. Bowles, H. Gintis and B. Gustafsson (eds), *Markets and Democracy: Participation, Accountability and Efficiency* (Cambridge: Cambridge University Press, 1993).

Aoki M., 'Monitoring Characteristics of the Main Bank System: An Analytical and Developmental View', in M. Aoki and H. Patrick (eds), *The Japanese Main Bank System: Its Relevancy for Developing and Transforming Economies* (Oxford: Oxford University Press, 1994).

Aoki M., 'Controlling Insider Control: Issues of Corporate Governance in Transition Economies', in M. Aoki and K. Hyung-Ki (eds), *Corporate Governance in Transitional Economies. Insider Control and the Role of Banks*, EDI Development Studies (Washington, DC: The World Bank, 1995).

Aoki M. and H. Patrick (eds), *The Japanese Main Bank System: Its Relevancy for Developing and Transforming Economies* (Oxford: Oxford University Press, 1994).

Asanuma B., 'Coordination Between Production and Distribution in a Globalizing Network of Firms: Assessing Flexibility Achieved in the Japanese Automobile Industry', in M. Aoki and R. Dore (eds), *The Japanese Firm: The Sources of Competitive Strength* (Oxford: Oxford University Press, 1993).

Babbage C., *On the Economics of Machines and Manufactures* (London: Charles Knight, 1832).

Berglöf E. and E. Perotti, 'The Governance Structure of the Japanese Financial Keiretsu', *Journal of Financial Economics*, XXXVI, 2 (1994) 259–84.

Bowles S., 'The Production Process in a Competitive Economy: Walrasian, Neo-Hobbesian, and Marxian Models', *American Economic Review*, 75 (1985) 16–36. Reprinted in L. Putterman, *The Economic Nature of the Firm. A Reader* (Cambridge: Cambridge University Press, 1986).

Bowles S., H. Gintis and B. Gustafsson, *Markets and Democracy: Participation, Accountability and Efficiency* (Cambridge: Cambridge University Press, 1993).

Braverman H., *Labour and Monopoly Capital* (New York: Monthly Review Press, 1974).

Chang H., 'Return to Europe? Is there Anything for Eastern Europe to Learn from East Asia?', in Chang Ha-Joon and P. Nolan (eds), *The Transformation of the Communist Economies. Against Main Stream* (London: Macmillan, 1995).

Coase R. H., 'The Nature of the Firm', *Economica* (1937) 386–405.

Coase R. H., 'The Problem of Social Costs', *Journal of Law and Economics*, III (1960) 1–44.

Cohen G. A., *Karl Marx's Theory of History: a Defence* (Oxford: Oxford University Press, 1978).

David P. A., *Technical Choice, Innovation and Economic Growth* (Cambridge: Cambridge University Press, 1975)

David P. A., 'Why are Institutions the 'Carriers of History' Path Dependence and the Evolution of Conventions Organizations and Institutions', *Structural Change and Economic Dynamics*, V, 2 (1994), 205–21.

Demsetz H., 'Toward a Theory of Property Rights', *American Economic Review. Papers and Proceedings*, II (1966) 347–59.

Dosi G., 'Sources, Procedures and Microeconomic Effects of Innovation', *Journal of Economic Literature*, XXVI (1988) 1120–71.

Earle J. S. and S. Estrin, 'Employees Ownership in Transition', in R. Frydman, C. W. Gray and A. Rapaczynnski (eds), *Corporate Governance in Central Europe and Russia. Vol. 2: Insiders and the State* (Budapest: CEU Press, 1996) pp. 1–62.

Earle J. S., R. Frydman and A. Rapaczynski, *Privatization in the Transition to a Market Economy. Studies of Preconditions and Policies in Eastern Europe* (London: Pinter, 1993).

Edwards R., *Contested Terrain* (New York: Basic Books, 1979).

Eldredge N. and S. J. Gould, 'Punctuated Equilibria: an Alternative to Phyletic Gradualism', in T. J. M. Schopf (ed.), *Models in Paleobiology* (San Francisco: Freeman Cooper, 1972) pp. 82–115.

Grossman S. and O. Hart, 'The Costs and the Benefits of Ownership', *Journal of Political Economy*, XCIV, 4 (1986), 619–91.

Hart O. and J. Moore, 'Property Rights and the Nature of the Firm', *Journal of Political Economy*, XCVIII, 6 (1990), 1119–58.

Hicks J., *A Theory of Economic History* (Oxford: Oxford University Press, 1969).

Hirschman A. O., *Essays in Trespassing* (Cambridge: Cambridge Univerity Press, 1981).

Hodgson G. M., *Economics and Evolution. Bringing Life Back into Economics* (Oxford: Polity Press, 1993).

Horiuchi T., 'The reference of Firm Status on banking relationship and Loan Syndication', in M. Aoki and H. Patrick (eds), *The Japanese Main Bank System: Its Relevancy for Developing and Transforming Economies* (Oxford: Oxford University Press, 1994).

Inkster R., *Science and Technology in History* (London: Macmillan, 1991).

Iwata R., 'The Japanese Enterprise as a Unified Body of Employees: Origins and Development', in S. Kumon and H. Rosovsky (eds), *The Political Economy of Japan. Vol. 3: Cultural and Social Dynamics* (Stanford, CA: Stanford University Press, 1992).

King N., 'Who's Steering?', *The Wall Journal Europe Central European Economic Review* (1996).

Koike K., 'Human Resource Development and Labor-Management Relations' in K. Yamanura and Y. Yasuba (eds), *The Political Economy of Japan. Vol. 1. The Domestic Transformation* (Stanford, CA: Stanford University Press, 1987).

Kreps D. M., *A Course in Microeconomic Theory* (New York: Harvester Wheatsheaf, 1990).

Kumon S. and H. Rosovsky, *The Political Economy of Japan. Vol. 3: Cultural and Social Dynamics* (Stanford, CA: Stanford University Press, 1992).

Jensen M. C. and W. H. Meckling, 'Theory of the Firm: Managerial Behaviour, Agency Costs and Ownership Structure', *Journal of Financial Economics*, III (1976).

Langlois R. N., *Economics as a Process, Essays in the New Institutional Economics* (Cambridge: Cambridge University Press, 1986).

Leijonhufvud A., 'Capitalism and the Factory System', in R. N. Langlois (ed.), *Economics as a Process, Essays in the New Institutional Economics* (Cambridge: Cambridge University Press, 1986).

Levine D. I., 'Demand Variability and Work Organization', in S. Bowles, H. Gintis and B. Gustafsson (eds), *Markets and Democracy: Participation, Accountability and Efficiency* (Cambridge: Cambridge University Press, 1993).

Littler C. R., *The Development of the Labour Process in Capitalist Societies* (London: Heineman, 1982).

Livingstone J., J. Moore and F. Oldfather (eds), *The Japan Reader 1: Imperial Japan* (Harmondsworth: Penguin, 1976a).

Livingstone J., J. Moore and F. Oldfather (eds), *The Japan Reader 2: Postwar Japan to the Present* (Harmondsworth: Penguin, 1976b).

Marglin S., 'What Do Bosses Do?', *Review of Radical Political Economy*, VI (1974) 60–112.

Marx K., *Capital* (New York: New York International Publishers, 1967).

Mayr E., *One Long Argument. Charles Darwin and the Genesis of Modern Evolutionary Thought* (Cambridge, MA.: Harvard University Press, 1991).

Milgron P. and J. Roberts, *Economics, Organization and Management* (Englewood Cliffs, NJ: Prentice-Hall International Editions, 1992).

Miyajima H., 'The Privatization of Ex-*Zaibatsu* Holding Stocks and the Emergence of Bank-Centred Corporate Groups in Japan', in M. Aoki and Kim Hyung-Ki (eds),*Corporate Governance in Transitional Economies. Insider Control and the Role of Banks* (Washington, DC: EDI Development Studies, The World Bank, 1995).

Morishima M., *Why Has Japan 'Succeeded'? Western Technology and the Japanese Ethos* (Cambridge: Cambridge University Press, 1982).

Morikawa H., *Zaibatsu. The Rise and Fall of Family Enterprise Groups in Japan* (Tokyo: University of Tokyo Press, 1992).

Nelson R. and S. G. Winter, *An Evolutionary Theory of Economic Change* (Cambridge, MA: Harvard University Press, 1982).

North D. C. and R. P. Thomas, *The Rise of the Western World* (Boston: Harvard University Press, 1973).

North D. C., *Structure and Change in History* (New York: Norton, 1981).

Pagano U., *Work and Welfare in Economic Theory* (Oxford: Blackwell, 1985).

Pagano U., 'Property Rights, Asset Specificity, and the Division of Labour under Alternative Capitalist Relations', *Cambridge Journal of Economics*, XV, 3 (1991a), 315–42. Reprinted in G. Hodgson, *The Economics of Institutions. A Volume of The International Library of Critical Writings in Economics* (Cheltenham: Series Editor, Mark Blaug, Edward Elgar, 1993).

Pagano U., 'Property Rights Equilibria and Institutional Stability', *Economic Notes*, XX, 2 (1991b) 189–228. Reprinted in J. Backhaus, *Systemwandel und Reform in Ostlichen Wirtshaften* (Marburg: Metropolis-Verlag, 1991).

Pagano U., 'Authority, Co-ordination and Disequilibrium: an Explanation of the Co-existence of Markets and Firms', *Economic Dynamics and Structural Change*, June (1992a). Reprinted in G. Hodgson, *The Economics of Institutions. A Volume of The International Library of Critical Writings in Economics* (Cheltenham: Series Editor, Mark Blaug, Edward Elgar, 1993).

Pagano U., 'Organizational Equilibria and Production Efficiency', *Metroeconomica*, XXXXIII, 1 (1992b) 227–43.

Pagano U., 'Braverman', in P. Arestis and M. C. Sawyer (eds), *Biographical Dictionary of Dissenting Economists* (Cheltenham: Edward Elgar, 1992c).

Pagano U., 'Organizational Equilibria and Institutional Stability', in S. Bowles, H. Gintis and B. Gustafsson (eds), *Markets and Democracy: Participation, Accountability and Efficiency* (Cambridge: Cambridge University Press, 1993).

Pagano U., 'Organizational Equilibria and the Japanese Model', in *Siena-Kyoto Symposium* (Kyoto: Kyoto University Press, 1994).

Pagano U. and R. Rowthorn, 'Ownership, Technology and Institutional Stability', *Structural Change and Economic Dynamics*, V, 2 (1994) 221–43.

Pagano U. and R. Rowthorn, 'The Competitive Selection of Democratic Firms in a World of Self-Sustaining Institutions', in U. Pagano and R. Rowthorn (eds), *Democracy and Efficiency in the Economic Enterprise* (London: Routledge, 1996) pp. 116–45.

Pistor K. and J. Turkewitz, 'Coping with Hydra – State Ownership after Privatization: a Comparative Study of the Czech Republic, Hungary and Russia', in R. Frydman, C. W. Gray and A. Rapaczynnski (eds), *Corporate Governance in Central Europe and Russia. Vol. 2 Insiders and the State* (Budapest: CEU Press, 1996) pp.192–245.

Putterman L., 'Some Behavioural Perspectives On the Dominance of Hierarchical over Democratic Forms of Enterprise', *Journal of Economic Behaviour and Organization*, III (1982) 139–60.

Putterman L., *The Economic Nature of the Firm. A Reader* (Cambridge: Cambridge University Press, 1986).

Reischauer E., *Japan. The Story of a Nation* (New York: McGraw-Hill, 1990).

Rostowski J. (ed.), *Banking Reform in Central Europe and the Former Soviet Union* (Budapest: Central European University Press, 1995).

Ridley M., *Evolution* (Oxford: Blackwell Scientific, 1993).

Samuelson P., 'Wage and Interest: A Modern Dissection of Marxian Economic Models', *American Economic Review*, 47 (1957) 884–912.

Thompson P., *The Nature of Work. An Introduction to Debates on the Labour Process* (London: Macmillan, 1983).

Williamson O. E., *The Economic Institutions of Capitalism* (New York: Free Press, 1985).

Yamamura K., 'L'industrializzazione del Giappone. Impresa, Proprietà e Gestione', in Chandeler A. *et al.* (eds), *Evoluzione della Grande Impresa e Management* (Turin: Einaudi, 1986).

Yamanura K. and Y. Yasuba, *The Political Economy of Japan. Vol. 1: The Domestic Transformation* (Stanford, CA: Stanford University Press, 1987).

Notes

* Università di Siena, Italy, and Central European University, Budapest, Hungary. I thank Fabrizio Barca, Gianni Fodella, Katsuhito Iwai, Lionello Punzo, Bob Rowthorn and Sandro Trento for useful suggestions. I have also

benefited from attending seminars and lectures on Japan given in Siena by Michio Morishima and Tsuneo Ishikawa. I am grateful for useful comments to the participants at the EU CompEcs conference held in Warsaw in September 1996 and to the participants at the CEU seminar held in Budapest in November 1996. The usual caveats apply.

1. According to Morikawa (1992) this is not correct: the *zaibatsu* companies were not involved in the raise of militarism in Japan and were opposed to the war against the United States.

2. See Pagano (1991a, 1991b, 1992b, 1993) and Pagano and Rowthorn (1994 and 1996). A brief and preliminary application of the 'organizational equilibria' framework to the analysis of the Japanese model was contained in Pagano (1994).

3. A similar characterization of the Japanese and American firms can be found in Aoki (1987a, 1989). Aoki (1993) clarifies how the Japanese firm is substantially different from a workers' co-operative and explains the role of external agents, such as financial institutions, in the solution of 'free-riding' problems. Aoki (1987b) explains the 'complementarity' between labour-market and financial institutions. Finally, Aoki (1992) introduces the 'duality principle'. According to this principle, under fairly general conditions, informational decentralization should be coupled with the centralization of ranking, which defines the hierarchy of the firm, whereas the centralization of information should be associated with the decentralization of ranking. Aoki (1992) identifies the Japanese model with the first case and the American model with the second. Aoki's view of the two models is not inconsistent with that advanced here. The decentralization of information, which characterizes the Japanese firm, is related to the existence of difficult-to-monitor and specific labour which embodies this information; the ranking centralization is equivalent to the complex system of rights which we claim to safeguard the Japanese worker independently of his present allocation within the firm. A similar 'equivalence' holds for the case of the A-model.

4. On this point see Iwata (1992), which also contains an interesting account of the historical origins of the system.

5. The New Institutionalist School stems from Coase (1937, 1960). It includes the contributions of Alchian (1984, 1987), Alchian and Demsetz (1972a, 1972b), Jensen and Meckling (1976), Demsetz (1966), North (1973, 1981), and Williamson (1985). They see the firm and the property rights structure of the firm as an efficient answer to the cost of using the market mechanism. From this point of view also Grossman and Hart (1986) and Hart and Moore (1990) belong to this school. Useful readers are Putterman (1986) which includes also 'radical' contributions and Langlois (1986). Pagano (1992a) considers the relation between the modern transaction cost approach and earlier approaches based on the disequilibrium costs of the market mechanism. The New Institutional approach is bound to change the structure of microeconomic theory: the firm must be seen as a 'market-like institution' and not simply as a 'consumer-like' agent. On this point see the last chapter of Kreps (1990) and the approach developed by Milgrom and Roberts (1992) in their book *Economics, Organization and Management*.

6. Alternative property rights structures can generate different 'technological trajectories'. On 'technological trajectories' see Nelson and Winter (1977) and Dosi (1988).

7. For instance, capitalist property rights may cause such a detailed division of labour (along the lines suggested by Babbage (1832) who contains an excellent summary of the principles of Taylorism) that the workers perform simple tasks which are easy to control and require only general purpose or 'generic' skills. On this point see Pagano (1991a, 1992c) where it is argued that 'classical capitalism' (such as that considered by Braverman, 1974) can inhibit the development of both 'general' and 'firm-specific' human skills and may only be consistent with the use of generic skills. These papers consider also the consequences of alternative kinds of capitalism on the development of the skills of the workers. Important criticisms of Braverman include Edwards (1979) and Littler (1982). Thompson (1983) and Pagano (1992c) survey this literature.

8. The idea of 'difficult-to-monitor capital' is not immediately clear but Alchian and Demsetz (1972a) show that it makes sense. Capital is 'difficult to monitor' when we cannot infer user-induced depreciation by observing capital before and after its employment. Some costly information on the way in which capital has been used is necessary to estimate user-induced depreciation.

9. It could be argued that the workers are not at disadvantage when they rent 'specific' capital because instead of renting machines, they can borrow money, buy the machines and use them as collateral. However, firm-specific machines are less valuable as collateral than general-purpose machines because it is more difficult to liquidate them in case of bankruptcy. In both cases, it will be more expensive to rent firm-specific capital than general-purpose capital. For similar reasons, difficult-to-monitor capital, like firm-specific capital, is less valuable as collateral than easy-to-monitor capital. In this case it will be more expensive for the lender to monitor user-induced depreciation. Thus, also in this case, borrowing money and buying machines may not be a solution to the problem of difficult-to-monitor capital.

10. An 'organizational equilibrium' can also be interpreted as a 'Nash equilibrium.' Organizational equilibria may be defined by the fact that 'producers' choose the technology that maximizes profits given the existing property rights system and by the fact that 'financiers' arrange such transactions that maximize ownership rent given the existing technology. Thus, the idea of organizational equilibrium is based on the assumption that 'financiers' have a perfect knowledge of the company's value for alternative owners using the existing technology but they are ignorant of the company's value under alternative technologies. This 'informational constraint' can be due to the fact that technology is not a 'menu' that is freely available to everybody but has to be created, developed and transmitted at certain costs in a given institutional framework characterised by certain property rights. When certain property rights are missing, much of the knowledge about the associated 'optimal' technology is also likely to be missing. On this point see Pagano and Rowthorn (1996).

11. Putterman (1982) and Levine (1993) consider alternative mechanisms by which property rights may reproduce themselves.

12. The concept of 'organisational equilibrium' is related to the Marxian notion of 'mode of production' which is also based on a close interaction between property rights (relations of production) and technology (productive forces). However, this relation may only hold subject to two qualifications. Firstly, our

analysis is related to what Hirschman (1981, p. 89) has aptly defined as 'micro-Marxism'. Hirschman observes that Marx 'oscillated between the grand generalization with which to characterize an entire epoch or process and the discriminating analysis of events which made differences between countries and subperiods stand out in richly textured detail'. The analysis is clearly related to the second approach. For example, we define as alternative 'organizational equilibria', or modes of production, Fordist-type firms and Japanese-type firms. Secondly, Marxist analysis has often oscillated between 'technological determinism' (technology invariably gives rise to a unique set of property rights) and 'property rights romanticism' (alternative property rights can invariably bring about an alternative technology). We hope that the idea of organizational equilibrium can clarify and overcome the limitations of these two extreme views. Chapter 3 of Pagano (1985) advances the hypothesis that the two Marxian views of history are related to the contradictions between two socialism models that are implicitly contained in his theory. However, in spite of these contradictions, the Marxian theory is an important ingredient to develop a theory of history. John Hicks (1969, p. 3) maintains that, besides the Marxian theory of history, 'there is so little in the way of an alternative vision which is available'.

13. These conditions are derived in Pagano (1993) and Pagano and Rowthorn (1996).

14. For a more detailed analysis of the properties of 'organizational equilibria', see Pagano (1991, 1992 and 1993a) and Pagano and Rowthorn (1996).

15. These additional agency costs will not only be paid when the workers rent high-agency-cost capital but also under alternative contractual arrangements where the workers borrow monetary capital and use high-agency-cost capital as collateral. On this point refer to footnote n. 9.

16. Attention is concentrated on a model with only two types of capital and labour. Likewise, only the extreme cases of 'pure capitalist' and 'pure labour' ownership is considered. This is done for analytical simplicity. Observe that the symbols could stand for different factors: this allows alternative interpretations of the model that could be used to study the outsider-insider problem in labour markets or the relation between financial and industrial capital. More complex cases, involving the 'unbundling of ownership rights' and their redistributions, characterize real-life economies. For instance, the Japanese economy can be seen as a case in which hiring and firing rights have been unbundled from traditional shareholder ownership rights and redistributed to the people using capital.

17. Thus the concept of organizational equilibria is based on the assumption that 'financiers' have perfect knowledge of the value of the company for alternative owners using the existing technology but they are ignorant of the value of the company under alternative technologies. This informational structure is based on the idea that technology is not a 'menu' that is available for free to everybody but has to be created, developed and transmitted at certain costs in a given institutional framework, characterized by certain property rights. When certain property rights are missing, much of the knowledge about the associated 'optimal' technology is also likely to be missing. Our point is consistent with the idea that it is very unlikely that an isoquant, describing all the production techniques, can ever be 'produced' and be known to all the

agents. The techniques that are currently used are likely to determine the 'piece' of the 'new' isoquant that is 'produced'. Property rights act similarly to factor prices and, indeed, affect these prices (when they include also agency costs). In this way, they influence the choice of the current technique and the set of new techniques that are going to be 'produced'. On the 'path dependency' characteristics of technological development see David (1975, 1994), Nelson and Winter (1982), Dosi (1988), and Inkster (1991).

18. For a more precise formal analysis of 'organizational equilibria' see Pagano (1993a) and Pagano and Rowthorn (1994 and 1996).

19. The elasticity of substitution has an important role in determining the multiplicity, the 'institutional stability and efficiency of organizational equilibria. On this point see Pagano and Rowthorn (1996).

20. For a complete analysis of the analogies between economics and evolutionary biology see Hodgson (1993).

21. However, as Mayr (1991) points out, even the 'speciational evolution', considered by Eldredge and Gould, is in some sense gradual. 'Such speciational evolution, because it occurs in populations, is gradual in spite of its rapid rate and therefore is in no conflict whatsoever with the Darwinian paradigm' (Mayr, 1991 p. 154). However, it is in sharp contrast with the view of some geneticists who see evolution as a gradual change of gene frequencies in populations and do not see the abrupt nature of speciation and the long periods of stasis that characterize the evolution of species (Mayr, 1991, p. 137).

22. If the hybrids between two species were at disadvantage, 'selection would act to increase the reproductive isolation because each form would do better not to mate with other and produce disadvantageous hybrids: speciation would be speeded up by selection in sympatry. The process is called *secondary reinforcement*. It is secondary if the reproductive isolation has partly evolved allopatrically, and is then reinforced on secondary contact. The process by which selection increases reproductive isolation independently of the history of the populations is simply called *reinforcement*' (Ridley, 1993, p. 412). Reinforcement is a necessary condition for the new species not to merge if they happen to share the same territory but it is not a sufficient condition for speciation. By contrast, 'the theoretical conditions for speciation to take place by reinforcement are difficult' (Ridley, 1993, p. 414).

23. Within the space of one generation Japan jumped from the condition of victim of western nations to the status of imperial power. The pressure to industrialize came from the fear of foreign domination. The steam-powered 'black ships' of the American Commodore Mathew C. Perry persuaded some samurai of the fact that only radical reforms could save national independence (see Reischauer, 1990 and Livingstone *et al.*, 1976a). Less than a century later, the Americans were again the most important external cause of the other major institutional shock of modern Japanese history.

24. The role of the samurai class and samurai ethos is emphasized in the 'orthodox' thesis on the industrialization of Japan. This emphasis has been somewhat mitigated by some recent studies on Japanese development. On this point see Yamamura (1986). Iwata (1992) traces the Japanese view of the firm as a 'Unified Body of Employees' to the business institutions of the Tokugawa period. On the role of Japanese ethos see Morishima (1982). Morikawa (1992) points out that many *zaibatsu* companies originated from

the 'political merchants' of the Togukawa period. While the differences
between western civilization and Japan have been the object of numerous
studies, there is one similarity between them that to my knowledge has not
received the attention that it deserves. Both middle age Europe and pre-Meiji
Japan were characterized by the coexistence and, often, the struggle between a
centralized spiritual authority (the Pope in the case of Europe and the Emperor
in the case of Japan) and a centralized 'temporal' political authority (the
Emperor in the case of Europe and the Shogun in the case of Japan). These
conditions were rather unique in world history and, perhaps, in both cases,
they favoured the development of the autonomy of the individual and,
indirectly, economic development.

25. The 'Yasuda Plan' of November 1945 suggested that, 'When the securities, or
other property transferred to the Holding Company Liquidation Company, are
offered for sale, preference to purchase will be given to employees of the
companies involved, and in case of corporate shares the number of such shares
that may be purchased by any single purchaser will be limited in order to insure
maximum democratisation of ownership' (Livingstone *et al.*, 1976b, p. 81).

26. Iwata (1992) points out that during this period this practice was not
uncommon. 'It was not rare to ask for the union's consent to nominees for
company president.'... 'Indeed, some union leaders were later promoted to the
presidency or other executive posts in their companies' (Iwata, 1992, p. 183).

27. See the readings and the documents collected in Livingstone *et al.* (1976b).

28. Berglöf and Perotti (1994) show that cross shareholding can support
collaboration also in situations where the simple loss of reputation could
not. In comparison to the reputation mechanism, cross shareholding is
characterized by the fact that other managers can apply stronger sanctions
because they can fire a shirking manager. In equilibrium, no manager has an
incentive to shirk and no sanction may be applied: it may well be impossible
for an outside observer to detect the implicit rules on which co-operation
relies. Even if cross holding could support co-operative outcomes in a wider
range of cases, according to Berglöf and Perotti the main bank system is a
fundamental 'complementary' institution that can rule out inefficient low
effort equilibria and discipline managerial behaviour.

29. The historical origins of the main bank system can be traced to syndicate loans
that during the war were formed to finance and monitor the risky business of
the munitions companies in the late 1940s. Since its formation, the major
participants – the main bank, other core banks, the bankers' association,
government authorities and the borrowing firms 'have shown dynamic
flexibility as power has shifted among them'. 'In each period, syndication was
made effective by the leadership with the highest bargaining power among
them' (Horiuchi, 1994, p. 292). Thus leadership was initially taken by the
Bank of Japan, and in the 1950s and later, by the Industrial Bank of Japan (IBJ)
and the bankers' association. MITI had also an important role for large heavy
and chemical industry firms. Lately, by the early 1980s, the initiative had
passed from lenders to borrowers and many large firms have taken banks'
willingness to lend for granted. As a result, as it has been shown most
dramatically in the bubble of the late 1980s and its aftermath, 'the main bank
system as a social device for corporate monitoring appears to be under severe
test' (Aoki, 1994, p. 137).

30. Thus, the interpretation advanced in this paper does not rely on Japanese cultural specific factors which could not arise in other countries. Japanese-like firms exist also outside Japan. The issue is not to attribute their nature to some unique Japanese character but to explain the conditions that have made them so frequent in Japan in a particular historical period. We share the criticism advanced by Asanuma (1993, p. 2) who argues that too many authors stop the analysis at a particular Japanese word (such as *keiretsu*) assuming implicitly that what is observed 'is in every respect to be ascribed to Japan-specific factors'. For a convincing criticism of the 'culturalist approach', see Koike (1987).

31. Amsdem, Kochanowitz and Taylor (1994) observe that one similarity between postwar Japan and the former socialist countries is the important role of extra-national agents in the reform process; in this sense, the World Bank has a role analogous to SCAP. However, according to them (p. 125), in Japan 'American occupying forces championed a more equal income distribution through land reform; in Eastern Europe, by contrast, the Bank has regarded the region's highly income distribution as a socialist artefact that would have to disappear with capitalist development. The occupying forces in Japan also championed democratization, trade union organization, and employee ownership of former *zaibatsu*, whereas in post-socialist Eastern Europe the Bank has regarded workers' organizations such as employees' councils with hostility, as blockages to change'. It would be a somewhat disturbing conclusion that it is better to be run by the occupation forces of your enemy than by the World Bank.

32. Chang (1995) observes that there were relevant similarities among postwar Japan (and the other successful East Asian countries) and the former socialist countries such as a high level of education of the population. East Asia should not be considered a 'special case' whose experience is not relevant for other countries.

33. The analysis of the links between the socialist past and the privatization processes of these economies is based on Earle, Frydman and Rapaczynski (1993). Path dependencies imply that, in general, insiders' and employees' ownership as well as indirect state ownership are quite common in transition. On these two points see respectively Earle and Estrin (1996) and Pistor and Turkewitz (1996).

34. However, according to a recent 'cover story' of the *Wall Street Journal Central European Economic Review*, by N. King (1996, p. 10), this outsiders' control is not working. 'The Czech experience argues loudly for why privatisation alone doesn't do it. Next must come active owners and a clear responsible market that rewards results and punishes the laggards. Both are lacking in Prague.' As a result of massive vouchers' privatization, 'most big Czech companies are ruled by investment funds, themselves often owned by Czech banks. Far from prodding managers to perform – or sacking them – the funds have grown plump on behind the scenes trading and their 2 per cent yearly management fees'.

35. In almost all cases employees have effective veto power on the corporatization of their company. 'The provision of the Law that allows the Prime Minister to force an enterprise to corporatize without obtaining the employees' consent has remained essentially unexercised, and the pace of corporatization has

been very low' (Earle, Frydman and Rapaczynski, 1993, p. 8). Moreover, the employees' councils and enterprise management have been very active in initiating privatization process through liquidation that involves the transfer of control to a group of insiders (mostly in the form of long term leasing with an option to purchase). According to Earle, Frydman and Rapaczynski (1993, p. 8), this 'has been the most common method of ownership transformation in Poland'.

36. The main bank solution is suggested by Aoki (1995) even if he is aware of the fact that the necessary banking skills may be lacking in the former socialist countries. Rostowski (1995, p. 34) observes that credit financing is impossible in those countries with very high inflation where the population minimises its holding of domestic and, therefore, the amount of real credit that is available in the economy. Thus, according to Rostowski, credit financing is a possible governance system only in a second phase of the transformation.

Subject Index

agriculture, restructuring of –
    simulation results, 189

bequest
    insurance, 113, 117
    optimal, 120, 125–6
    strategic, 111, 113
bequest/care exchange, 111, 121, 125
bureaucracy
    hierarchical, 96
    rational, 93
    size of, 96, 101
    supranational, 92
bureaucratic reform, 88–9, 91–2
business service, 67, 79, 80–2

capital-to-labour
    long-term optimum values of the
        ratio, 179
    ratio, 182–4
    simulation results, 192, 195
cost disease, 73
country risk, 7, 10
    interest differential, 8, 10
cross shareholding, 219
currency risk, 7, 11, 35
Czech Republic, 223–25

deregulation, 95
dichotomization thresholds (cut-off
    values), 153–4, 163
dynamic discontinuities, 38–9

effect
    dimension (absolute), 156
    proportional (relative), 156
employment
    actual and optimum – simulation
        results, 189–90
    structure – simulation results, 187
European bureaucratic integration, 87,
    98, 104
European Central Bank, xiii

European Monetary Union, xiii

forward discount, 7, 8, 10–1
Framework Space, 42, 45

governmental intervention, 88
growth cycles, 38

Harrodian corridor, 45, 51
hierarchy, hierarchies, 87, 90, 95–7,
    99–103, 105
Hungary, 223–25

inventory
    changes, 184
    desired level of, 184
input-output
    approach, 151
    regional tables, 151
institutional infrastructures, 135,
    137–8, 145
labour
    market, 185
    productivity – simulation results, 188
lean government, 87–9, 93, 96
innovation
    local system of, 131–2, 140–1, 143–5
    national systems of, 131, 133, 135–9,
        144–5, 148
insider control, 219
insurance
    legislation, 113
    long-term care (LTC), 111–8, 120–2,
        124–5, 130
    optimal (perfect) coverage, 120–1, 126
    perfect, 122, 124–5

long-term care (LTC)
    costs, 112, 114–6, 122
    risk, 111–2, 114–5, 121
loss function, 16, 19, 20–2

Maastricht Treaty, 104
macroeconomic policy, 180

Author Index